THE SALLY AND TOMMY JOHN STORY

The Sally and Tommy John Story

Our Life in Baseball

SALLY AND TOMMY JOHN

Macmillan Publishing Company

NEW YORK

Macmillan Publishing Company
866 Third Avenue, New York, N.Y. 10022
Collier Macmillan Canada, Inc.

Library of Congress Cataloging in Publication Data
John, Sally.
The Sally and Tommy John story.
1. John, Tommy. 2. Baseball players—United States—Biography. 3. John, Sally. 4. Wives—United States—Biography. I. John, Tommy. II. Title. III. Title: Our life in baseball.
GV865.J58J63 1983 796.357′092′4 [B] 83-5429
ISBN 0-02-559260-2

10 9 8 7 6 5 4 3 2 1

Designed by Jack Meserole

Printed in the United States of America

To the children and
to the fans

ACKNOWLEDGMENTS

Our special thanks for all they have done for us: to His Eminence, Terence Cardinal Cooke, for his love, prayers, and great advice; to C.D. Higginbothom and Harry Strohl, Tommy's great Little League coaches; to Bill Welch, Tommy's confidence builder in American Legion ball; to Howard Sharpe, friend and Gerstmeyer High School basketball coach; to John Valle, for guidance and leadership as Dean of Boys at Gerstmeyer; to all Tommy's athletic coaches and trainers, who offered great assistance and guidance while at Indiana State; to Jim Henson and the Muppets, for the time, gifts, and love to Travis; and to David Hartman, for his friendship and thoughtfulness.

We would also like to take this opportunity to thank the many people that were involved in making this book possible: to our parents, Opal and Jerry Simmons, for all the love, encouragement, and hours of baby-sitting, and Ruth and Tommy John, for their love, support, and prayers; to Fifi Oscard, our literary agent, for all of her time and effort; to Kevin McShane, for his hours of work and patience; to our dear friends, Chuck and Carol Schaefer, for their unending love; to Jerry Reed, Sally's sister, for loving and helping; to all the doctors and nurses in Pediatrics at New York University Hospital and Point Pleasant Community Hospital, for their love and intelligence; to Bob Smith, without whose contribution this book could not have come about; to Dr. Stuart and Linda Siegel, for their love and friendship; to Carol and Larry Haggerty, for their love and support; to Betty Ann Smith and Jane Byrnes, for taking excellent care of our children; to Lois Esposito, for the hours of love, guidance and encouragement during our four and one-half years in New Jersey; to May and Larry Kohan, for being great and helpful neighbors, and for the love and guidance they gave to our daughter Tami; to Jackie Donovan, for setting an excellent example of loving and sharing for our children; to Pastor Donner Atwood, for his love and guidance during Travis's injury; to Pastor Bob Duncan, for helping us immediately in Point Pleasant; to the town of Franklin Lakes and Mayor Vichiconti, for their love, prayers, and encouragement in Tommy's baseball career and for our family; to the teachers of Woodside School, in helping Tami during the trauma of Travis's injury; to Hilda Godding, for everything; and to my special friend, Mary Nagelvoord, for being there and for setting such a great example for our children. And let us not forget our editor, George Walsh, who was always understanding and helpful.

PROLOGUE

On August 13, 1981, Travis, our littlest boy (at that time), fell from a third-story window and struck his skull on the pavement. Both of us, and nearly everyone else who was nearby at the time, were convinced that the fall had been fatal.

The fact that Travis, after a protracted and harrowing stay at the New York University Medical Center, came back to us not merely alive but fully recovered and as active as ever, is a miracle for which we shall continue to give worshipful thanks, not only to the gifted doctors Fred Epstein and Sol Zimmerman who attended Travis, but for all our lives to the Loving Father who watched over him, whose boundless love sustained us, and whose goodness made itself felt in the kindness and devotion of the many hands and hearts that contributed to our beloved son's recovery.

But once the horror of the event had begun to recede we discovered another cause for gratitude to God. For in sustaining us through this tragedy, He provided us both with what we now feel was miraculous vision of our own lives, of the world around us, and of a world we had never before known existed. He gave us, as we contemplated His ineffable Goodness and Loving Kindness, a new understanding of ourselves, of our love for each other, and of the Christian Love that bound us to our neighbors.

Sitting together by Travis's bed, waiting for him to return to us from the depths of that frightening sleep, we had time to look back over our lives together and to see them with a wonderful clarity. It was as if this sudden and potentially shattering tragedy had driven from our minds all the petty selfishness, the secretly nourished prejudices, the false pride, the jealousies, the spite, and the self-righteousness that too often cloud or distort our vision, and we were able to sort out in our lives the trivial from the significant or the pure gold from the dross. There is nothing like a face-to-face encounter with death to cast a stark light on all the concerns of this world. And we did indeed look death in the face. For more than just a few hours nearly everyone close to Travis held only the thinnest thread of hope for his recovery. I don't think any of us at the time expressed this feeling of despair more effectively than did our young friend, Betsy Schaefer, then thirteen years old, who wrote this poem that her mother found weeks later in Betsy's room:

> I feel bad
> and oh so sad.
> So many days have gone by
> When I want to just sit back and cry.
> Is there any hope inside?
> Should I crawl in a hole and hide?
> Can anyone show me how to be strong?
> Tell me how long can this last? How long?
>
> The sky is turning black now.
> Please show me how.
> I feel so helpless.
> How can I be fearless?
> Travis is gone.
> Travis is gone.

By the time this verse came to light we were all giving

thanks to God that Travis was *not* gone. And now we give thanks to God for the lessons He helped us learn.

We learned for one thing how to couple our prayers with a firm resolve to accept God's will. And we learned that there is a very real world beyond the one where we have lived in comfort and security, a world where sorrow and suffering are the daily fare, where children cope with hourly pain and loneliness, where some parents just watch their little ones fade away before their eyes, where hope is measured in days or even hours, and where the comfort Christ has offered the heavy-laden is constantly sought after.

But of course in re-assessing our lives we recalled the brighter moments too—the joys and mishaps of courtship and marriage, the small triumphs on the baseball diamond, the half-forgotten folk of Tommy's minor-league days, the quarrels (all seeming rather comic now), the seemingly impossible recovery from a major accident, the "characters" who used to brighten stadium and training camp, the crazy ups-and-downs of contract negotiations, the joyous moments that marked our little boy's gradual return to full health, and the love and concern expressed by thousands of people all over the land whose faces we never saw.

Because each of us learned from this experience in a special way and each applied the lessons to our own lives in a special degree, we have chosen to share the experience with you, the reader, through our separate voices. That is why the story that follows is divided into what Sally has to tell and what Tommy wants you to know of the changes this miracle made in our lives, our work, the strength of our faith, and our ways of looking at the world.

SALLY JOHN
TOMMY JOHN

Spring, 1983

ONE

Sally:

I still feel a stab of anger when people ask me: "Don't you have guilt feelings about it?"

Guilt because my little boy was almost killed in a fall? Of course I have guilt feelings! What mother wouldn't feel responsible no matter how many precautions she had taken? I can still experience the horror that surged through me when I saw Travis lying on the cement walk, and the way the bottom seemed to drop out of the world when I held him in my arms and his little head rolled loosely as a blossom on a broken stem. And I can remember the wild anger that boiled up in me—anger I later felt ashamed of and that caused me to scream: "Where is she?" I meant the baby-sitter who had been left for just *five minutes* with my two boys and warned not to let them out of her sight for one second. But I am sure I was angry at myself, too. I think any mother will always feel, when one of her children is hurt, angry at herself for not having been there to prevent it—even if the accident takes place a thousand miles away. A feeling of total responsibility seems built in to motherhood.

I did feel, of course, that I had taken every sensible step to keep the boys from getting hurt—one grownup for each child, and a well-recommended and responsible baby-sitter as back-up when one grownup or another had to leave for a short time. But I had no energy right then for vain regrets or for anger. Travis was hurt and I wanted to *fix* it! I had picked him up instinctively to comfort him and keep him from further harm. Now I had one purpose only—to make him well. Nothing in all the world was going to distract me from that job. But—oh Lord!—what if he should die?

He didn't die. But it was many, many hours before we were sure he would live and many weary days and nights before we knew he would walk and talk again.

If I ever feel any other guilt, it is a very mild attack, perhaps not guilt at all but just a slightly uncomfortable feeling for being glad about the baseball strike that had made the weeks preceding the accident among the happiest I had ever known. It was the first time in our married life that we had been together as a family all through the best days of the year, from June to August. We had dinner together *every* day. And we had it not at two o'clock in the afternoon, with Tommy having to rush off at once to the stadium, but at a proper hour, with the whole long evening ahead of us. And there were no more endless days of separation while the club was on the road, or life apart from the kids when I accompanied Tommy on a long trip. Of course, I love baseball and will always be grateful to baseball for the life it has given us and the security we feel. But those months without baseball were truly bliss. I think Sundays were the best. We would all go together to church, the whole happy tribe, Big Tommy, Little Tommy, Tami, and Travis, then come home together to a real family dinner with time to relish every moment. Then afterward Tommy and the boys would stretch out before the TV, while Tommy watched a golf tournament or some such alleged entertainment and I would peek in later to find Tommy sound asleep on the carpet with the two little boys nestled in his arms. That's a picture I'll hold in my heart as long as I live.

We had time to go everywhere that summer: trips to Vermont where we could swim and take the kids fishing; visits to relatives in Indiana we almost never had time to see in the summer months; family picnics whenever the weather invited us. What better way to spend a summer than just to idle the weeks away together as a loving family in a comfortable home with no harsh schedules to keep, no long separations, none of the fears that distance always brings? So I blessed that baseball strike, even though I felt like a traitor when I did so.

Perhaps if I had been superstitious I'd have told myself that it was all too good to be true. Naturally, it had to come to an end with the settlement of the strike and with Tommy pitching another "season opener"—probably the only time in history a pitcher ever worked two opening games the same year. But I had no premonition at all, unless a bad dream I had could be called a premonition, and I don't for one minute believe in such nonsense.

It was a dream from which I awoke screaming. I had seen little Travis, my two-year-old, drowning out of my reach, sinking helplessly in the water with no one to save him. I jumped from my bed, still more than half-asleep, and called out for Tommy to help me. We *did* have a pool. But the gate there was always locked. Still, I rushed into Travis's room and caught him in my arms and held him tight for more than a minute, until I came fully awake and realized it had been just a nightmare. Afterward my doctor told me this sort of dream was not at all uncommon in pregnant woman (I was six months pregnant); it was merely a sign of the natural increase of the protective instinct.

If there were any premonition at all—and of course there was none—someone might have seen it in the fact that, when I drove to the beach that day, with my sister and her family following in her car, I moved my car from where I first parked it and, in order to leave room for my sister to unpack without standing in the road, pulled it right up close to the house. For that move, the doctor told me later, undoubtedly saved my little boy's life.

But tragedy was far, far from my thoughts on that golden August day. We had all come down to Bay Head, New Jersey, to visit our friends, Chuck and Carol Schaefer, and to give the kids, big and small, a day at the beach. (My sister Judy brought four of her five children, Kathy, nine, Rick and Rusty, both eleven, and Leslie, sixteen.) I had made painstaking preparations for the trip, even bringing the baby-sitter into the house three days in advance so I could be sure she understood what the job was going to be. It was *not* to be a vacation for us, I told her. We were to watch the little ones every second and *never* lose sight of them.

I must tell you that Travis had always been a full-time job all by himself, and I thought long and hard before deciding to bring him along. At one point I had made up my mind to call in the pediatric nurse I often hired to look after him and leave Travis behind in her care. For Travis was the sort of small boy people tell stories about. Inquisitive, bright, active, and self-willed, he seemed forever bent on poking into something that awakened his curiosity and sampling anything he was warned not to touch. (My mother tells me I had the same nature when I was Travis's age.) While Tommy, the oldest boy, was self-disciplined beyond his years, to the point of refusing candy that his parents did not approve of, Travis was a boy to whom forbidden fruit was always the most precious. And instant gratification was his constant aim. On Halloween, when out trick-or-treating, Travis would accept the treat with proper gratitude, then promptly sit down on the steps (or on the floor!) and consume it.

Perhaps you can understand then why we felt little Travis had to be under constant guard. We had even installed an intercom in his bedroom so we could hear his breathing and make note of any unusual movement. Eventually, we took to turning the lock on his door at night lest he scamper out on the bridge-balcony that spanned our living room before we could head him off.

Still, it seemed cruelly unfair to deny Travis his share of a day at the seashore. Surely, with two of us watching, he could be kept out of danger. I am sure I was as concerned about the dangers as any mother would be, so I took extra pains to explain to our baby-sitter that we were here not to romp in the sand but to watch over my little boys like a couple of hired bodyguards. For I was truly *scared* of what could happen on a beach. On the way down I told Travis of the dangers that lay in the high waves, the strong tides, and the shifting sand. And when he remained unimpressed by all of these, I told him of the *sharks* that might bite his toes. *That* seemed to shake him a little.

As it turned out, Travis had very little interest in the water. Instead, he devoted himself to sand castles and to taking an imaginary trip on a "raft" the boys had made on the sand. Then he spent a thrilling twenty minutes examining a live crab some boy had found on the beach. His shrieks as he watched this weird creature wave its claws and scuttle this way and that must have carried all down the shore. But he was never out of our sight for a second and I began to tell myself I had been foolish to have made people so uneasy about a simple trip to the seashore: The day was so golden bright, the kids all so caught up in the wonders of the sea, and all of them, big and little, getting along so happily together.

Then a thick haze began to form along the water, moving in to dim the sun and make the beach less dazzling. There was no hint of rain but it seemed like a good time to hurry back to the house and make ready for a trip along the boardwalk, where there were rides of all sorts that the kids were eager to try, goodies to sample, and new sights to see.

The house, when we returned, was redolent with the smell of roasting turkey. There would be thirteen of us for dinner that night and the fragrance of a turkey in the oven made it seem like Christmas in August. It was, as a matter of fact, August 13, 1981. All that was lacking to turn this place into a minor paradise, for me at least, was Tommy's presence. But he was with the Yankees in Detroit and was not scheduled to return for a week. All the same, I had not forgotten my promise to myself to keep devoted watch on my two active boys. There was still the beach to be scared of and I was not about to relax my vigil, vacation or no. After bathing and dressing the boys, who were wriggling with excitement at the prospect of sampling the marvels of the boardwalk, I took them downstairs and told the baby-sitter, in my firmest voice: "The boys are *yours* for five minutes. Don't let them out of your sight for a single second. If you must go to the bathroom, take them with you. I'm just going to throw on some clothes."

Throwing on clothes is about what I did. I had no time to primp or fuss. In these surroundings every moment when Travis was out of my sight was a moment of near-panic. But I had been upstairs hardly two minutes when I heard Tami, my six-year-old daughter, screaming:

"Mommy! Travis fell out the window!"

The window! The third-story window! Oh God! I hope not a broken arm! If he landed in those bushes his little face will be scratched to pieces! In less than a minute I was down the stairs and just flying around the corner of the house. And there Travis lay, not in the bushes, but on the concrete driveway, with his head pillowed on a step, his little body sprawled out like a discarded doll. I am sure I began to scream at once. "Oh my baby! Oh Travis! Oh God!" Forgetting all I had been taught about leaving an injured person undisturbed, I caught him up in my arms and held him to me. He was not breathing! I held him at arm's length and his head rolled as loosely as if it were held with string. Blood trickled from one ear. "He's dying!" I screamed. I looked up at the window and thought I saw the stricken face of the baby-sitter. Travis's eyes were open to slits and his lips, too, were barely parted. I could see that his little tongue had rolled back into his throat, shutting off the air passage. I tried to pull his mouth open. I hadn't the strength. Desperately I looked about for a stick, anything! Then I realized I still held in my hand the tiny bottle of nail polish I had been ready to drop in my purse. It had a long tapering top, like a tiny steeple. I worked this into the side of Travis's mouth and with all my strength I pried his teeth apart far enough so I could get one finger in and pull the little tongue free. The air rushed in with a sort of gravelly gasp, as if I had punctured a vacuum can. Then he began to breathe steadily. God be thanked!

Carol and Betsy Schaefer were at my side. "Do something!" I screamed. "My baby is dying!" Almost instantly I realized that an oversize policeman was standing beside me. Someone had called a police car—undoubtedly one of the neighbors had heard my screams—and it got there before the ambulance Carol had called. The policeman, acting of course according to procedure, told us, "Don't move him! Don't touch him!" But I had already moved him and was holding him tight. "Get him to the hospital!" I insisted. "Is there a hospital here? What is this place?" I had forgotten where we were staying. There was a hospital close by, at Point Pleasant, they told me, but we would have to wait for the ambulance.

"Forget the ambulance!" I screamed. "My baby is dying! Take him in the police car!"

The oversize policeman looked at Carol. "Get the mother out of here!" he yelled. "She's hysterical!" Undoubtedly he had noticed I was pregnant. I had actually forgotten it. "I'm not hysterical!" I told him. "Get my baby to the hospital!"

One of the neighbors was hustling forward with an ironing board to use as a stretcher. But I had no time for that. The policeman carefully put Travis on the back seat of the cruiser but held me back when I tried to get in with him.

"I am *not* leaving my baby!" I told him.

My sister Judy spoke up like the voice of authority: "The

mother goes with the child!" This must have sounded to the policeman like a quote from a book of rules, for he allowed Carol to shove him aside so I could climb into the front seat. Almost instantly we were on the way, with the siren howling. I turned to see Travis and I was dismayed to find him closed off from me by a heavy guard screen. I clawed at the screen and wept. Travis was moving spasmodically and had started to moan.

"Mommy's here!" I cried to Travis. "God loves you! God will help you! I love you Travis! Oh please God, help him!" All the way to the hospital I sobbed and kept seeing again that dreadful scene on the driveway—my little baby wearing the look of death. The police car rolled to a stop, caught in a mass of commuter traffic at a red light. The siren howled in vain. No one seemed willing to make way.

"Get up on the sidewalk!" I screamed. "Drive on the sidewalk! For God's sake keep going! Hurry! Hurry!"

Perhaps the man in back was convinced I was hysterical but the young driver, after a brief glance behind him, drove the car up on the sidewalk, sped along the pavement to get around the backed-up cars, and then rocketed away unimpeded to the hospital.

It seemed as if half the staff of the hospital were outside to meet us—nurses, orderlies, guards, Lord knows what, rushed forward, transferred Travis gently yet swiftly to the stretcher, then took my arms and tried to guide me to a wheelchair. I shook myself free. I needed no wheelchair! It was only much later that I realized I had forgotten I was pregnant while they must have been concerned with it immediately. But right now I wanted to stay with Travis. I hurried along behind the rolling stretcher and saw the emergency room doors swing back to admit it. Then bam! The big doors were shut in my face. I stood there, tears on my cheeks, bewildered and desolate. If only *Tommy* were here! Someone led me to the desk where a crisp unemotional voice asked me meaningless questions: My Social Security number. My phone number. My insurance carrier. Who had time for such nonsense? I wanted to reach my husband! Fortunately my friend Carol Schaefer and my sister Judy were able to supply all the proper passwords. (Carol and Judy had come speeding after us in another patrol car.) I looked frantically around for a telephone. There was a booth right outside the emergency room door and I ran to it. As I approached, the guard stepped firmly in front of the door to the emergency room, arms folded, barring my path. I snapped at him angrily:

"I am just going to phone my husband!"

What to do? He was in Detroit, and right now must be at the ball park. I took a firm grip on my voice and called information for the ball park number. I dialed that with extra care.

"I am the wife of Tommy John, the Yankee pitcher," I told the voice that answered. "I have to speak to him on a matter of life and death. Please connect me with the visiting team clubhouse right away!"

"Hold on," said the voice. And I held. There were clicks and hums—and then . . . the dial tone! I had been cut off! And of course I had not memorized the number. My hands were shaking. Try again. Dial information. Get the number once more. Meanwhile, I was conscious of activity around me, for I had kept the door to the booth open so I might know if anyone came out of the emergency room. Now the guard had left his post and hastened off—undoubtedly to spread the word that Tommy John's family was at hand. This irritated me a little but there was no room in my mind for petty worries. I had the ball park again. "Don't cut me off!" I shouted. "This is Tommy John's wife. Please connect me with the clubhouse right now!" So they promptly cut me off again. This time I remembered the number and got them right back.

Some annonymous voice—it must have been the clubhouse attendant's—answered and told me flatly that "TJ's on the field" as if that meant he was unreachable.

"This is an emergency!" I screamed. "Get him! Please!"

He muttered something I could not understand and another voice came on the phone. "This is Jeff Torborg. Is that you Sally?"

"Yes! Yes! Please, *please* hurry!"

"Okay!"

It seemed to take an hour to bring Tommy to the phone and I was trembling all over. Actually it was only five minutes before I heard his voice. Relief flowed through me at the sound.

"Travis had a fall," I told him. "I think his neck is broken!"

I could hear his gasp. He didn't want to believe what he had heard.

"Are you sure? Where are you?"

"Yes! Yes! I'm at Point Pleasant Hospital in New Jersey. Please come right away!"

"I'll be back as soon as I can get a plane. Now don't worry. I'll get hold of Doctor Bonamo and we'll find the best orthopedist in the country. I'll call you and tell you when I land. Don't worry! I'm on my way! I love you!" (Doctor Bonamo was the Yankee team physician.)

When I left the phone booth I was suddenly overwhelmed with attention. I wanted word of Travis. No report yet. The public relations man for the hospital, Bill Eastmond (whom Tommy will always describe, correctly, as a super person), came to tell me where Tommy might land if he should arrive in a chartered plane and he promised to have a police car there at whatever hour to speed Tommy to the hospital. Then two nurses appeared at my side to ask if I might like to go to the chapel. Judy and Carol joined me and together we went along to the lovely small chapel where just a few pews faced an enormous cross. It was a still, almost enchanted place. But a lump rose in my throat as if I had come into the immediate presence of death.

Oh, not my little Travis! Not that lively, happy, little blond imp with the loving heart and the quick smile! So helpless now, so pale, so far beyond my reach! I dropped almost instantly to my knees. "Oh God," I prayed, "don't take Travis! Touch him, God, and mend whatever's wrong!"

I cried aloud and shook my head in helplessness. Carol, at my side, urged me to repeat the Lord's Prayer. Never before in my life had I prayed so earnestly. But when I came to the words "Thy will be done," they stuck in my throat.

"Oh, no!" I sobbed. "Not *Thy* will! Please! *My* will! Don't take my little baby! Please God, let it be Thy will to save Travis!"

The three of us, Carol, Judy, and I, wept and prayed together. Wept aloud. There seemed no comfort. My little Travis, sinking deeper and deeper into unconsciousness, his little eyes staring at nothing. No one to hold him back. I went out and sought word from the emergency room. Nothing yet. But they needed my signature now on a paper to permit them to operate. I can't commit my baby to death, I told them. I know nothing about brain operations. I have to talk to my husband.

It won't wait, they told me. We must move at once to relieve pressure or he could die. I signed with a trembling hand. I had a desperate need now to talk to someone. In all the world, besides Tommy, there were only two people I felt sure could offer me some aid. They were the two pastors we had known in California: Pastor Lareau Lindquist and Pastor Gene Ongna. Pastor Lareau had moved to Rockford, Illinois. Pastor Gene had christened Travis and had watched our children grow up when we lived in Yorba Linda, California. He was close to them all and close to Tommy and me. So I called Gene first. The very sound of his voice comforted me. I told him in every detail what had happened to Travis, choking back my sobs as I went over the dreadful story again. I could hear the heartbreak in his voice as he answered me.

"Sally," he said, "trust in God. I will call right now and start the prayer chain through the entire church. All of us, all the friends that know and love you, will be praying for Travis! And remember, Sally, we love you!!"

The strong yet gentle tones gave me immediate comfort and even now my heart is full when I remember how this kind and, yes, holy man succeeded in transferring to me the abiding faith that guides him. Almost at once I felt new strength flowing through me, clearing my mind, quieting my heart, assuring me I was not alone. There are all those people out there, I told myself, who love me, who will join in my prayers for Travis. And I have God. God I know will keep Travis safe. For the first time since I had seen that limp little body lying there, I began to feel at peace. Then I called Pastor Lareau but could not reach him. It was a long time later that he called me and his dear voice too, so full of love and compassion, brought me added comfort.

"Put Travis in God's hands," Pastor Lareau told me. And I was able to do that—for a little while. But it was just not humanly possible to turn my mind away from what might be happening in that silent emergency room. Was he even still alive? Would someone come out soon and tell me Travis was gone? I looked out the windows to the green living trees and the grass, still bright in the fading sun, the people moving by so unconcerned, so deep in their own affairs, so *alive.* And here in the hospital everything seemed so bare, so sterile, so eloquent of illness and death.

They had given us a room where we could be by ourselves. News of the accident had already been broadcast by Phil Rizzuto, who was reporting the Yankee game on the air, and telephone calls were pouring in. But the hospital operator and the public relations office had been monitoring them carefully, calling me only for the ones they knew were urgent. (Of course I was receiving VIP treatment and I was grateful beyond words for all the kindness and concern and the manner in which everyone in the hospital seemed to take extra pains to protect me from annoyance and worry. But afterward I could not help asking myself, "What if I had been just plain Sally Simmons? Would someone whose husband was not a 'name' be treated quite so tenderly? Shouldn't *everyone* in such deep trouble receive this sort of treatment?" I wish I could believe that they would.)

I could not be still. I could not lie down and "rest," as I was so often urged to do. What mother could rest whose little boy might be dying . . . might already be dead? I went in and out of the chapel, praying with all the earnestness I could summon. I sat down. I stood up. I pestered the nurses for word, for some explanation of what might be going on behind those grimly silent doors. And the nurses were all so patient with me, answering my endless questions quietly, gently, as fully as they could. He is in the best possible hands, they told me. Trust the doctors. Two of the best neurosurgeons in the area had just happened to be making rounds and they had taken over. But of course they could tell me nothing definite. Nurses are not allowed to give opinions about the progress of an operation. All I could learn was that the doctors were operating on Travis's skull. Could I see him? Not yet. Not yet. Wait until the doctors are through. Well, I *knew* that!

The doctors are certainly the gods in a hospital. But as anyone knows who has ever been a patient or has had some dear one lying sick, the nurses are the angels. It is they who bring comfort and solace, who seem to share your concern, who try to shield you from the terrors that can rise from just not knowing what is going on. One nurse in particular will have a place in my heart as long as I live. Nor will I ever forget the truth and sincerity that shone from Mrs. Bergman's blue, blue eyes. Perhaps because she was a mother herself she knew just the words I needed to calm my fears.

She was in and out of the operating room several times, bringing me each time—not specific reports of what was happening—but at least the news that all was well, that I need not fear, that my Travis was still alive. And then finally—God bless her!—she came swiftly out of the room wearing the most beautiful smile I ever expect to see this side of Heaven. She took me right in her arms and hugged me tight. "He's all *right*!" she told me. "He's come through fine!" Naturally, not being a doctor, she could not impart any prognosis. But she did not need to. I had already read it in her smile and felt it in her joyous hug. Travis had made it. He had survived step one. Could I see him? No, I would have to wait until he had been moved to the recovery room. That seemed to take half the night. But actually it was only minutes later that I was taken into the room. "Room" indeed. It was more like a closet, with lighted screens and machinery taking up almost every inch of the space around the bed. But there was my little boy, alive, with tubes, it seemed, attached to him everywhere. His little head shaved bald and swathed in the most incredibly enormous bandage I had ever seen. "He won't know you," the doctor warned me. "He won't know what you are saying."

But his eyes were open, the pupils no larger than poppy seeds. And the tubes and wires surrounding him. His arms waving spasmodically. It was a grotesque sight I suppose but to me it could not have been more beautiful. My little boy was *alive*. They told me then that I could check his condition every twenty minutes and I followed that schedule to the second, so that the nurses declared they needed no clock to measure the intervals. When twenty minutes were up, there I was.

At one o'clock in the morning Tommy arrived. By this time, there was a crowd of reporters at the hospital doors waiting for Tommy. He had to push his way through. "How's your son, Tommy? What's the latest?" Tommy just shook his head. "I don't know any more than you do," he told them. “I’ll talk to you later.” They made way then quickly and he saw sympathy in all the faces. “Good luck, Tommy!” they called after him.

When he came in the door, I was at the other end of the hallway, and I raced down like a child to meet him. He had stopped for a brief word at the desk. Then he held me in his arms. “Travis will be okay,” he murmured. “God loves him!” Oh what a blessed relief to shed that awful weight of worry onto those broad shoulders. He was so strong and confident. I loved him so. And he was my very best friend in the world.

I’ll let him tell his part of the story now.

Tommy:

I’ll tell you the truth: I thought Travis was dead. All the way back to New Jersey I was bracing myself for the word I was almost sure was waiting for me—that my little son had died.

When Sally called first I was in the bullpen down the right field line. I was not scheduled to pitch that night but I was out there loosening up and I had just begun to get into my rhythm. It’s a good feeling when the whole machine seems to be working smoothly and I was in no hurry to stop. So when the batboy trotted out and told me I was wanted on the phone in the clubhouse, I just told him to get the number and tell them I would call back. Somebody wanting to talk to me about an endorsement, or about free tickets, I figured, and I just put it out of my mind. But the next minute out came Jeff Torborg. He was running and seemed agitated.

“It’s Sally!” he told me. “Sounds like she’s in trouble.”

I broke into a sprint then and got to that phone in seconds.

“Travis’s neck is broken!” she said. I couldn’t believe it! Was he alive? Was he in the hospital? How could his neck be broken?

"Are you sure?" It was a dumb question, of course. I just didn't want to believe it. I was trying to think of someone who could help. Dr. Bonamo, the Yankee doctor, was an orthopedist. He would know about broken necks. But I knew I would have to get to where Sally was and get there *quick*. Point Pleasant, New Jersey, Sally told me. Wherever that was! I'd find it. I told her I'd be there, just as soon as I could get on a plane. There was no questioning the fear in her voice and no doubt that Travis had been critically injured. How long could a little boy live with a broken neck? I didn't want to hear the answer to that. Not right now. I would ask Ed Oley, an old friend now working in Detroit, whom I had known since I was with the Dodgers at spring training camp in Vero Beach, to drive me to the airport. I would just have time enough to wash off the ball field dirt and get into street clothes. Ed got me out there in a matter of minutes, in plenty of time for the next nonstop to New York. Except there weren't any flights to New York! We had forgotten about the air controllers' strike.

I could, they told me, get a flight to Boston that would enable me to get to New York on the shuttle. And when would that get me there? Oh, about 2:30 A.M. And I would still have to find my way to New Jersey. That would be about ten hours from now! We could *drive* there in less time than that. Ed and I figured that with two of us driving we could average over eighty on the thruway and get to New Jersey in no more than eight hours. Should we try it? Well, I had one more idea. There was Bob Zankl, a golfing partner who had an auto agency here, and he and I had just been talking on the golf course about the private plane he owned. Maybe I could borrow that? I called Bob at his agency. His plane was in use, he said. But he knew a fellow who had a plane available right here in Pontiac, just a short ride down the road from Bob's office in Roseville. Why didn't we come over there? We sped there and learned that the plane was all gassed up and ready. Just a matter of getting clearance, of making sure there would be an airport open. I called the Point Pleasant Hospital then and learned that Monmouth County Airport was nearest, that they would see that the airport was open, and that there would be a police car there to speed me to the hospital. Travis? He was still alive and in surgery. Oh, hold on little boy, I prayed. Hold on for Daddy! Sally came on the line and she groaned when she learned I was still in Michigan. "Oh, hurry! Hurry!" she cried. "Travis is in *critical* condition! I don't know if he'll *last*!" With that thought lying heavy on my heart, I climbed into the plane—a two-engine Cessna—and we were off on what seemed the longest flight of my life. For much of the time in the air I shut my eyes and prayed just as hard as I knew how that God would spare my little boy, that Sally would hold up until I could get her in my arms, that my little boy would not be suffering, that he might last at least until I could see him once more. I took time, too, to get myself ready for the moment when they told me Travis was gone. Would they tell me when I got to the hospital? Would they try to soften the blow? I would have to take it as calmly as I could, for Sally's sake.

The trip seemed to be taking all night, yet it was only two and a half hours later that we reached Monmouth. The police car was waiting, just as promised, its lights all ablaze, and an officer ready to lead me to it as soon as I could get out of the plane. A quick thank you to the pilot, a half-sprint to the car and we were off, with the siren blasting the birds awake. Now my heart really got up there into my throat. I knew he was dead. I *knew* he was dead! Or did I just keep telling myself that to make ready for the shock?

There was a small cluster of people outside the hospital door. Reporters! They must have been from the networks and wire services, for I saw no familiar faces. They moved close but they did not get in my way.

"How is he, Tommy?" "How's your son?" "Is he all right, Tommy?"

I shook my head and told them I didn't know any more

than they did. How could I? I would talk to them later. There were murmurs of sympathy all around. "Good luck, Tommy!" one man said in my ear.

In the hospital I went right to the desk. I wanted the news *before* I talked to Sally.

"His condition is guarded," said the lady solemnly.

Now what did that mean? It meant he was alive at least. I felt the tension in my chest let go. Now we would get him well. With God's help, we would get him well.

I turned and saw Sally at the far end of the hall and she raced up to meet me. While we hung on to each other I told her: "Travis is going to be all right. God loves him, Sally. He'll be all right." She seemed to sag into my arms as if she was shifting all the weight to me. That was all right. That's what I came for.

The nurses brought us into the intensive care room to see Travis. There he lay, his head shaved, all wired up like a mechanical toy, with monitors blip-blipping all around. The room was barely big enough to hold us, just a make-shift arrangement while they completed alterations on the regular unit. Little Travis was trussed to the table to keep him from thrashing about. Of course he did not know us, although his eyes were open. But it was enough for me to see that he was really alive, breathing, moving, with the blood flowing through his cheeks.

It turned out his neck was not broken at all but that there was real danger of brain damage. Because his fall had been broken, he did not hit the concrete with full impact. (Sally told me that, after first parking the car just inside the drive, she decided she must leave room for Judy's car and so pulled her car tight against the house.) They had drilled four holes in his little skull to ease pressure on his brain. And now the room was cold as a refrigerator to lessen the chance of edema, or swelling of the brain. The doctors who, Sally told me, had promised to be here to talk to me when I arrived had long ago gone home and the nurses could not say much more than that

Travis was "doing okay." We must have heard that phrase two hundred times before the ordeal was over. Of course it meant no more than that he was alive and we knew that already. But that's the way it is in medicine. Nurses aren't supposed to be as smart as doctors and are never allowed to give opinions. Still, it was possible to learn something from a facial expression—a quick smile was always good news. But we lived in dread of seeing someone come forward with a solemn face. Fear, believe, me, was thick as soup in that tiny room.

Sally, while I was on the way, had had a call from a doctor friend in California, Stu Siegel, who was the chief doctor of hematology and oncology at Children's Hospital in Los Angeles. He and his wife Linda had become very close to us through the golf tournament I sponsor there for the benefit of cancer research at the hospital. Stu had gotten all the details of Travis's injury from Sally—and believe me she had noticed and remembered everything, down to the amount of blood trickling from Travis's ear.

How Stu happened to call is a story by itself. He had been driving home on the freeway about 10:45 P.M. after an evening meeting when he heard on the news broadcast that "the son of Tommy John, the Yankee pitcher," had been injured in a fall.

"I almost swerved off the road," he told us later. But he kept going, a good deal faster now, and reached home in ten minutes. When he told Linda what he had heard she urged him to call us right away, that night, to offer whatever help he could give. But it was after 2 A.M. in New Jersey, he told her, and he had no idea where Travis had been hospitalized. Then call the sports people at the Los Angeles *Times* and ask them to find out, she urged him. Stu called and at first ran into a blank wall. Whoever the fellow was who answered, he knew it was not policy to give out such information. But when Stu explained he was a physician and a personal friend who wanted to give medical advice if it was needed, the guy agreed right away to find out what he could. He came back in a minute or two with the name of the hospital. Stu got that number and called right away. Another blank wall. The hospital operator would not put the call through to Sally. After Stu had identified himself and explained his purpose, there was another long time out while the operator verified his identity through some official sources. Finally, they put the call through to Sally in the intensive care unit and Sally was able to provide all the details he needed to get at least a rough idea of Travis's condition. (Why is it, I wonder, that men are so often stymied by rules and regulations—They aren't allowed to do that! It's too early in the morning! That guy won't know the answer!—while women often go straight to the goal? Thank God, anyway, for Sally and Linda, who were not going to be put off by any petty obstacles.)

While we were waiting to hear from Stu Seigel, a call came in from Dr. Bonamo's office, whom I had called before leaving Detroit, and I told them the latest—that Travis's neck was not broken but that there was danger of brain damage. In a very little while they came up with the name of the doctor whom Bonamo and his staff rated the very finest pediatric neurosurgeon in the country—Dr. Fred Epstein at the NYU Medical Center in New York. Then Stu Seigel called and said *he* had the name of the best pediatric neurosurgeon in the land: Dr. Fred Epstein. And he urged me:

"Get Travis out of there, Tommy! Get him to a *medical center* where they have a CAT scanner and all the facilities right at hand. Don't take no for an answer. He's got to be moved to where they can get everything they need in a hurry! I'm sure Travis will make it through the night now. But move him in the morning!"

Sally and I—after a long, long talk and a lot of hard thinking and praying—decided then that we would move him, provided Dr. Epstein would accept the case. It was now three-thirty in the morning. We got the telephone number and Sally was all for calling him at once. What's the point? I said. He won't answer the call until he gets up anyway. Let's wait until a decent hour and then put it to him and hope he agrees. Sally would wait no longer than seven-thirty so I put the call through to the answering service at that time even though I knew full well no doctor was going to check his calls until after he'd had his breakfast. That's where I was wrong. It was just seven-forty-five when Dr. Epstein called, listened to our story and said immediately that he would accept the case.

(He told us much later that he had heard about Travis's accident on the radio at eleven-thirty that night and, being completely exhausted from an extra long day in the operating room, had actually told himself: "Thank God I don't have *that* job!")

Dr. Epstein now had to talk to the doctors in charge at Point Pleasant. And *I* had to persuade Sally to make the move *now*. Sally dug in her heels. It was *dangerous* to move Travis so soon! How would they ever get him all the way to New York City? Helicopter, I said. A helicopter? He's got all that machinery hooked up to him. What if something breaks? What if a tube gets disconnected? If there was anything Sally feared more than spiders it was helicopters! What if it fell?

Listen, I said. Helicopters don't fall. Dr. Epstein is the best in the country. He wouldn't suggest moving him if there was *any* danger. And we have got to get Travis to where he can get the very best help. We take a bigger chance by leaving him here after Stu Seigel and Dr. Epstein both say he should be moved. Now, he's going to be moved and that's all there is to it. Sally saw the point—or was relieved to let me make the decision. And now we had to break the news to the doctors in charge here. They were strongly against it. And, believe me, I knew exactly how they felt. Nobody wants to be yanked out of a ball game when he feels he has everything under control. These were two of the best doctors in the whole New York area and they were not going to grant that somebody else could step in and do better. One of them had been a classmate of Dr. Epstein's in medical school and felt, quite naturally, that he had learned just as much as Epstein had. But Sally and I were the Steinbrenners of this game and if we thought it was time to call in a reliever that's what it was going to be. And anyway, had they not already arranged to have Travis moved to a Toms River hospital, a twenty-minute ambulance ride away, to have a CAT scan done?

The doctors finally gave in with a solemn warning that they would not guarantee that Travis would survive the trip. Bill Eastmond, my idea of what every public relations man ought to model himself on, then took over, arranging for a small police helicopter to transfer Travis and necessary medical people to New York City. With the greatest tenderness and care the hospital personnel moved Travis, with all the life-support paraphernalia, to the ambulance and then to the waiting helicopter, while we watched in something like dread.

The scene at the airport resembled a shot from "Emergency!"—one tiny bandaged and wired-up figure, surrounded by bearers, Dr. Weinstein, a neurosurgeon from Point Pleasant Hospital, and life-support people, being handed up into a muttering helicopter on a stretcher, along with a respirator and a mess of machinery. The doctor had decided there was absolutely no room on the helicopter for Sally and me, so Bill Eastmond had quickly laid on *another* helicopter to carry Sally, me, and Carol Schaefer, who had left her own kids at home to see us through, as she had promised.

What a ride that was! Completely unreal! More and more like a scene from a movie, one clattering helicopter trailing another across the sky. We flew right over the Schaefers' house where all the kids, Carol's, Judy's, and our own, stood and gaped at us. Our machine had no pontoons so we could not take the short route over the water and had to let the other copter veer away from us, almost out of sight while Sally pressed her face against the glass, watching Travis's copter vanish, and prayed out loud that he would get there alive.

Is this really happening? I asked myself. It was too much like a TV show with all the familiar scenery below—even the Statue of Liberty, the Empire State Building, the East River bridges, all looking just as they did in the movies. The beautiful sights I had loved all seemed so meaningless now, almost unreal.

Travis's helicopter came into sight again and we closed in on it, so by the time we came in view of the Thirty-fourth Street pad we were back in formation—too close for me! For a time it seemed as if those whirling blades might lock into each other. Sally was not the only one who prayed out loud right then.

As we hovered over the landing pad, I could see a crowd waiting for Travis's copter to land. My God! It was a crowd of reporters again, only twice as many this time, along with movie cameras, TV cameras, TV trucks. Sally screamed: "You can't take pictures of my baby! Not Travis! He may not be alive! Oh, get them *out* of there!" Carol Schaefer started shaking our pilot by the shoulder: "Oh do something!" she yelled. "Don't let them take pictures!"

"Nothing I can do up here," said the pilot, who was right then trying to maneuver for landing. I reached out and, as gently as I could, took Carol's hand away from his shoulder.

By the time our copter landed I knew what I had to do—quick! I had drunk something like thirty cups of coffee through the night and at that moment what I wanted most in the world was the men's room. We put down, gently as putting a baby to bed, right beside the enormous oversize trailer, or whatever, and I took off, ducking low to keep my head from being sliced off by the slowly swinging blades. First I got word from Travis's attendants that he was still alive. I spotted the men's room then and headed for it without a glance right or left. But just as I got through the door I realized that Sally and Carol had come trotting along behind like two little trained ducks. One glance at the unfamiliar plumbing and with one voice they let out a tiny shriek and plunged back outside. They were standing there, looking foolish, when I came out.

The guys with the cameras surrounded us, trying it seemed for shots from every angle. I saw Carol heft her pocketbook as if she would belt a camera out of somebody's hand. Fortunately, her good sense took hold and we got out without violence. When we started out the gates of the heliport, two cops held us up and assured us we were not going anywhere. "That's my son in that ambulance," I told them. Their expressions underwent a quick change from hostile to concerned. "Sorry, Tommy!" they chorused and showed us to the waiting police car. But even in the car we were not secure from reporters and photographers. Some of the cameras were shoved right against the closed windows while reporters kept yelling stupid questions. But before I could snarl any kind of response Sally said, very coldly: "Please, let us be with our son." That seemed to chill a few of the people and enough fell away so the car could move.

NYU Medical Center was just around the corner and in about two minutes we rolled to the emergency entrance right behind the ambulance that was carrying Travis. Getting inside the hospital was like finding dry land in a flood. Guards kept the press people away from the doors, while the public relations people fended them off until we could get through. They led us through the emergency room and up to the "Pediatric Intensive Care Waiting Room," a barren white cubicle looking as sterile as an operating room, with stainless steel tables, a lone TV set, and X-ray viewers along with a few straight chairs. We slumped into chairs and Sally laid her head right on the cool table top. She was going strictly on adrenaline now. We had tried to get her to eat something at the Point Pleasant Hospital by telling her she had to keep up her strength for the baby she was carrying. But all she had been able to choke down was a single bite of a roast beef sandwich. The weaker sex! That day she had the strength of a lioness.

We waited there in silence, each of us, I am sure, more than half-scared of what news an opening door might bring us. The door did open at last and I was amazed to see—not a solemn-faced doctor in a long white gown but a pleasant-looking guy in a neat dark tropical suit with a blue-striped shirt and matching tie. His greeting was as informal as if we ran into each other every day and he told us his findings without preliminary.

Travis had come through the trip in good shape. They had completed the first tests and could see no indication of irreversible brain damage. (Sally and I hugged each other at that news.) There were more tests to come. They would have to make one more opening in the skull. Then it would be a long time for recuperation. How long? No telling. Maybe months. The next twelve hours would tell. (That assurance was to be repeated again and again—the next twenty-four hours, the next seventy-two, the next week.)

Sally had a dozen questions to ask, questions I would never have thought of. Were there any broken bones? No, his fall must have been softened somehow (the hood of Sally's car!). What about internal organs—the spleen? the pancreas? Dr. Epstein answered every question as patiently as a teacher dealing with a child, with no superior smiles or know-it-all airs. Sally was much taken with this man. So was I. I felt as if we were in the hands of an All-Star. I asked him if there were any machines or implements needed that were not on hand here and assured him that we would get *anything*, regardless of expense. No, he said, all the necessary equipment was right here and all the tests could be done swiftly.

Now Sally took a deep breath and asked the big question: "On a scale of one to ten, what are Travis's chances of getting out of this undamaged?" Dr. Epstein thought for a minute or so. "I would say about a seven." Well that was good! That was *damn* good! Sally and I had the same thought now: Thank God we are at NYU! Thanks to God for guiding us here.

While we were still in conversation with Dr. Epstein, in

walked two of the finest people in the world—Jerry Murphy and Betsy Leesman from the Yankee front office. Jerry had come, he said, to see what we needed to have done. How about a hotel? No, I thought we would stay right here. Well, you need a room to change clothes now and then, wash up, to take a nap. I'll get it! The Yankees will pay for it. We agreed to this and Jerry made a reservation at the Grand Hyatt, just a few short blocks up Lexington Avenue. He made the reservation in his own name to keep us safe from reporters and photographers. And he got a room for Carol too, when he found she was determined to stay by Sally's side. (Somebody has to be there all the time, she said, in case of bad news.)

Betsy had reports to give us about the flood of phone calls that had been keeping the Yankee switchboard lighted up all day. David Hartman—an old friend from my days with the Dodgers—had called to say he and his wife Maureen were badly shaken. Richard Nixon had called. Fans from California had called. We were really strengthened by news of all this friendship and concern. As for Betsy herself, I only wish I could believe that George Steinbrenner knows what a prize he has in her—a beautiful, unaffected, sincere young lady, completely unselfish, as warmhearted a person as you'll ever meet. What did we need, she asked us. Anything! We'll get it for you! She went to Travis's bedside and looked at him with tears in her eyes. "He's so beautiful," she whispered. "And I *know* he'll be all right. He's in God's eyes."

Calls were coming into the hospital, swamping the phone operators. And people were coming in by the dozen. This had its unpleasant side, for there were, the public relations people warned us, a good percentage of wackos among them—guys with some crackpot remedy to offer, nuts who wanted to give Travis magic potions. But in general the visitors and the callers were generous, kindly people who were honestly concerned. Some brought enormous bouquets. Some carried whole bunches of balloons, all with get-well messages on them.

It's hard to keep track of all the things that happened on those first few days. Travis had his ups and downs—sometimes opening his eyes, sometimes seeming to sink away from us. Sally and I stayed right by Travis's bedside until finally the doctors and nurses ganged up to insist that if Sally at least didn't get some sleep they would have another patient to find a bed for. But before Sally would agree to go to the hotel she extracted a promise from Dr. Epstein that he would stay right there all night. Carol and I managed then to drag Sally to the hotel. There was a limousine waiting for us, ordered by the Yankees, but between us and the limousine were a handful of reporters and photographers from the New York newspapers. Sally broke into a run and jumped into the limousine before they could intercept her. But I had always found the New York reporters a pretty decent bunch and I just told them: "Some other time please. Sally and I are exhausted." Their papers, they told us, had been swamped with calls from fans of mine all through the area who wanted to know how Travis was doing. Weary as I was, the realization that so many people cared about us gave me a sudden lift. I told the press people thanks and, even though they must have been waiting for hours, they fell back without any protest. The limousine had us at the hotel in less than five minutes and we were too weary to exchange a word. Both of us were so done in, we were just barely able to put one foot ahead of the other. The hotel people were as considerate as could be, assuring us that they were all praying for Travis. It was all I could do to murmur my thanks but Sally had a word for everyone.

Carol Schaefer had been given a room near ours—and that was another weird story, to go with some of the far-out happenings that had made this whole time seem like a crazy man's dream. When she first checked into her room she carried nothing but her purse, which she took with her when she hurried back to the hospital. Then when she returned at about three in the morning she opened her door and saw two eyes staring at her from her bed. She let out a scream that must have awakened the whole corridor. It sure put some life back into my limbs. I reached her room—just down the corridor—in about two jumps. There was some guy in his night-clothes in her bed, and insisting that she had no right in the room.

"What on earth are *you* doing in this lady's room?" I yelled at him.

I was about ready to strong-arm this seeming weirdo right out into the hallway when I happened to notice that the long white garment lying on the bed was a wedding dress! And before I had completely absorbed this fact, the bathroom door opened and a young lady in her nightgown joined the company.

"What's going on?" I gasped. "Is this your . . . ?"

"It's our wedding night," said the man on the bed. "And I want to know how she happened to get a key. . . ."

We straightened that part out in a hurry. The management found Carol a room on another floor (finding no baggage in her room they had assumed it had been vacated) and the happy couple were left in peace.

Sally had little peace however. She flopped into bed and right away dialed the number Dr. Epstein had given her.

"How is Travis?"

"Just the same as when you left him an hour ago, Mrs. John." Later on, I woke out of a sound sleep to hear the same conversation. But I'll let Sally tell about it.

Sally:

It was only forty minutes between my first call from the hotel and my second. I thought it was an hour or more. "Get some sleep," they told me. "You need it."

"Do I bother you by calling?"

"Not at all," said that blessed nurse. "But we're worried about you. You *must* get some sleep!"

I did get some sleep, perhaps a whole hour, before I reached for the phone once more. Tommy, now dead to the world, did not even stir as I murmured into the phone and again heard the answer: "The same, Mrs. John."

"What time is it?"

"It's four A.M."

"O.K. I'll sleep."

This time I slept for two hours. There was light in the sky when I dialed again and Tommy was still deep in dreamland.

"How's Travis?"

"The same. But he moved his left arm and leg a little."

He moved! I slid out of bed, dressed quickly, pulled the covers up over Tommy, kissed his cheek, scribbled him a note, called Carol, found a taxicab and reached the hospital at half-past six. I ran full speed into the Intensive Care Unit. "He moved!" I cried.

"Yes," they assured me. "But please don't get too excited about it. Comatose patients often make these movements." There will be peaks and valleys. Dr. Epstein had warned me. Don't despair at the valleys. Don't let your hopes get too high at the peaks. Was this a peak? I sat with Carol at Travis's bedside for two long hours and the little body did not even twitch. Then I recalled I had seen a policeman standing outside the door of the Intensive Care Unit. How come? I wondered.

It turned out that the hospital had received kidnapping threats and that one strangely acting character had tried to make his way to the room. But they did not tell me this right away. They were just "making sure" that no unauthorized people came in. I am convinced there was much more to this than we were ever told, for the hospital authorities must have decided I had worries enough without this added fear. Tommy actually did see one of the "characters" who tried to reach Travis's bedside. He was a very intense-looking man wearing a black coat and a hat, Tommy said, that looked as if it had come out of a circus, who told the guard that he knew a way to "take care of" Travis. The guard hustled him out and later told us that he had been carrying "a weapon." Just what sort of weapon they never said and I did not want to hear. It sickened me that there could be people in the world who would want to do harm to a little boy who lay near death.

But the world was full, too, of people who kept Travis in their thoughts and prayers, and people who tried earnestly to make things easier for us. While we had not lived in the Jersey area long enough to make many friends, there were two neighboring families who opened their hearts to us. The Irv Paulus family, knowing that Judy, my sister, had more than both hands full taking care of her own brood and mine as she tried to make ready to drive back to Indiana, took the car to the garage, had it fully serviced and filled with gas, and brought it back ready to go. And the Larry Kohans offered to take the children into their own home and to provide whatever transportation we needed back and forth to the hospital and to bring anything we asked for. Tami flew back from Judy's to stay with the Kohans so that she could start school on time. Ed, who ran the local gas station, called to offer a hand and to assure us that Travis was in his prayers. So did Bruno, the tailor, and Sal, Tommy's favorite barber. Mayor Vichiconti of Franklin Lakes sent us a beautiful letter offering his help. What a sense of strength and support this gave us! I realized then—not for the first time—that while God may not always give you what you pray for, prayer does give you a knowledge of God's presence—within you and all around you—a realization that you are not alone in your troubles, that your cares are His cares, and that you are, though small, an important part of His Great Plan.

I had asked my sister Judy to call our mother and father. I did not want them to hear about Travis over the radio, or in the course of the baseball game. And Dad was addicted to baseball broadcasts. He had had some bad times with his heart and I feared any sudden shock. Judy did call and found Dad home by himself, so she tried to make the call sound casual. She found out where Mom was, then asked him: "Were you listening to a baseball game?"

"No. Damn it all. I can't seem to get Detroit on this radio. Why? Is Tommy pitching?"

"Oh, no. I just wondered. I'll call Mom later. I love you." Judy immediately called Mom at the house Dad said she was visiting and told her please to get home and be with Dad. Travis had had an accident, she told her, and was in surgery. "We don't know much," said Judy. "Just pray and stay with Dad."

What we did not know was that the news had been broadcast all over the country and an old friend of Dad's in Houston called right after Judy did and broke the news rather abruptly. Dad took it well enough but this added one more worry to our store.

But, of course, the worry about Travis overrode everything. The first week or so, I simply lost track of time and to this day I cannot be sure just what the exact sequence of events was. Travis did indeed experience those peaks and valleys Dr. Epstein had warned me of. And he sank into one "valley" that really scared us all skinny. I awoke about five-thirty in the morning at the hotel and, as was my habit, immediately called the hospital. Again the word that Travis was "just the same"—*but* (and she seemed to try to make this as casual as possible) they had had to put him on a respirator. Wasn't he *breathing?* Oh, yes. This was just a precaution. Oh BULL! I told myself I am not quite *that* dumb! I had got into the routine of climbing into my clothes like a fireman. Just fifteen minutes later I was in the Pediatric Intensive Care Unit and I was aghast at what I saw. All this machinery surrounding my baby! The ominous blip-blipping of the monitors, the dreadful sighing of the respirator! Dr. Epstein had told me earlier: "His breathing without help is a good sign." But he was *not* breathing without help! I was shaken right down to my shoes. I was actually watching my dear baby slip away from me. I sat close by his side and begged God not to take him away. And I begged Travis to hold tight to life.

"Please, *please* be strong," I beseeched him. "Don't give up! You are a tough little boy. Your brother Tommy and your sister Tami love you and miss you and want you to come home and play. They want you to be with them when they watch the Muppets. (The Muppets were his favorite TV people and he would watch them right through without fail. He had memorized "The Rainbow Connection" and would pretend to be strumming his guitar, just like Kermit the Frog.) Mommy and Daddy love you and want you home. Don't quit! You're a fighter, just like your daddy!"

As I prayed God not to take my baby, I put my hands on Travis's little suntanned arms, so limp and lifeless now, and I stroked those sturdy little legs and wept at the softness, the *innocence* of the skin. Carol Schaefer joined me then and I saw her face turn white at the sight of the respirator. She had no chance to speak before Dr. Zimmerman, the head pediatrician, and perhaps the most brilliant man I ever met, came in and I turned to him with a cry: "What does this mean? Truly? Will my baby live?"

Dr. Zimmerman explained that it was "precautionary" and when I grimaced at that term, he went on to say that Travis had weakened but he had *not* stopped breathing. And to prove it, he turned off the respirator and let us see that Travis's little chest rose and fell on its own. But the monitor showed how weak the respiration had become. The respirator would help ease the strain. It would also cause Travis to "hyperventilate," to breathe harder and faster, and this would diminish the carbon dioxide content of his blood.

I think I must have asked Dr. Zimmerman a hundred questions, seeking some reassurance. And he answered me specifically, patiently, graciously, just as Dr. Epstein had done. He was comforting. But there was a look in his eye—

was it doubt? sympathy?—that scared me. I knew my little boy was in dangerous condition.

Carol and I both felt a powerful need to do *something*. Perhaps there was some treatment, some apparatus, some medicine that would help. Carol took to the telephone and called everyone she knew or had heard of who had any connection with medicine. She called Columbia Presbyterian Medical Center, and Yale University Hospital, I can't begin to name them all. Of course, it seems foolish now for us to think that we could have uncovered anything these great doctors had not heard of. But it relieved the awful strain to be making an effort to help.

Tommy came in while we were still busy with this search, and I ran and hugged him tight. He always seemed so capable and confident, his mere presence made this easier to bear. But he turned pale too when he saw the breathing machine and it was my turn to offer reassurance by telling him how Dr. Zimmerman had demonstrated that Travis could breathe on his own. But we could not rid ourselves of the fear that our baby was gradually slipping away.

We sat together then on opposite sides of Travis and, as we prayed together for God's help in making our baby well, we began to move his legs and arms gently, and to massage them, and to move his fingers and toes. We both knew that this sort of thing was important in maintaining tone in immobilized muscles.

I had already told myself that I would never leave my baby's side as long as there was breath in his body. If he stayed in a coma for months, as I knew he might, I would stay right here to keep these little arms and legs mobile. Tommy of course had his job to occupy him, and I knew by this time that it was far more than a job. I had seen the pain, the strain, the endless labor he had gone through after a severe injury to make his way back into baseball. I recalled how he had lent himself with such fervor to a regime that anyone with less faith and less determination would have been simply unable to stick to—dreary exercises, painful repetition of efforts to make useless muscles work again, daily disappointments, skepticism of those around him, even ill-concealed pity and clumsy efforts to help him get "adjusted" to finding another way of making a living. But Tommy, spurred by his faith that "nothing is impossible with God" (words quoted to him by our beloved Pastor Lareau) kept plugging, even inching along toward his single goal—to get back into baseball again and earn his way. And I shared the almost delirious triumph when he not only reached that goal but went on to place himself at the very top of the profession.

It was not in my heart to ask Tommy to abandon all that he had so dearly won. I knew that I would devote all *my* waking hours from now on to seeing Travis through to health again. And of course I wanted Tommy by my side all through it. But I had been a baseball wife long enough to become adjusted to long road trips, night games, and sudden disruptions of home schedules. When I told Tommy my plan to stay by Travis's side for as long as he was hospitalized, it was really not my plan to try to talk him into staying with me. But he looked me steadily in the eye for a time, then said: "I'll stay with you at Travis's side no matter how long it takes. He may be six months in a coma, maybe eight months. Maybe it will take a year for him to recover full use of his muscles. It doesn't matter. If it means giving up baseball, I'll give up baseball. I am sure God intends for me to be with you and Travis. We can sell our house and take an apartment. We can put Tommy in a nearby nursery school. We can find a private school for Tami. As for the new baby (remember, I was six months pregnant), why the maternity floor is right above us and we can keep the whole family right here. Whatever it costs in time or money, I think we should pay it. Nothing is more important to me than getting Travis back to health. Even if it is only one chance in a hundred, we'll take that chance. Let's have faith that God will show us the way."

Up until that moment I thought I could not possibly love Tommy John more deeply than I had for the years of our marriage. Now suddenly I was simply inundated by a love so overwhelming, so all-encompassing, it could never be expressed in words. Oh, Tommy! How perfectly you have set our goals! What a fine, what a selfless person you are! And how I love you! I tried to speak. Instead, I simply put my face in my hands and wept.

TWO

Tommy:

As far as I was concerned there was never any choice. How can you choose baseball—or any job, or any profession—ahead of your little boy? If ever there was a time that Travis needed his family right at his side, this was it. Could I ever sleep at night with the thought that I had shirked the job of bringing my little son back to full health and strength? And how could I ask favors of God, if I was unwilling to sacrifice my own ambition? Sally and I both knew, from our own bitter experience, how vital it was that paralyzed limbs be exercised and massaged regularly if ever they are to return to normal. So we pledged ourselves to the tasks of keeping those little muscles from deteriorating, of never-ceasing effort to get through to that little mind and start it functioning normally again, and to offer devout and regular prayer at Travis's side to beseech the constant intervention of the God who had been our ever-present aid in all our previous (and now seemingly minor) difficulties.

Sally and I maintained our vigil together, with our friend Carol Schaefer often on hand to help. (She had vowed to Sally: "I am going to stay with you through all of this!") We massaged the seemingly nerveless arms and legs. We moved each tiny finger and toe. We spoke constantly to Travis of our love and need for him. Carol and Sally sometimes sang to him in low tones: "Amazing Grace" or "I Come to the Garden Alone."

After several days, when Travis's condition began to stabilize and the real question was how soon, if ever, he would be able to walk and talk, Sally and I would spend our long vigil hours reliving our lives together. Baseball was far from our minds most of the time but inevitably we talked about the part it had played in our lives. I know that when we met, Sally was about as ignorant on the subject of baseball as a young person born in America could ever be. If someone had told her, when we met, that the Chicago White Sox were a hockey team sponsored by a hosiery company, she'd have believed it. The only baseball players she knew about were Pete Rose, from nearby Cincinnati, and Mickey Mantle, and she wasn't sure what club Mickey played for or what position he played. Still, she picked up the fundamentals of the game quickly because, despite all its complications and mystifying statistics, baseball is essentially a simple game that probably derived originally from a game of tag. Almost every American child, I think, has played some sort of game where you kicked or threw a stick or a ball as far as you could and then tried to get to a base and back before the object could be retrieved and either placed back in position at the "home" base or used to tag the runner "out" before he reached the safety of a post or base, or circle in the dirt.

When baseball was first played in this country, it was not much more complicated than that. The runner, in the early days, and even many years later in some parts of the land, could be declared out if he was hit with the ball while he was not safely in contact with a base. The great Rube Waddell, who became a famous pitcher for the Philadelphia Athletics in the early twentieth century, one time in a big-league game forgot himself and "plugged" a runner with the ball when the runner was between bases. "That's *out*, where I come from!" he declared.

But it was not "out" in the leagues then, or now. Now you have to lay the ball on the runner with your hand, or get it to the base ahead of him.

Originally, too, the pitcher was about the least important player on the team. His job was simply to serve the ball up, underhand, for the batter to hit and he had to keep tossing them up until the batter found a ball he liked and hit it. Finally, when people got tired of the endless waiting for the batter to see something to his liking, they began to put restrictions on him—to call "strikes" if he did not swing at a fair pitch or if he swung at it and missed, and to call "wides" or "balls" on the pitcher if he did not get the ball reasonably close to the area where the batter could hit it. Eventually they settled on the present plan of calling the batter "out" if he swung at and missed three pitches, or let three good pitches go by. The umpire of course had to decide if a pitch was good enough to be called a strike, or if it was a "ball." And four "balls" would allow the batter to go to first base free. Then it was up to his mates to push him around all three bases until he got "home" and a run was scored for his side.

Under this scheme, the pitcher became the most important man on the team, for it was up to him to throw the ball up so that the batter would miss it, would let it go by, thinking it was no good, or would hit it so poorly that someone in the field could catch it on the fly or grab it up and throw it to first base before the runner got there. And that, to shorten the tale, is why I became a pitcher—and why I became so hooked on baseball that I have stayed in it for twenty years and hope to stay, in some capacity, for another thirty, at least. (Connie Mack, owner-manager of the former Philadelphia Athletics, stayed in professional baseball for sixty-four years.)

What attracted me to pitching, I guess, was simply that the pitcher is in charge of the ball, obviously the most valuable player on the field. But what keeps me hooked on it is the cat-and-mouse game the pitcher must play every day, with every batter. This keeps the game always new, always tantalizing, always demanding new ways of thinking and new ways of working. Once it became the pitcher's job to *prevent* the batter from hitting safely, baseball became a grown-up game that can involve both players and watchers completely.

My basic theory is that the pitcher must keep the batter guessing, keep him off balance, by delivering the ball faster than the batter expects—or more slowly.

Of course, if a pitcher can propel the ball at a speed of better than ninety miles an hour—as pitchers like Nolan Ryan and Goose Gossage can—he can get by on his fast ball alone because *every* pitch will reach the batter sooner than he expects it to, and sooner than he can get ready for it. But a fast ball doesn't last forever. Even the guys with the most smoke reach an age when the muscles just can't deliver the ninety-mile speed and the fast pitch begins to come up a little short. Many a pitching coach, in my hearing, has said about a fast-ball pitcher: "He'll learn to pitch when he loses his fast ball," meaning that then, to stay in his job, he will be forced to develop some sort of off-speed pitch that will make the batter, who is looking for the fast ball, lose his timing, start to swing too soon, and be unable to get his full strength into the swing or be unable to meet the ball squarely.

But why should a pitcher wait until his fast ball is gone? Every successful pitcher, any pitcher, that is, who has managed to stay on top season after season, has ultimately turned to an off-speed pitch to keep batters off balance. Sandy Koufax, who could throw about as hard as any pitcher I ever saw, made constant use, at the end of his career, of a fork ball—a ball thrown, that is, from the "fork" made by spreading the first two fingers, so that the grip is much looser and does not impart the spin that makes a ball with back-spin travel so fast. Throwing the ball without much spin is the purpose of all sorts of trick pitches—the knuckle ball, the illegal spitball, the palm ball, and even the illegal but still occasionally used Vaseline ball. When a batter tries to hit a palm ball, because the body and arm motions of the pitcher look just about the same as they do on any other pitch, there is a real illusion that often causes the batter to swing at empty air.

But a pitcher can change speeds without resorting to trick pitches. By shortening or lengthening his stride, or by dragging his back foot over the mound instead of pushing off the mound with full strength, a pitcher can slow down his delivery just enough to upset the batter's timing by a fraction of a second.

Preacher Roe, whose fast ball would not black your eye, owed his effectiveness to his ability to slow down his pitches so that by contrast his "fast" ball, when it came, seemed to be traveling ninety miles an hour. The Preacher also confessed to deluding batters sometimes by using saliva to make the ball slippery so it would not spin. This "spitball," long against the rules, was originally called a "thumb ball" because only the thumb provided any spin. The pitch, slipping off the two top fingers, would then rapidly drop from the friction of the thumb. This change in aerodynamics, giving the ball a different spin, would cause the ball to fall away from the batter.

Even Goose Gossage, who can throw his fast ball through the side of a tank, has developed an off-speed pitch lately—a slider that, because it is thrown rather like a football, with the fingers on the sides of the ball rather than top and bottom, fades a little as it approaches the plate and moves away from the batter. The batter, after telling himself perhaps that he has finally timed that fearsome fast ball, starts his swing too soon and is unable to meet the ball with full strength—if indeed he hits it at all.

Robin Roberts, one of the real power pitchers of my early days and one I idolized when I was a youngster, fooled the batter by his easy, apparently effortless motion, from which his pitch seemed to explode. It was like a high-speed projectile suddenly booming out of a popgun. Tom Seaver, now back with the New York Mets, has a motion almost exactly like Roberts's.

Of course there is a good deal more to pitching than just changing speeds in this manner. Batters, being just as smart (sometimes) as pitchers are, scheme right along with the pitcher, trying to get him into a spot where he has to throw the pitch they are looking for. One of the facts of life that a professional pitcher, who faces the same batters season after season, has to face is that batters can improve, not just from year to year, but from game to game and sometimes even from inning to inning. For instance, when Brooks Robinson first started in the American League with Baltimore, he was known as a man who had a hard time hitting a curve. But after seeing—and making out on—all kinds of curves, Brooks gradually made himself into one of the best curveball hitters in the business, particularly with runners in scoring position or with the pitcher ahead on the count. Although I never faced Gene Woodling, famed Yankee outfielder, I know that he had the same experience—seeing curves so often that he developed unusual skill at hitting them, although he had been an almost sure out on a good curve when he started.

A really seasoned batter, like Graig Nettles, can go to school on a pitcher in a game, taking note of the pitch the pitcher may have made him look bad on, and getting ready to see that pitch next time at bat, or when the situation is such that the pitcher *has* to get Graig out. And perhaps after two or three looks at it, he can figure out how to nail it—and make the pitcher sorry he had tried it just once too often. They say that Ty Cobb, called by many people the best hitter who ever lived, would sometimes make himself look bad on a pitch, just so he could be sure of getting that pitch when a hit was needed to bring a runner in to score.

Naturally, batters can learn to hit other pitches besides

curves, if they see them often enough. Power hitters are supposed to dote on fast balls. Mickey Mantle, who still holds the record for home runs in postseason games, used to have Bob Turley let out with a piercing whistle whenever Turley caught an indication that the pitcher was going to let go a fast ball. Mantle would then get ready to swing with full strength. (Turley is probably the best there ever was at "reading" a pitcher's intent by noticing differences in the way he wound up or held his hands, or moved his head or feet.)

But other heavy hitters, from seeing so many off-speed pitches—curves, which are usually noticeably slower than fast balls, fork balls and such—develop skill at timing them and hitting them squarely. Reggie Jackson is one of the best at hitting off-speed stuff—the "hanging" curve, the mediocre fast ball, or a knuckle ball that "hangs"—i.e., fails to break.

That is where the cat-and-mouse aspect of the game comes in, with the cat—the pitcher—trying to tease the batter into going after a pitch he can't hit safely, and the batter—the mouse—trying to anticipate the pitcher's strategy or trying to fake the pitcher into making the move that will let the batter get safely on base. Playing this game over the years, I have developed some ideas of my own on how to get batters out and I do not always agree with the conventional wisdom of the game—the "wisdom" that is often preached by men who just have not had the experience of working on all sorts of batters game after game.

One bit of conventional wisdom I do not accept is a theory that I heard preached recently, after I joined the Yankees—that is: "Throw a good pitch to the batter's weakness and a bad pitch (out of the strike zone), to the batter's strength." I suppose that the idea behind this theory is that, in this way, you will either make the batter swing at a bad pitch (because it is "to his strength") or force him to swing at a pitch he cannot hit (because it is too good to pass up). To me that seems completely backward. If my strength is a low pitch and the batter is one who hits low pitches well, as some do, am I going to avoid using my best pitch when the going is rough? What if the bases are full and the count is 3 and 2 (three balls and two strikes)? One more bad pitch will force in a run. Do I throw a bad pitch to his strength? Or even if the count is 2 and 2, and another bad pitch will put me in a hole. Do I stick my head in that noose? No, I think the contest then should be strength against strength. I'll go, that is, with the pitch that is working best for me that night (or afternoon). There is too much luck involved in the placement of pitches for me to take a chance on giving the batter any extra advantage. For instance, if I am facing Jim Rice, I do not need to be reminded that he is an exceptionally good low-ball hitter. I once saw him just flip his bat at what I thought was an outstanding sinker of mine, a pitch that dropped below his knees and outside the plate. Yet Jim, with what seemed like a flick of his wrists, drove the ball on a line about six feet off the ground right to the left-field wall, where Piniella caught it head-high. Jim's weakness is a high fast ball, inside. A good fast-ball pitcher can get Jim out with a strong pitch, up and in. But my fast ball is nothing like Gossage's or Guidry's. If I pitch a high, inside fast ball to Jim Rice, and miss my mark by a few inches, Jim is likely to put the ball out of the park. No. I'll challenge Jim, or any low-ball hitter with my own best pitch and take heart from the fact that even the very best batters will hit safely only three times out of ten.

I also disagree with the standard formula of "wasting" a pitch when you have the batter down by two strikes and no balls. I know the basis for that theory is that the batter, under pressure not to let a good pitch, or anything that might be called a strike, get by him, may swing at the waste pitch and make out on it. But if you have a batter at your mercy, why let up on him? Why not get him out of there with the pitch you know is your best? If you waste *two* pitches, trying to tease him into hitting into an easy out, you may suddenly find yourself even in the count, and then behind in the count, with the pressure on *you*. I'd rather have it the other way around.

You do, however, have to make sure your best pitch is working for you at that time. More times than it should, your best pitch may desert you suddenly. I have known times when my best pitch was working fine as I warmed up and suddenly left me when I reached the mound. I don't pretend to understand why this happens but I know it does. And it works the other way, too. You may have decided in the warm-up that your curve is "hanging," i.e., failing to break down and away from the batter as it should, only to discover when the pressure is on that it is breaking beautifully down and across the far corner of the plate. How things like this happen I don't know. Batters have a similar experience, when they hit better with men on base than when there are none. It may have something to do with the pulse rate, or concentration. But it is one of those facts you have to deal with as you plan your part of the cat-and-mouse performance. And it is one reason why your catcher is so important to you. He has to be able to tell you what your pitches are doing and build your confidence in the one that is working best. Of course, you don't throw a pitch just because the catcher signals for it. It is bad news to throw any pitch you don't firmly believe in. You signal the catcher, with a shake of your head or a brush-off motion with the glove that you want to throw a different pitch. It is vital that you have a positive attitude when you're pitching, that you don't throw a pitch just hoping it might be the one that will work. If you shake off a catcher's signal too many times, he may come to the mound and tell you what his reasons are for calling that pitch, but he has got to convince you. There should not be anything halfhearted about your pitch.

Still, a young pitcher should not get the idea that he has the entire game in his hands, important as his part may be. I know I had trouble at the very start of my career because I thought it was up to me to get every batter out. When I was reminded, by Steve Jankowski, a veteran who was a player/coach with Charleston, West Virginia, in the Eastern League, that I had eight other guys on the field to help get batters out, I began to work with the idea of making batters hit—hit low pitches that would turn into ground balls that could be gobbled up by fielders and thrown to first to make the putout. I heard a story about Dizzy Dean—one of the truly great names in pitching history—that illustrates this simple truth. Once when the shortstop playing behind him practically stood on one ear to stop a ground ball and fired it off from an impossible stance to rub out the runner by half a step, someone said to Dizzy: "Wasn't that a brilliant stop your shortstop made?" Dizzy displayed no emotion. "That's what they're *supposed* to do," said he.

Not that you shouldn't be grateful for every out your fielders make for you. Indeed you should. And you should tell them so. But you should remember that they are out in those positions to do their own jobs—and you should let them perform, too.

A pitcher has to deal with a lot of second guessers. I don't believe there is any game in the world that lends itself to second guessing more than baseball. You are ahead of a batter with a count of two strikes and no balls and he gets a hit off your pitch. The manager growls at you when the inning is over: "How the hell can you let him hit an 0 and 2 pitch?" Of course what he means is that you should "waste" a pitch at that point. There isn't much you can say unless you want to explain that you don't believe in letting a batter off the hook when you are two strikes ahead of him. And that may be contrary to his philosophy. But one thing you never want to do is second guess yourself. Throw the pitch you *know* is the one you want to throw at that point. And if you're wrong, console yourself that good batters are bound to get *some* safe hits. There are not too many managers who have been pitchers. And at any rate *you* are the one who is out there with your won and lost record—the figures that may be used as the basis for your future income—on the line. You make the decision and have faith in your own judgment.

Another thing that makes pitching fascinating to me is the difference among batters. Every batter is a different job, and, for that matter, every batter *has* a different job. On the New York Yankees for instance, Willie Randolph's job is to get on base. Dave Winfield's job is to hit the long ball, and drive Randolph (or anyone else who happens to be on base) across the plate to score. Batters at the lower end of the order are not necessarily just people who can't hit very well. They may be specially adept at using the bat in a particular way—at bunting to advance a runner from first base to second (called a sacrifice because the batter "sacrifices" himself to put the runner in a position where he may be brought home with a safe hit) or at hitting to right field, a useful art when there is a man on second base (with no one out) who can move on to third while the enemy is busy putting the hitter out at first. (If the batter should hit to the left side of the field, the ball [and the play] will be in front of the runner and he may possibly be put out at third base more easily than the hitter can be at first base.) That will put the runner on third base, where he can run home to score on a long fly ball, after the ball is caught, still leaving one out to spare.

On the California club, Rod Carew is a handy man with the bat, whom we count on to get on base frequently. Reggie Jackson, Fred Lynn, and Doug DeCinces are the long-ball hitters who will be trying to bring in the runners.

Knowing what a batter is probably trying to do helps you in pitching to him, just as it helps to know what sort of pitch he likes to hit. If the batter is planning to bunt (and a batter setting out to make a sacrifice bunt will usually turn to face the pitcher with his hands well apart on the bat) you may want to pitch him high and inside, because a high ball is somewhat harder to bunt and sometimes results in a pop foul that is easily caught for the out. But one thing you do not want to do is to try to keep him from bunting by offering him pitches he cannot reach—and that will count as "balls" if he lets them go by. A free walk to first base for the batter is even more damaging than a successful sacrifice bunt. So you let him bunt. But you have to have an understanding with your infielders as to just what each man is going to do. This is usually indicated by a sign from the manager in the dugout. Most likely the first baseman, or the third baseman, or both, will come charging toward the plate, to snatch up the ball in hopes of having time to throw it to second base soon enough to put the leading runner out, and thus frustrate the purpose of the sacrifice. And you must have a previously agreed on signal the first baseman can give you so you will know he is leaving the base. Otherwise, you might decide to try, before you pitch to the plate, to pick the runner off first base—and find no one there to take the throw, and a wild throw or balk will result.

And that is another aspect of the pitcher's trade that requires study and practice—the art of deceiving the base runner, so that he may think you are about to fire the ball to the plate when you are really going to throw to the first baseman, who is ordinarily standing there ready to tag the runner as he tries to regain the safety of the base. Some runners take good long leads off first base, so as to shorten the distance to second, and you can make them cut down their leads by keeping them guessing about when a pick-off throw may be on the way.

This job is complicated by the "balk" rule, one rule that many spectators (and even a few ballplayers) have trouble understanding. A "balk," originally, was a fake pitch, just a motion with the hand as if you had started to pitch, followed by a quick throw to first in the occasionally vain hope that the runner would be faked into starting for second base, leaving himself halfway down the base line, at the mercy of the man with the ball. Such a move was outlawed early. But over the years, as pitchers worked out different devices for making it look as if a pitch was coming, the rule has had to be extended to cover all sorts of motions and to force the pitcher to halt his pitching motion for a moment, so that a throw to first cannot be part of his "stretch," the over-the-head reach of the hands that is about all the "windup" a pitcher takes when there are men on base. Now, if you so much as move your front foot forward, or striding foot back across the rubber—that is, breaking the imaginary plane of the pitching rubber—you must go through with a pitch to the plate or the umpire can call a balk and allow all the runners to advance a base. Or if you interrupt your pitching motion, once begun, and do not get your feet immediately off the rubber slab marking the point from which you are required to pitch, you could be charged with a balk, even if you do no more than stop to hitch up your pants, rub the baseball, or brush away a fly. Most of the time the umpires will not call a balk if they determine you are not trying to deceive the batter or runner with this movement, but it is best to be careful. And when you move off the rubber, you must lift your contact foot off—*away* from the plate.

That does not cover the balk rule completely but it may give you an idea of why pitchers spend a seemingly inordinate amount of time trying to perfect a "move" that will keep the runner guessing and will still not cost a balk penalty. Some pitchers have managed to incorporate hesitations and gestures into their regular motion so completely that umpires have allowed them to commit apparent sins against the balk rule just because the questionable move belongs in their regular routine. Luis Tiant, for instance, when pitching from the "stretch" position, brings the ball down to pitching height in a series of hesitations that somewhat resemble the way a man might adjust the height of a reading lamp. If you or I tried such a move in a game, I think most umpires would promptly signal "balk!"—because of our failure either to come to a full stop as required, or to deliver the ball after the first stop. Everybody knows, however, that that's the way Luis pitches.

Luis is different. And batters are different, too, which is one more reason why pitching, while it may tire your brain, will never anesthetize it. Because the strike zone—an imaginary oblong area the width of the plate and extending from just above the batter's knees to just under his armpits—quite naturally differs with every batter. Some batters shrink the strike zone by the way they stand at the plate. Some extend it because they are so tall. So you have to keep adjusting your sights to find the area into which the ball should go if it is to be called a strike. My father—who may very well have been the perfect father for a boy to own—set out to teach me what every young boy should know about the strike zone when I was about eight years old. He was not one of those fathers who will try to force baseball down a kid's throat just because it was a career he wanted for himself. Dad had been a good semipro ballplayer and he naturally wanted me to enjoy the game as much as he had. But to him the key word was "enjoy." There were no houndings or scoldings or temper tantrums, such as I have seen some fathers indulge in at Little League games. But as soon as he was convinced of my devotion to the game, he put in many extra hours helping me improve my play. (I think he became thoroughly convinced when he looked out the window and saw me—then eight years old—trying to manhandle a wheelbarrow load of dirt across the yard, and spilling most of it. Why? To make a pitcher's mound!)

He then built me, out of long stakes and string, a target representing the "strike zone" on an imaginary batter and I worked and worked at firing baseballs through that target. As a result, by the time I was ready to play school baseball I had at least somewhat better than average control. I also developed a curve ball sooner than many young pitchers do because I had a good teacher, a guy from Terre Haute named

Arley Andrews, a friend of my father's. Arley had been a minor-league pitcher with the Philadelphia Phillies organization. He had never made the big team but he did learn how a big-league curve was thrown and he showed the secret to me. What I recall chiefly was his insistence that the curve be thrown—not with a sidearm throw as most schoolboy curves are pitched—but with an overhand motion. "Pull down," Arley told me, "just as if you were pulling a bell rope or a window shade—straight down!" It took me a long time to learn that—to pull down with wrist and arm to provide the spin that makes a good curve break down and away. But I mastered this science eventually and with it, plus my fast ball (my best weapon), I managed to win a string of high school victories that ultimately attracted a number of big-league scouts. All the same, I felt my high school record was flawed because, after I had won every game I pitched during the season, I lost a game to Danville High, a school with a history of great baseball teams. And that was the one game we always wanted to win, because Danville was a strong rival. And I *lost* it, in front of all those big-league scouts. The coach was convinced I blew the game because I threw too many curve balls at the wrong time and he told me angrily that if I threw one more curve ball for his team, I was *finished*. "Those scouts don't come here to see you throw curves," said he. "They want guys that throw *hard*."

I listened politely. But I had no intention of obeying him. I thought my father was a better coach anyway. And, just as my father taught me faith in God, he taught me faith in myself. "The heck with that idea," I said to myself (or something like that). "I'm going to keep right on throwing that curve the way Arley showed me."

The irony of this episode was that when the day came (very soon) that the Cleveland club talked to me, Gabe Paul, the general manager, said: "You've already got a big-league curve ball. As you grow bigger and stronger, your fast ball will come along."

Before this ever happened, however, I had a number of offers to think about—offers from colleges to play basketball! I was a really good basketball player too, although I had managed to conceal that fact most of my time in high school, because I did so poorly in practice. That's a mystery I will never solve, because I have always been a believer in the theory that lousy practice means a lousy game. But I think what I really mean is that halfhearted practice means a lousy game. My practice was never halfhearted. But it sure was lousy. I don't believe I could have sunk a ball in practice if the basket had been on the floor.

As a freshman at Gerstmeyer High School, where fine basketball teams were a tradition, I found myself far down on the coach's list for "playing time." The junior varsity coach, Bill Welch, had nothing to go by, of course, other than what he saw in practice, and what he saw of me stirred no hope in his heart. Although I *knew* I could play the game and felt sure I was going to be good at it, I simply could not demonstrate any skill in practice. By the time of the first game I seemed destined for a season on the bench and I sat through the entire contest as an unhappy spectator.

But my career turned around suddenly during the second game. We were playing an all-black team from Crispus Attucks High School in Indianapolis and seemed likely to be blown off the floor. In desperation—or perhaps in the conviction that the cause was hopeless anyway—Bill Welch sent me into the game. Almost instantly I started to pop in baskets from every angle, grab rebounds, and move the ball up the floor as if I had been playing the game all my life. We did not win the game, but I know that my second-half play brought joy to Bill Welch's heart. After that, my name was near the top of the list for playing time. But I still had rotten practices. How come? I have asked myself many times. Is it like the hitter who surpasses himself when there are men on base? More adrenaline? Faster pulse? That's a phenomenon I think I'll have to leave to the scientists. Whatever the reason, I became an area star and began to enjoy the attentions of college recruiters from more schools than I can remember.

I wanted to go to college, for odd as it may seem for a boy who concentrated so hard on sports, I was really a good student. I *loved* mathematics and would have liked to investigate the upper reaches of that study. I think it is just possible that if I hadn't talked to the right man, I'd have postponed baseball and taken one of the many offers of full college scholarship I received. There were even baseball clubs who would arrange for a college scholarship for me (at a school, naturally, that played baseball) if I would sign with them. And my high school teachers were urging me to give my intellect a chance to develop along with my muscle. My parents were going to leave it up to me.

I traveled one Saturday to the University of Illinois, which had offered me a scholarship, and talked with their baseball coach, Lee Eilbracht. I think he gave me the soundest and most unselfish advice I received from anyone on this question.

"We'd love to have you come here and play basketball and baseball for us," he told me. "But it really comes down to what a college education is worth in hard cash. I'd say four years full scholarship would come to about twenty thousand dollars. If you can get an offer from a ball club for more money than that, my advice is to grab it."

During my senior year at Gerstmeyer High, college basketball coaches were calling me nearly every day. One morning, just as I was about to leave for school, Wack Hyder, basketball coach at Georgia Tech, called to explain to me on the telephone what a splendid school Georgia Tech was and how I could make their fine basketball team even finer. He urged me to come visit the school during Easter vacation. Soon afterward, Dave Strack, the basketball coach at the University of Michigan, called me to invite me *there*.

It was fun, believe me, for a seventeen-year-old to be getting calls and letters like this, every invitation sounding more tempting than the one before, until I was ready to accept them all.

But one recruiter was different and his invitation fell flat. That was the great basketball coach from the University of Kentucky, Adolph Rupp, who showed up at our door one day in May along with his assistant, Harry Lancaster. He made it plain at once that he had not come all the way to Terre Haute just to talk to me. He and Harry had spent the previous week in Indianapolis trying to persuade the famed Van Arsdale twins, Tom and Dick, to come grace the basketball court in Kentucky. And when he failed to persuade them, he thought he might as well give me a try. I was not there, however. I was out playing golf. They had to make their pitch to my dad. Dad was not a man to go all starry-eyed in the presence of Adolph Rupp. And Rupp, very early in the discussion, struck a sore spot on Dad's hide, when he belittled my skill at *baseball*. Dad had told him I might skip college altogether and have a try at professional baseball.

"Why," Rupp declaimed, "we have major-league scouts down looking at some of our baseball players all the time. Tommy might not even make the *team* down there." That remark would have earned the great Coach Rupp a flat F, for flunk, in Dale Carnegie's course in How to Make Friends and Influence People. When you are trying to win an athlete's father to your side, you don't do it by belittling the son's ability.

Hardly had the words left Rupp's mouth when my dad was on him like ugly on an ape. He had never been an admirer of Adolph Rupp's coaching methods nor of his personality and he set out, in scorching phrases, to make his feelings clear to the man's face. And as for the University of Kentucky—well Dad had some comments to offer on that institution as well, remarks that would never have fit into a valedictory speech down there. Dad wound up his own oration by reciting my basketball stats to the astounded coach:

26 games played, 20.3 points per game, and 17.5 rebounds per game.

"Don't let the door hit you on the way out, Mr. Rupp," my dad urged. "And the next time you feel like recruiting my son, you'd better allow more than an hour left over from missing out on recruiting the Van Arsdales."

I feel sure Adolph Rupp had never hearkened to such talk since he had ascended the throne in Kentucky. He slammed out of the house growling to himself and was never heard from again.

There were no player-agents in my day—or none in my area that I knew of. My dad was my agent and it was not in his nature to bargain or shop around or get one club bidding against another. The Cleveland scout, John Schulte, an old-time catcher, said he could offer $35,000—but would have to get the approval of his boss, in Cleveland—and his boss would want to look at me first. Well, that was about twice what my father could earn in a year. And it was about a hundred times as much as I had ever seen in one place in all my life. And I had been earning money during vacations and after school for a long time. Selling doughnuts, for one thing!

Off we went to Cleveland by rail to face I knew not what, two rubes right out of the country. For all I could tell I was headed for an inquisition. Instead, I was welcomed as if I had come with a bag full of goodies. They handed me a brand-new big-league uniform, not quite my size, but good enough, and sent me out on the diamond with the bullpen catcher, Al Jones. Al greeted me with the friendliest of grins and began to talk to me about home—about high school, about my family, until the last flutter in my stomach had been stilled. Then I went to the mound and threw for some fifteen or twenty minutes, with Al calling encouragement with every pitch. I wanted to make sure my arm was running on all cylinders before I tried to impress the brass. Gabe Paul, general manager of the club (and now the owner), and Bob

Kennedy, assistant director of minor-league operations, stood by when I was ready and watched every pitch. They at least looked satisfied. But they wanted to have Hoot Evers, the farm director (who at the time was down in Mobile signing a kid named Tommie Agee) to size me up, too. I had heard about Hoot Evers from some of the other Cleveland players, and I did not look forward to the meeting. He was, I had been told, a tough, mean, hard-nosed old coot whom nobody could please. He looked tough too—tall as I was, lean, cold-eyed, red hair going slightly gray at the edges, stony face, aloof manner—and I was more uneasy about my second "audition" than I was my first. I needn't have been. Hoot Evers loosened up quickly after we had talked awhile. And Gabe Paul, as I have already noted, told me I was throwing a big-league curve. So the offer stood.

There was just one catch. Dad had a close friend in Terre Haute named Bruce Connatser, a scout for the Philadelphia Phillies, who had been watching me pitch since I was a Little Leaguer and Bruce had asked for a chance to meet any offer I might get from a big-league club. Dad called Bruce and told him the size of the Cleveland offer. Bruce called back promptly to say that the Phillies could not lay out any such sum, having just blown $100,000 on a young pitcher named Bruce Gruber who came up with a sore arm. Dad told Gabe Paul that if they would boost the offer to $40,000, we'd sign. They boosted and we signed.

Hoot Evers and I had a long friendly talk. He described the long-range goals of the Indians, named the players already in their minor-league system, and explained what I might expect when I joined the farm clubs. He had good advice to offer on pitching, too, and one special bit of advice for my first season in professional baseball. How to get my arm in shape? How to throw sliders? No. How to eat!

"Don't eat to save money!" he warned me. "Eat plenty of vegetables, especially greens—salads and the like."

Good advice from a warm-hearted, considerate man.

There wasn't much danger of my saving money on a $700-a-month salary, even though hamburgers in that day (1961) were still only a quarter. I wanted to send money home, and I had rent to pay, clothes to buy, and movies to see now and then. The Indians had two farm clubs in Class D—one in Alabama and one in Dubuque. They sent me to Dubuque because they wanted me to be as close to home as possible. I had just turned eighteen. Also, they wanted me to be with Merrill (Pinky) May, manager of the Dubuque club, who was a fatherly type, particularly good at helping teenagers make the adjustment to the pros.

While Dubuque itself was over 300 miles from Terre Haute, there were Class D clubs in Kokomo, Indiana, 100 miles from Terre Haute, and in Decatur, just 90 miles from home. Both places being in easy reach of my parents, I was assured of seeing a friendly face now and then.

There were no friendly faces at the hotel, the first hotel I had ever stayed in and the only one I ever did know that had for a fire escape a knotted rope coiled on a spike in each room. The thought of trying to shinny down that rope at midnight was not one I wanted to dwell on. The Cleveland club preferred that I not stay more than a day or two at the hotel, for they wanted to place me in a home-like atmosphere as soon as they could. Gabe Paul, Hoot Evers, and Bob Kennedy all seemed concerned with making the lives of their young ballplayers comfortable. They found me a room with Mr. and Mrs. Matt Olansky, two gentle folks in their sixties whose own kids had long since left the nest and who were happy to have a teen-aged lad for company. Matt was one of those short, sturdy, bald, and beaming Jewish gentlemen who always make you feel as if you'd known them for ten years. His wife was just as pleasant, honestly glad to have me in her home and considerate of my need to sleep late after a night game. While my deal with them did not include meals, Matt often would call me into the kitchen when I got up and invite me to share fried-egg sandwiches or latkes, a Jewish pancake that I had never met before and to which I easily became addicted.

The atmosphere at the ball park was different, believe me. I was a stranger there and the other guys, most of them in their early twenties, did not let me forget it. My arrival had meant the release of another pitcher who had been a buddy to some of them and the resentment was thick as butter. Not that anyone was openly disagreeable or mean. But the short answers and cool glances made it clear enough to me that I was meant to keep my distance.

Two guys were different. One left-handed pitcher, Art Siefert, a middle-sized, stocky type with a permanent glad-to-meet-you expression, really had more reason to resent me than most of the others. He had been three years in the minors, was still hoping to make it up the stairs, and here was a left-handed bonus baby come to take his job away. But he just couldn't *help* being nice to people, so he was nice to me, helping me most of all in knowing what I was supposed to do. "Now we go out and shag (chase fly balls)" he would tell me. Or "Come on, time to run!" And I would follow his lead until I caught onto the routine. He showed me where to eat and told me who the people were who hung around the park. Being from Cincinnati himself, Artie was almost like home-folks to me.

Then there was Tommie Agee, who arrived from Mobile the same time I did and had actually lived at the same hotel until the club was able to find him a "nice black family" to stay with. People in all parts of the country in that day still wanted black people to stay with "their own kind." Well, Tommie was my kind—a rugged, good-natured guy, a few months older than I was, who was built like a halfback and could run like a wide receiver. Tommie had as much raw talent as any ballplayer I ever met and he was always good company, ready to go anywhere and not given to quarreling. We often ate our meals together and I guess found comfort in sharing the minor irritation of both being objects of resentment for the first few weeks. After a while, of course, despite the fact that eight out of the ten other pitchers on the roster were earnestly wishing me the worst luck in the world, we all began to get along together easily enough. A ball club just has to develop some sort of family feeling. And in Class D it comes more naturally, because we actually shared the same "home"—our clubhouse, where we had to split all the chores, sweeping and cleaning, washing out our sweatshirts and underwear, polishing our shoes, and hanging our laundry out to dry. No "clubhouse kids" to wait on you in that league.

We were all at the park early anyway, for all of us, hitters, pitchers, fielders, were bent on getting in as much practice as we could, so as to be sure that when choices were made, we would be up front.

I had a special urge. I pitched my first professional game against the Quincy club and not even for an extra year's salary could I now recall just how that club rated in the league or even what the score of the game was. I know I pitched hard, that I walked a number of batters and that, by the sixth or seventh inning, I was so weary I was heaving baseballs almost everywhere except into the strike zone. I was "wild high"—the sure sign that I could no longer get my legs into the pitch. But I had struck out a good many batters, too, and the manager took me out soon enough to save the victory—and that went into my "win" column. Still, I felt that I had failed the test. According to my book, pitchers were paid to go nine innings. I didn't know for some time that professional ball clubs kept a supply of relief pitchers in the bullpen for the sole task of finishing up ball games for tired starters. I decided I *had* to increase my stamina, and I undertook to accomplish that by running and running and *running*, every afternoon. I would run for forty-five minutes every day—sprinting and walking, foul line to foul line—until I felt I was getting stronger.

One thing I did not do was learn how to make sense out of the "pitching charts" they handed me before the game, showing me where in previous games Quincy batters had hit the ball, what sort of pitches they hit, what the ball-and-strike count was when they hit it and so on. I took one long look at that batch of utter confusion and told myself, "I'll *never* learn this job! How can I memorize all that stuff?" As a matter of fact, I never did learn how, not to this day. I don't believe that sort of statistic does a thing for a pitcher in getting batters out. A pitcher has got to go by what comes naturally, maybe not his instinct but his *reaction* to different situations, a reaction that is the result of long experience and steady practice. Try to keep those charts in your head and you won't be able to concentrate on pitching.

Away from the park, life in Dubuque was small-town life at its best or at its worst: a minimum of excitement, not too much privacy, plenty of pretty girls, a narrow choice of recreation and restaurants, a rash of "boosterism," friendly greetings from strangers, a tumbledown slum area, and a general air of informality in clothing and in manners.

The booster club that supported the baseball team named itself the Packer Pals, and was made up largely of the owners of small businesses—a sort of sports-oriented Kiwanis. But the moving spirit was the widow of a local baseball backer named Luckritz and called "Lucky." Mrs. Luckritz, who had a fourteen-year-old son who was a baseball addict, used to devote a lot of her time to keeping the ballplayers well-fed and entertained. She took a group of us to lunch now and then and she staged picnics occasionally for the whole team out in the countryside.

Most of the time, however, when not playing or practicing, the players simply hung out at the Hollywood Grill, a "moderate-price" restaurant owned by a man with the interesting name of John Thomas. This was where you could nurse coffee and rolls for a couple of hours at a time while ribbing your teammates and arguing baseball with some of the steady fans.

Like most small cities in the Midwest League, Dubuque

had a crowd of devoted fans. The Hollywood Grill was their standard gathering place, where they would replay the game of the night before and try to decide what was coming next. The Cleveland Indians being the parent club, the fans would replay the Cleveland games too, reciting statistics and arguing strategy until the tenth cup of coffee had grown cold. The fans were addicted to making imaginary trades too—swapping off players who were having bad years for players on the other clubs who might strengthen the Cleveland lineup.

I suppose the only really unpleasant aspect of this life was the dreary bus rides, particularly tough on a guy with legs as long as mine, that would land you in Kokomo or someplace with just barely time enough to suit up and get out on the diamond. But there were other minor disasters from time to time that were really comic to remember—like the time a game was called off on account of flies. Flies, for Pete's sake! Big buggers called fish flies that swarmed so thick around the lights they put the whole field in darkness.

All in all, my stay in Dubuque was a happy one, thanks largely to people like Art Siefert and Tommie Agee and the Olanskys and Mrs. Luckritz—and to a frisky ten-year-old batboy who used to play pepper (fielding bunted ground balls and tossing them back so the batter could bunt them again) with all of us, and who really had obvious baseball talent even then. That was little Milt May, who has grown up to be a rugged catcher with the San Francisco Giants. His father, Pinky May, our manager, was once third baseman for the Phillies.

But the best part of my stay was the fact that I posted a record of ten wins and only four losses, enough to earn me a move right up to Charleston, in Class A, just two notches below the big leagues. Next spring, only a year and a half out of high school, I was facing some really savvy batters. And I also learned something new about pitching.

The fact was, I really *did not* know how to pitch. I was rearing back on every pitch and firing with all my strength at the strike zone. As a result I kept getting behind in the ball-and-strike count, often running it to three balls and no strikes, so I just had to put my fast ball right over the plate and get it *creamed*. The worse things got, the harder I would try to throw and, as had happened in Dubuque, I became wilder and wilder. The man who saved me from myself, as I've already explained, was Steve Jankowski, the player-coach. He simply reminded me that I was not the only man on the team, that there were eight others in the field to help me put batters out.

"Back off," said Steve. "You don't have to come in with a hundred percent of your strength every time. Give them something they can hit and let the other guys put them out. Use about eighty percent of your power and save some for the later innings." From then on, I think, I was a real pitcher, or learning to become one, because Steve's formula worked. Not only did I get more batters out, I actually improved my control. I could get my curve into the strike zone. I could put my fast ball where I wanted to.

While I was at Charleston, the Indians sent in a young pitcher they had recruited in Mexico who had developed a sore arm. That was Luis Tiant. And Luis and I were to keep running into each other for the rest of our careers. Luis was a wizard even then. He threw the ball from four or five different angles and wound up like a dervish about to go into a spin. To have him turn his back on the batter, as if he were going to pick the ball off a table behind the mound, and then explode a whistling fast ball out of almost anywhere, apparently without even looking at the plate, would loosen up the stance of some of the toughest hitters.

At the end of July, when I had won six games and lost eight, I was suddenly promoted to Jacksonville in the International League. That was Triple-A ball, one step below the major league. Here I suddenly felt more than a little out of place. Many of these guys were seasoned players, five, six, even ten years older than I was. But I did find one welcome and familiar face—Al Jones, the catcher who had caught my schoolboy throws the previous year when I had put on the demonstration for the Cleveland brass. Al was a coach here and he made me instantly welcome in his warmhearted way. Just throw what the catcher asks for, he told me. And that is what I did. I had two wins and two losses in the remainder of the season but I embellished my record with two wins in the play-offs, just pitching what the catcher wanted.

What made life enjoyable here—among the older players who were inclined to treat me like a child—was the friendship of a sports writer, Rex Edmondson of the Jacksonville *Times-Union*. Rex was another one of these people who seem put in the world to look after young fellows. He used to take me out to eat, to make sure I was getting enough to eat. He would go out of his way to find me a ride to the ball park and he saw to it that I got a discount rate at the hotel. Al Jones would eat with me at the coffee shop just to help me develop the conviction that I was one of the team. But Al will never know how great it made me feel to have a knowledgable coach spend time talking baseball to a rookie. I had no other special pals at this time. In off-hours I would go to the movies alone. The high-stake card games the older guys liked to devote their spare time to held no lure for me. I was still sending a good chunk of my salary home, pocketing only a few dollars each payday to keep me in meal and movie money. A few dollars bought a lot more in those days. I felt sure I would become a regular. In 1963, my second season at Jacksonville, my friend Al Jones was gone and I was left to the mercies of the manager, Ben Geraghty, whom I hardly knew, even though I had played for him part of a season.

I was proud of myself that spring. I had gone back to school at Indiana State University, in the winter, to study math some more, and I had worked out every day with the Indiana State coaches, jogging, playing badminton or basketball, refereeing a game or two, even announcing play-by-play on radio and TV, so when I came to Jacksonville I was ready to set a few pitching records. We had won the championship the year before and I could see no reason why we shouldn't do it over again. But I had forgotten about the manager, Ben Geraghty. And he had certainly forgotten about me. Geraghty was a soft-spoken Irishman with a face so deeply graven you could have planted corn in the wrinkles. To me, at nineteen, he looked as old as my grandfather. Yet, come to find out later, he was not even fifty years old! He just looked bent and discouraged and worn down. And he was the sort of guy—and I met a number of them in my youth—who thinks young fellows are natural objects of scorn. Instead of trying to teach the young players the many things they needed to know—simple things like what part of your game needed most work at the moment—he would just look right through you and let you go your own way. He concentrated on the older players, who needed no instruction at all, and many of whom were really just trying to squeeze a final season or two out of their aging frames. But Geraghty wanted to win baseball games, not teach young ignoramuses the three R's of baseball. I think that to Geraghty we were simply nuisances wished on him because Jacksonville had made a working agreement with the Cleveland Indians. In all the time I was there, he never spoke to me more than a half-whispered and obviously grudging word of greeting. I can see him sitting in his bare office, the open door of which was right opposite my locker, legs crossed, gazing across some invisible outfield as if I wasn't there, hungrily devouring a cigarette. I might be the only player in the locker room. But I still rated no more than half a nod. Sometimes after a game, he would sit there silently for an hour in his baggy long johns and sweat shirt, smoking, smoking, smoking, gulping a swallow now and then from a can of beer, and seeming to play all over again in his mind a game we had lost. Geraghty, I was told later, was really a fine manager and once had been a first-rate instructor. But he had been riding a bus one day in which two or three of his ballplayers were killed and he had never seemed able to get his full heart into the job thereafter.

He pitched me simply out of necessity. In 1962 he had only three starting pitchers. The fourth starter would be somebody out of the bullpen—no telling who until the day came. This year, 1963, he had a whole string of starters, most of them older men who needed no directions from him. In the first month I pitched only two games. I was really writhing inside from inaction. I used to sit there in the bullpen and stare out at Geraghty, who, like all managers in that league, served as third-base coach, wondering when he was going to notice me. But when our club took the field, he would just plod, head down, back to his cozy spot on the bench and retreat behind his cigarette. If he *did* need a pitcher, he would take one of his old-timers.

It saddens me now to think that Ben Geraghty then was counting off the last few weeks of his life. He died of cancer in June 1963. By that time I had left the club to go back to Charleston. My guardian angel, in the person of gaunt Hoot Evers, had flown into Jacksonville a short time before to break the news that I was going to be "sent down" to Charleston in Class A. If Hoot thought I was going to be in need of consolation, he was far off base. I was delighted to learn I was going where I would have a chance to pitch more than once every two weeks and I drove northward with a light heart.

There were friends waiting for me in Charleston—Don Schaefer, Pete Olson, and Luis Tiant, among others—and I felt almost as if I had come home again. I was now one of the old-timers and on that basis (and because I could type) I was given a job, along with two other pitchers, Olsen and Schaefer, of writing up the game reports for manager John Lipon. We had to report on every player we saw in the league, so the parent club could use this information in making trades and moving players upstairs.

Still, life was rough in Class A, doubly rough I imagine on the older players. We were allowed two and a half dollars a day for meals, plus a half a buck that the Cleveland club kicked in. That was pretty close to starvation for most of us. But we did have one kid on the roster who belonged in a book by Ripley. He actually *saved* twenty dollars in two weeks. I still can't figure out how he did it. The rest of us had to get by partly on our wits. One guy would actually wander around a restaurant and swipe tips from the tables so he could eat. That, to me, was about as low as you could get.

There was one hotel on the circuit that served a free "Continental Breakfast," consisting of coffee and rolls. We loved that place. We would get to the counter early in the morning, drink six to eight cups of coffee and gobble up as many rolls. Then we could get by without food until after the ball game. We were addicted to White Towers then, for in those golden days (1963) they would occasionally have a special: twelve hamburgers for a dollar.

In the Eastern League, what with the long travel and the lack of meal money, I found it difficult to follow Hoot Evers' advice about diet. But I always took a little extra money on long trips so I would not have to go without my greens.

The bus rides were probably the worst aspect of the job. We had trips of fourteen, fifteen, sixteen, and seventeen hours. You would leave one town at midnight and land in the next spot late in the afternoon or early evening, with a game scheduled for 7 P.M. The roughest trip of all was the one from Charleston to Springfield, Massachusetts. Twenty-four dreary hours in a bus seat! Once we made a trip to Springfield that got us into town about six in the morning—just in time for one of those great continental breakfasts. If we had had any sense, or less addiction to golf, we'd have gone right to bed. But one of the guys—either Don or Pete—had an American Express card. We knew that the United States Open was being staged at The Country Club in Brookline about eighty miles away, with Julius Boros, Arnold Palmer, Jackie Cupit, and all the great names of the era scheduled to play. We rented a car on the credit card, took off for Brookline, and followed the leaders around the course all day long, then hustled back to Springfield just in time to get into uniform for the game. I wasn't tired. How could I get tired watching golf? I was exhilarated. I shut out Springfield 5 to 0.

By this time we had learned how to civilize the bus rides a little by playing bridge until we fell asleep. It was a sort of floating bridge game, with a score that began to mount into the millions. It had a sudden happy ending for me when word came from Cleveland that I was going back to Jacksonville under the new regime there—on the strength of my nine wins and two losses at Charleston and my stingy earned run average of 1.61 every nine innings. Of course there was a radical change in the character of the ball club at Jacksonville. Instead of a bunch of case-hardened veterans looking to win a minor-league championship, we were going to be transformed gradually into a proper "farm" club, where new talent could be cultivated and shipped to the big market in Cleveland. For a start we added a bushel of new pitchers, including Mike Cuellar, who was destined, within a few years, to star for Baltimore; the indestructible Luis Tiant, whose sore arm was now a memory; Sam McDowell, who would eventually lead the American League in strikeouts for five different seasons; and of course, ambitious Tommy John, the realization of whose ambitions was fated to be frustrated for another season or two—chiefly because I still had a great deal to learn, and some things to unlearn, about pitching against the good hitters.

But it seemed to me that I reached my immediate goal at the end of that season when Birdie Tebbets, the Cleveland manager, called me to say I was coming up to the big club—not next year but right away. It must have taken me the better part of fifteen minutes to pack my gear and make ready to go.

I had seen this Cleveland park before, but never with all

these people in it. The tenderly tailored outfield, the trim infield, the carpeted clubhouse, the kids to run your errands, all these together made a vision that just about set my head afloat. I was sent at once to the bullpen, but that bothered me not at all. I was in the Big Leagues! And I wasn't even twenty-one years old!

My first game brought me an unexpected rush of panic. Not because I doubted my ability to pitch to these batters, not because I was intimidated by the crowd, or by the consciousness that several pairs of skeptical eyes would be assessing my performance. No. It was because when they called for me to come into the bullpen, we were in Washington, where I had never played before, and I couldn't get the *gate* open! The fence was ten feet high and I could not see where the latch was on the gate. For Pete's sake, was I supposed to *climb* this thing? The notion of making a fool of myself before this park full of people really reddened my neck. The squawk box behind me was asking, "Where the hell is T.J.?" In desperation I grabbed the big gate and shook it. And lo! the latch fell open and the gate swung back to my shove. Just as the Lord had promised—shake (or was it knock?) and it shall be opened unto you. I trotted onto the field with my heart pumping—not with fear but with pride. My first game!

I had only two innings to pitch and I got through with just a single unearned run. I pitched twice more in relief again that season, both times against Minnesota, and I gave up no runs at all. My only start came against the California Angels, with Dean Chance pitching. Maybe, if this had come sooner, I'd have been all aquiver. But I had already pitched in the big-league games, all the butterflies had fled from my stomach and we were barely edged by the great Dean Chance, 3 to 2. That season I pitched only twenty and a half innings and I was charged with two losses. But I had started to learn to pitch and had gotten my feet wet in the big leagues. I had a nice earned run average of less than three runs per nine innings. I wasn't entirely satisfied with the record. But I wasn't downhearted either. I could look back and see spots where I could have done better. And I knew I was going to have to learn a lot more about keeping runners from getting too good a start off first base. My pick-off throw had about as much deception as a steamboat whistle. I was more relieved than surprised at the end of the season when Birdie Tebbets told me he wanted me to go to Puerto Rico for winter ball. That meant steady paydays for the winter and a chance to work on my weakness with the man who had been my manager at Charleston, John Lipon, former shortstop with Detroit. After about six weeks of pitching in Puerto Rico I came up with a stiff arm—not just a sore arm but an arm so weak I could not even lift it high enough to brush my teeth. I had heard about sore arms and was not too much worried. The local doctor told me I had tendinitis and needed two weeks' rest. But when the two weeks were over, I still could not throw a ball with any strength. And it hurt day and night. Lipon and I agreed that I had better go back to Cleveland and see an orthopedic specialist.

On the trip to Cleveland I had plenty of time for gloomy imaginings about never pitching again and I was really in the dumps when Bob Kennedy met me at the airport. We sat and talked about what could be done and Bob suggested I see the trainer of the St. Louis Cardinals, Bob (Doc) Bauman, who was supposed to be the best in the business in restoring sore arms to health. I returned to Terre Haute and called Doc Bauman from home. He invited me to come right to St. Louis. After a careful examination of my ailing arm, he sent me to the team orthopedist, Dr. I. C. Middleman.

Dr. Middleman gave me a good going over and told me the bad news: I had torn some fibers that would take a long time to heal. A shot of cortisone eased the pain. But when I left the doctor's office I was deep in gloom—not because of the prognosis, because I was always optimistic about such things (having of course no premonition of the disaster to my arm that lay far in the future)—but because of what the doctor and I had just heard on his radio: President Kennedy had been shot in Dallas and was dying. It was my very first sharp reminder that "in the midst of life, we are in death," and it made my own woes shrink suddenly to their proper size. At least I was alive! and I would get better!

I did get better too, thanks to some exercises with a "baseball" made of lead provided for me by Bob Bauman. (This was not my first nor my last chance to observe how unselfishly baseball people would help out even their rivals when real trouble struck.) But I still had not overcome my difficulties with the pick-off throw. And other more serious difficulties lay just ahead. For one thing, Birdie Tebbets, the Cleveland manager, was sick in bed when the 1964 season opened and my only adviser was Early Wynn, the pitching coach, and the man of whom it was once said he would "knock down his own grandmother with a pitch if she ever came to bat against him in a pinch." (Early did once deck his own son—by accident—with a pitched ball.) Early complimented me on my pitches but insisted that I needed to learn *one* more to be the complete Big Leaguer. He taught me how to throw a slider—the "nickel curve" that had just recently come into wide favor. I learned it fairly quickly—and I was overjoyed with it, for it seemed easy to control and I began to get strike after strike. The only trouble was, that by neglecting my fast ball, I began to lose control of it and with loss of control I lost my confidence—which is really the number one asset of any ballplayer, pitcher, hitter, or fielder. The pitcher has to *know* he can make his best pitch work; the batter has to *know* he can hit what any pitcher may toss up; the fielder has to *know* he can handle any ball that comes his way.

With Birdie Tebbets still laid up from his heart attack, it was up to Gabe Paul to decide what to do about me. He had been around long enough to know that the only thing that will build a pitcher's confidence is winning ball games, so he decided to send me down where it would be easier for me to win a few—down to Class AAA, this time in Portland, Oregon.

The only thing I could be glad about in returning to Class AAA was that Johnny Lipon was manager there now—and he knew my strengths and weaknesses as well as anyone alive, including me. Almost the first thing he told me, after seeing me work, was "forget the slider!" He reminded me that my best weapons had always been fast ball and curve. "Stick to those and forget everything else," said John. And I realized that somewhere along the line, since I had ignored that coach's advice to stop throwing curves, I had lost my faith in my own judgment. It didn't take long, with John Lipon's help, to get it back. I also developed, or rediscovered, another skill at Portland—my hitting ability. In a game against San Diego, I not only hit a grand slam home run, good for four runs, but hit another, with two men on base, good for three runs, and then hit a long, long sacrifice fly that brought in another run—eight runs batted in, in a single game—a record of some sort for a pitcher. On the basis of all this slugging, John used me as a pinch hitter in a game against Seattle. And, lo and behold, if they didn't give me an intentional base on balls—maybe the first time in *that* league that a pitcher had been walked on purpose. Talk about confidence! I felt, for a few days, like the next Babe Ruth. Babe, you may recall, had started out in professional baseball as a pitcher, the best in the league one season. But I knew my own ability too well by this time to hold on to any illusions about leading any league in home runs. I would follow John's advice and forget everything except fast ball and curve.

There was one unhappy aspect about my return to Portland that I did not tell about. The news came to me when the club was in New York, just after I had been shelled off the mound in Kansas City. My mom and dad had long planned a trip to New York to see me mow down the Yankees and they had already left when I was told I was headed for Portland.

They had not told me what hotel they were staying at and I could not get word to them, so they did not learn until game time that their son, the left-handed pitcher, was winging his way back to the minor leagues.

When the Indians sent me back to Portland, they asked for a rookie in return, a young kid named . . . Luis Tiant. Luis had really been scorching the Coast League that season—fifteen wins and one loss. But when word was given out that he was going to start against the Yankees, in the second game of a doubleheader, Whitey Ford, who doubled as the Yankee pitching coach, told himself: "This kid will be so nervous, pitching his first big-league game in Yankee Stadium, he probably won't last three innings. *I'll* pitch the second game." Too bad for Whitey! Luis was in such exquisite form that day, pitching sidearm, overhand, three-quarters, and turning away from the plate so far in his windup it looked as if he might decide to heave the ball into center field, that the great New York batters never *could* get their balance. Luis shut the Yankees out 1 to 0 and struck out a dozen.

But here I was out on the Coast, and headed for Hawaii, a place I had sometimes dreamed about. The club was going there for a whole week of playing the Hawaii Islanders. But I got off to a bad start. The traveling secretary (also our trainer) offered us a choice—either fly up to Los Angeles or take the bus. Well, I had had a belly full of bus rides by this time so I chose to fly, and so did my pals. But the club had a surprise for us.

In my innocence, I had imagined that we would fly to Hawaii in big-league style—first class—or coach at the very least. But, having chosen to fly up from San Diego we now, we were informed, had to "make up the money" for the San Diego flight by flying "Super Economy" class from Los Angeles to Hawaii. The most stunning feature of the Super Economy class was the fact that *no food would be served.* And I had started off from San Diego with nothing more in my stomach than a bowl of cereal! The flight to Hawaii would take six hours. Six starving hours! Along the way I did manage to cadge a few rolls from somebody's dinner tray but long before we reached the Golden Isles my stomach had forgotten all about that trifle and was insistently begging for mercy.

The Beaver-Rooters, fan club of the Portland Beavers (that was our name) were financing this trip and they had also offered a prize for the player that came back from Hawaii with the finest tan. (Tommie Agee felt that was outright discrimination.)

Even some big-league managers might have put the kibosh on that little P.R. event, but Johnny Lipon was all for it. He told us that he wanted us to enjoy this trip because many of us might never get another chance to see Oahu. The very first day he urged us to get out and see the sights, have fun on the beaches, and just take care that we did not get ourselves so sunburned we could not play ball. Johnny Lipon treated us like grown-ups, assuming that professional ballplayers had sense enough not to cripple themselves deliberately. I know a few big-league managers who could have taken lessons from Johnny Lipon in how to handle athletes and I often marvel that Lipon never managed in the big leagues himself.

Anyway, thanks to our manager, we all took our fill of the joys and the sights of Hawaii and came home thoroughly tanned. (I forget who won the contest.)

Come September, when our season was over, several of us were called up to the Cleveland club, Tommie Agee and I among them. Tommie owned an automobile and he suggested we drive to Cleveland together, taking turns at the wheel and sleeping in the car. Steve Hargan, a big right-hander, about my own age and size, who lived in Fort Wayne, Indiana, asked if we could give him a ride home. As Fort Wayne was on our route, we happily agreed.

A local restaurant, that season, had been awarding tickets good for big buckets of Kentucky Fried Chicken for every home run. Agee still had three tickets and I had my three.

Agee, always thinking, suggested we pool our tickets, collect our buckets, and thus avoid even having to stop for food along the way. Great idea! We all climbed into Tommie's magic carpet and set off for Cleveland.

We met our first obstacle somewhere about the first night—a road construction job that stalled us long enough for us to do away with two buckets of chicken. Then we sped smoothly on through Idaho. It was late at night. Tommie was driving and I was deep asleep in the back seat. I woke up to a devilish turmoil—yelling, cursing, horses stamping—and I looked up into a regular nightmare: a whole gang of men on horseback carrying shotguns and flaunting badges and flashlights. Two of the guns were pointed straight at me.

"Out!" I was ordered. "Get out with your hands up!" It was like a scene out of "Gunsmoke." But the guns were real and the men were not playing games. They lined the three of us against the car and gave us a quick frisk, then looked inside the car. It was a sheriff's posse, it turned out, looking for three men who had just held up a motel in Twin Falls. They were convinced they had nailed the right guys and listened very sourly to our story of being three nice innocent boys who played baseball for the Cleveland Indians. But we couldn't have looked more like escaped convicts if we had made up for the role—clothes that had been slept in, faces that hadn't been washed or shaved for a day and a half, and buckets of cold chicken that had obviously been bought a few days earlier. Still, after each of us had dug through our luggage to display enough Cleveland Indian insignia and correspondence to make our story sound plausible, they very reluctantly let us proceed. So reluctantly indeed that about a half hour later we were stopped again at a roadblock by another group of lawmen who had been warned by the first gang that we were coming. Apparently they were not sure but what we had managed to con them on the first search by fake documents and fast talk. This time they really combed us over and let us go only after a lot of growling among themselves. We just *looked* so guilty.

I took over the driving then and at the very first truck stop we came to, I wheeled right in.

"What are you doing?" Agee cried.

"I'm going to *stay* here," I replied. "And I'm going to *shave*. And so are you! We just look too much like escaped cons."

We put in, and got ourselves cleaned, and shaved off that two-day crop of whisker. Then we looked each over before we went in to eat. We were still rumpled and weary-looking but we were clean.

"Now," I said, "at least we don't look like convicts."

"We're not!" Agee yelped. "We're Indians!"

THREE

Sally:

I think my worst night at the hospital was Saturday, August 15, when, for the very first time in my life, I realized what it was like to put everything in the hands of God. It was the most difficult decision I had ever made—almost physically impossible, harder even than allowing some other person to decide if you should live or die. Because this time it was the life of my little boy, a life far dearer to me than my own.

I know Carol tried to shield me from what was happening that night but I sensed something was terribly wrong the moment I entered the Pediatric Intensive Care Unit. Despite the hum and blip-blip of the machinery, there was an unnatural stillness. Everyone, it seemed, was moving on tiptoe. Drapes were drawn about cubicles. And then, to my utter dismay, I saw what was happening. I peeked into the next cubicle and saw them wrapping a little four-year-old girl from head to foot, in white, like a tiny mummy. She had died only minutes earlier. I began to tremble. Tears welled up. This *couldn't* be happening! Oh God! Those *poor* parents! I held myself tight to keep from sobbing aloud. Then I hurried to Travis's side, almost as if by hovering over his bed I could fend off death. I could *feel* that chill presence. "Oh Death," I whispered. "Leave me *alone*!"

Who would be next? How could this be happening to these helpless babies? There were so many here with such terrible ailments. How could God permit such things? But my Christian faith took hold, and despite the dreadful wrench in my heart, I made myself say: "God knows best. Oh, God, Travis is in your hands." I believed in God. I trusted in His will. But I was so terribly afraid! No, no, no, I kept thinking. Not Travis too! I sat and prayed quietly by his side.

Travis, of course, came safely through the night. But I must have called up every hour or two all night long. Then on Monday I had another fright. They told me, when I came to the hospital, that Travis was being moved to a different cubicle in the Intensive Care Unit. They showed me the cubicle and, while I was there, the electrician came in to "service" the monitor they would use for Travis in his new bed. The monitor certainly looked as if it needed servicing. It was altogether different from the one he had at the time—obviously older, less compact, even slightly tarnished. I was dismayed. What if this decrepit machine broke down? Travis was still deep in a coma. There would have to be someone at his side every second. I asked Dr. Epstein, the neurologist, who was now "Fred" to us, why this had to be. Well, there was a little boy just coming out of open-heart surgery and they felt that he had to have the modern machine.

"But this machine is so old!" I said. "Can't you find another one—a good one?"

Fred was really shocked.

"This *is* a good one," he insisted. "You should know I wouldn't put Travis on a machine that was not in proper shape."

I felt embarrassed that I had ever questioned his decision. But he completely understood my concern and fear.

Well, the monitor proved sufficient at least, although the electrician had to come in to "service" the machine several

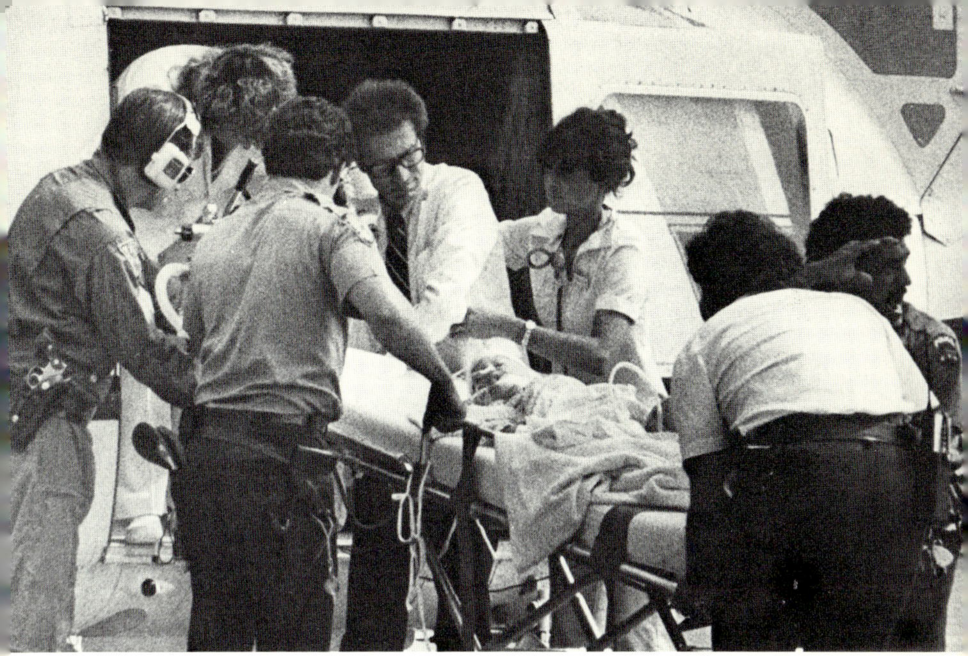

The injured Travis is rushed to a New York hospital by helicopter. *(UPI photo)*

Travis in the early days of his coma *(Chuck Schaefer)*

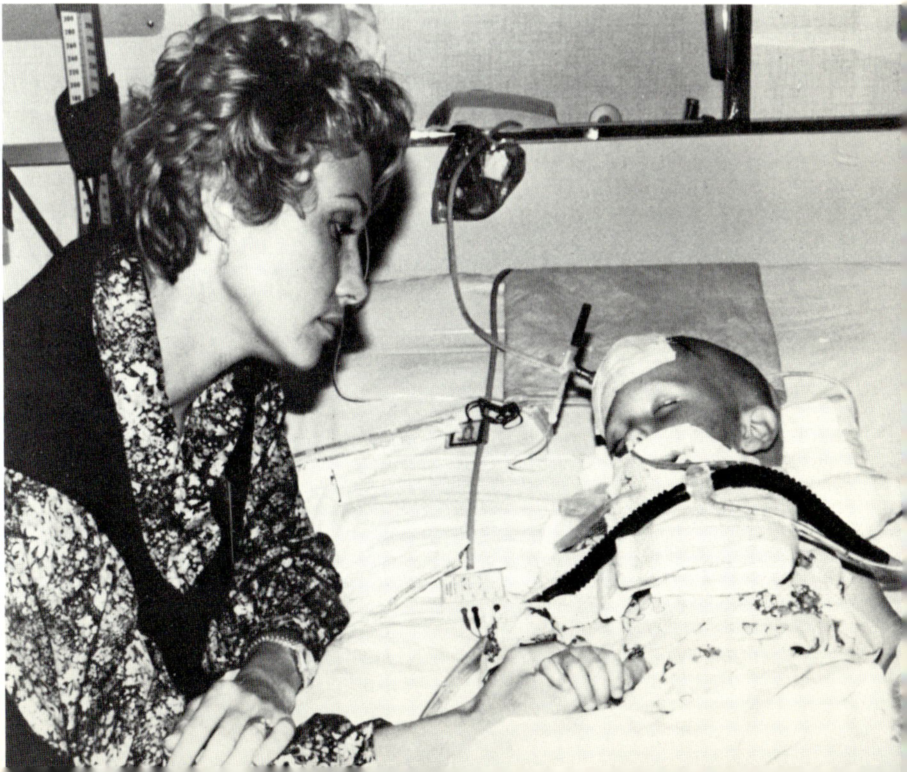

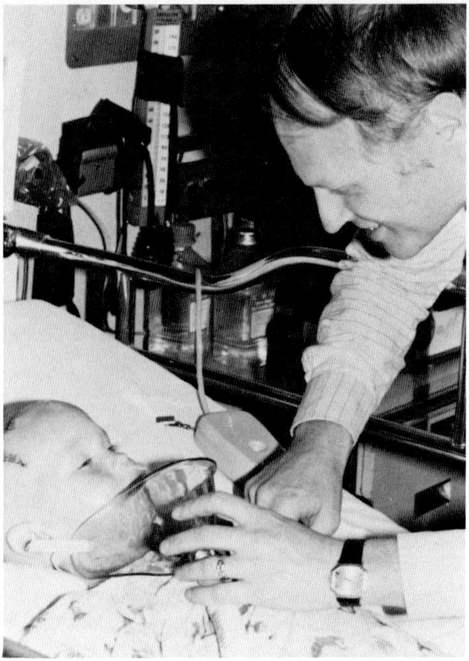

Travis, his eyes now open but still in a coma, with Dr. Fred Epstein *(Chuck Schaefer)*

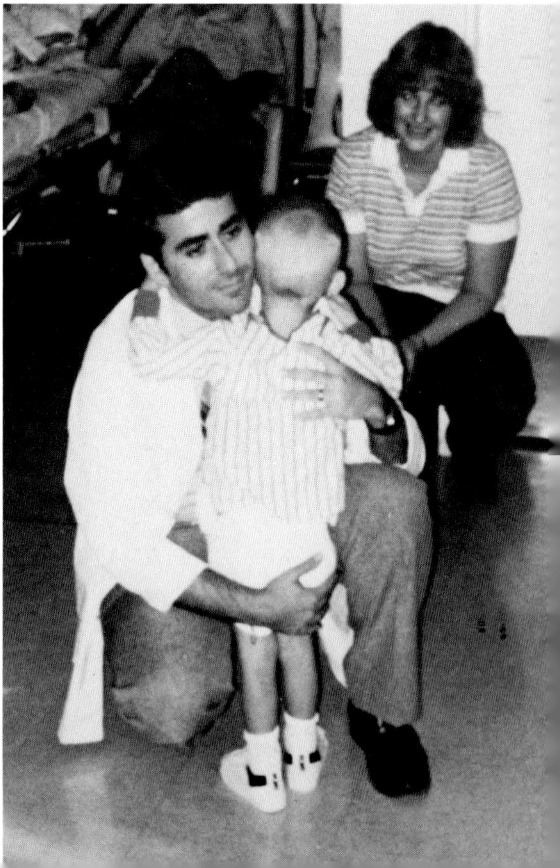

With Dr. Sol Zimmerman *(Chuck Schaefer)*

Travis offers grace. *(Chuck Schaefer)*

With visitor Bucky Dent of the Yankees *(Chuck Schaefer)*

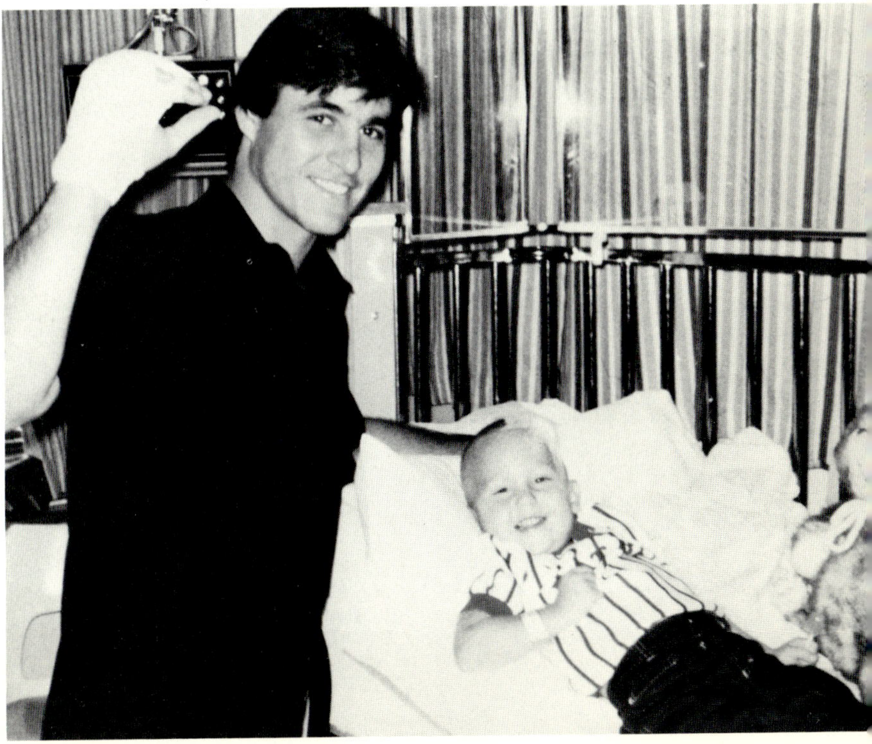

A hug for Dr. Stu Siegel *(Chuck Schaefer)*

Playing ball with Tommy in the hospital

Answering mail

A red-letter day: Travis leaves the hospital with Mommy and Daddy and family friend Carol Schaefer. *(UPI photo)*

Back in Yankee uniform

While a Yankee Stadium crowd cheers, Travis throws out the first ball of the evening to catcher Rick Cerone while Reggie Jackson coaches. *(Courtesy of* The Daily News)

Now in Angel uniform *(Susan Gaedy)*

Sally's parents, Opal and Jerry Simmons, with Travis and the Johns' three other children, Tami, Taylor, and Tommy

Sally's sister, Judy Reed, (*lower center*) with her husband, Russell, and their own five children (*clockwise from left*) Kathy, Leslie, Linda, Rick, and Rusty *(Olan Mills)*

Tommy's parents, Ruth and Tommy John, Sr., with the four John children, at their home

Travis, fully recovered

times, sending me each time into moments of terror. It was not until a year later that I learned that NYU did indeed need *new* monitors of this sort, and other machines that could help keep children alive. Much of the machinery is badly out of date and funds are tight. So Tommy and I are right now planning a fund raiser of some sort to buy new machines for the Pediatric Intensive Care Unit and the operating room. What if some child dies for want of a functioning monitor? What a price for some family to pay! Dr. Epstein is now performing surgery on spinal cord tumors with a borrowed "Cooper Laser"! There are no funds to purchase this for him. He has saved the lives of sixty children when other doctors had said that the tumors were inoperable.

The presence of so many little ones, suffering such fearful ailments, and the frightened parents, not knowing which way to look for help or comfort, seemed to create a sort of family feeling among us all. We actually took strength from each other and often in praying together we achieved a real consciousness of God's presence that provided another source of strength.

And the children themselves were a source of comfort and love. Here they were, suffering from the most terrible afflictions, cancer, brain tumors, crippling diseases, yet they had loving kindness enough to send all sorts of tokens to the Intensive Care Unit—cards, hand-drawn posters, balloons, toys. One young lady, Stacy, a lovely sixteen-year-old who had had twenty-nine operations on her spine and who would never walk, sent in a beautiful silver balloon with this message written across it: "I love you Travis." Travis, of course, could not see it, but it really wrung our hearts and inspired us, too, with the realization that here in this totally unreal atmosphere of suffering and sorrow, real love could still flower freely, unselfishly and, as the Bible says, vaunting not itself. I think Tommy and I both began to feel and share this presence and to derive strength from it.

Of course, there were messages from the "real" world

too, such an outpouring of sympathy that it nearly overwhelmed us. From President Reagan, President Nixon, President Ford, from Frank Sinatra in Rio de Janeiro, from baseball club owners, from baseball players on just about every club in both leagues, from Don and Barbara Rickles, Tom and Nancy Seaver, the entire Cleveland ball club, the USC athletic department, the Oak Ridge Boys, Angie Dickinson, Bill Anderson, senators and congressmen, Tom and Jeanne Weiskopf, Andy and Debby Bean, and Curtis and Sara Strange. David Hartman phoned again and again. But I think the one letter that moved us most was from Buzzy Bavasi. Tommy and Buzzy had exchanged some bitter words and the episode had rankled with us both, like a sore spot that keeps getting rubbed.

It had its origin, as so many quarrels do, in a misunderstanding for which neither side was really responsible. Tommy, unable to reach an agreement with the Dodgers in 1978, had chosen to try free agency, expecting two or three offers and hoping for bids from Cincinnati, the Angels and perhaps the Yankees. He received thirteen offers that he and Bob Cohen, his attorney, spent some time evaluating. The best offer came from the Yankees. We would have liked to stay in California where we had a comfortable home, dear friends, and a church to which we were devoted. But the offer from George Steinbrenner was many hundreds of thousands of dollars ahead of all the others. The trouble was that the Yankee offer, because of George's occasional preference for the devious and round about, had to be disguised in such a way that the guarantee from the Yankees would not look so lavish in the official report to be rendered to the Commissioner and the other club owners. When time came to sign, it was revealed that almost all the "deferred payments" were to come, not from the Yankee baseball club, although guaranteed by the Yankees, but from other enterprises George controlled so that, even though the "consideration" Tommy promised was still playing baseball for the Yankees, the total payment from the Yankees was diminished.

As a result of this bit of hocus-pocus, the "offer" as it was spelled out in the official report looked like a good deal less money than the California Angels had offered. Buzzy Bavasi immediately took personal offense. He wrote an angry note to Tommy that he made a point of putting into Tommy's hands himself at their next meeting. Among other things, the note said of Tommy that he was "a phony with a capital P." That was not the sort of charge that could be laughed off by anyone like Tommy, who, never afflicted with an inability to express himself, responded with a number of salty comments of his own. And I was quoted in the papers as declaring that "Tommy should punch Buzzy Bavasi in the nose." I don't recall saying anything like that. But perhaps I did. I was angry enough.

Now here was this letter from Buzzy—brief, sincere, obviously from the heart, offering us deepest sympathy and prayers. Until Tommy saw that note, I had not realized how much Tommy must have mourned the end of this friendship. He read that letter again and again, treasuring every sentence and probably reading in it the deep emotions that prompted it. As for me, I found some New York Yankee stationery in my purse and sat me down there in the hospital to write an immediate reply. "It took a very big man to write this," I told Buzzy. "I sincerely hope you and Tommy can put your troubles in the past. Maybe (was *this* a premonition?) Tommy will be an Angel someday. . . ."

Tragedy, or near-tragedy, can really open people's hearts, make them better and kinder, I sincerely believe. I know that Tommy and I, from being thrust into this world we could never have dreamed existed, came out with a better understanding of what woes other families had to deal with and with a strong feeling of kinship for all the children and families that were sharing our troubles. We began to understand, too, that God's all-embracing love expressed itself through the hearts and minds of all of us, His children. Words that we had sung or recited or listened to with no more than passing comprehension suddenly became full of vivid meaning. "Love Divine! All Love Excelling!" How better to describe the feeling that flowed back and forth among all of us, the stricken, the sorrowful, and the frightened, who dwelt in that unreal world of beeping monitors and panting respirators, of tubes and anesthesia, and reeking medications, harried nurses and tired doctors, of the sounds of pain and labored breathing, and of long hours of silent dread.

We were, in some ways, so much more fortunate than most. There were children there hundreds of miles from home, whose parents could not afford to be with them. There were some without relatives or friends to comfort them. There were families who had no one to share their fear or sorrow and none to offer sympathy. But we were deluged with expressions and offerings, many from people we hardly knew, or knew only by name, many from total strangers, and, of course, even more from friends and kin who were dear to us.

Reggie Jackson sent us the most spectacular floral piece I have ever seen outside a parade—and I like to think of it as a symbol of the warmth of Reggie's heart. It was a dog—a poodle—life-size and made entirely of flowers. We simply gasped at the sight of it. And—because Travis could not have seen or enjoyed it—we had it brought immediately to the pediatric floor where it prompted such cries of joy and excitement that they would have brought tears to the eyes of a lead soldier. And there were other gifts, some lavish, and some priceless only because of the love and care that were obviously poured into them—stuffed animals enough to complete a toy zoo, books, games, and Lord knows what, that would have foundered a delivery wagon. Tommy and I soon decided how best to distribute them. I would write cards "from Travis" and Tommy would take them to different little patients and tell them that Travis right now was too sick to come see them but that he sent this present with his love and just as soon as he got out of bed he would come visiting. To see the rapt and joyous expressions of some of those pale small faces would have given anyone an instant understanding of why toys were invented. There are not many medicines that can match a teddy bear.

But for the first week or more we were so consumed by our own fears, we simply lacked the heart to involve ourselves with others. Our little boy lay there with only the blipping of the monitor to assure us that he was alive. His small face held no expression. His eyes, now open, showed no hint of life. On the eighth day, I could take no more. I asked both doctors, Doctor Zimmerman and Doctor Epstein, to come talk to me in the conference room. I had heard all I wanted to hear of "He's doing okay" or "He's in as stable a condition as we could hope for." What I wanted to know was: Is my little boy going to be a little boy again, or just a creature without sense, or feeling, or emotions, unable to talk or to smile or to understand? If that was what his fate would be, then I didn't *want* him to live. And I didn't want to live either.

When I sat down with the doctors in the conference room, I found I could not speak. I leaned over and put my head in my arms upon the table and sobbed. When I was finally able to talk without sobbing, I laid right into them. They had not been telling me the truth! They had been trying to soften the blow because I was pregnant. My little boy was not getting better. There was no spark of life or recognition in his eyes. His face was blank. His little brain was not working! He would never be normal—and they knew it! This was not what I meant by living. I didn't want him to go on and on like this, just a lump of flesh or a vegetable.

Dr. Zimmerman laughed aloud.

"I knew you'd break, Sally," he said. "It will do you good. It just wasn't possible for any human being to continue under that strain and get as little sleep as you've been getting. But really, Sally, Travis is getting better. Progress is very, very slow. It does not show overnight. But all the same there's definite progress. Time now is the only cure."

I had heard *that* before! I was not dumb enough, I told him, to believe that. But he and Fred Epstein came and took my hands. Believe us, they said. We are not trying to deceive you. Travis has a 97 percent chance of full recovery. There is positively no trace of irreversible brain injury. Please, please believe us.

But I want him to walk and talk, I told them. I don't want him just alive. I want him *perfect.*

Fred Epstein looked me steadily in the eye. He will walk and talk, he told me solemnly. It may take four months. Maybe six months. But he will walk. It may take four months for him to talk. But he *will* talk. We guarantee that. You have got to believe that, Sally. We have no reason not to tell you the truth. I cried for an hour and felt much better.

It was different when I looked again at that expressionless little face, those unseeing eyes. But at least it was a hope I could cling to, with a little effort, and I tried hard to make myself believe it. And I did have Tommy with me, to share his strength and faith, to help quiet my fears, and to join me in massaging that little body, in trying to pierce the veil that shrouded that little brain. I used to look at Tommy sometimes and recall the day I first set eyes on him. And I would smile to myself sometimes to think that I had once refused a chance to go out with him. No *sir*! I had said. I want no professional athletes in *my* life!

My mental image of a professional athlete in those days was an oversexed, egotistical, "swinger"-type who either owned a cocktail lounge or spent all his off-hours in one. I looked at this gentle, caring, thoughtful man across from me and wondered how I ever could have classified him as one of those. And I winced a little to think how close I had come to sending him out of my life altogether. But who could have known just to look at him, that he could be so strong, even fierce at times, or at least fierce-looking when he faced a batter, so confident, so self-assured, and at the same time be so modest, so unfailingly kind, so tender in dealing with kids—so just plain *good* in every way.

I saw once again, almost as vividly as if it happened the day before, the scene at Indiana State Homecoming, 1968, when I first set eyes on Tommy John. Only I didn't know who he was and really felt no urge to find out. But he did stand out from the crowd that day and I could recall exactly what he was wearing. I, as a member of the Blue Berets, a group of men and women students who were charged with the job of escorting VIPs out on the football field to receive Distinguished Alumni Awards, had been assigned the task of escorting Senator Birch Bayh's father out to the microphone at midfield. I had looked over to the sidelines and immediately spotted this strange figure there. A tall, slender man with a striking outfit on: orange turtleneck, black-and-white sports jacket, black trousers and *white* shoes. At a football game in Indiana on an October afternoon! White shoes! He must be a Hollywood character, I decided. Or possibly a big-city sports writer. Whoever he was, he seemed out of place here. I must have looked at him a little longer than I meant to, for I realized suddenly that he was staring back at me, intently. I looked quickly away. I just could not keep from glancing at him once or twice more. He seemed so clearly a creature from another world—a world that held no interest for me.

My nickname at that time, strangely enough, was "Space," awarded me, I supposed, because of my standard act of being always a little light in the head, never knowing a serious moment, given to flip talk and lots of laughter. A girl really has to have an act of some kind at that stage in life, when the boys you go out with are so often trying to get "serious"—serious about sex, serious about romance. I had a lot of life and no intention of getting "serious" about any young man, so I used my "spacey" act to keep them safely at arm's length. A few days after the game, I heard someone calling to me: "Hey, Space!" It was John Knox, the football captain, himself a slightly off-the-wall type, who had been a good friend of mine for a long time.

"How'd you like to meet Tommy John?" he asked.

I am sure I was supposed to recognize the name but I didn't. It sounded almost make-believe. Who the heck was Tommy John?

"He's a pitcher for the Chicago White Sox!"

Still I failed to register any thrill.

"What are the White Sox?"

John registered mild disgust.

"Oh, for Pete's sake! The baseball team! Tommy pitches for them."

"A professional baseball player?" Visions of Joe Namath and Mickey Mantle! "No thanks!"

"But he was at the game last Saturday. He wants to meet you."

"Not that guy in the white shoes?"

"Right!"

"He's *old*! I don't want to go out with him!"

"He's only twenty-five."

"That's old! My sister Judy's twenty-five and *married*."

"Well, Tommy's not married. And he's a nice guy. He really wants to meet you."

"Well, he's a professional ballplayer. And I don't want to meet him."

How close that came to being the end of it! I was nineteen and had no desire to see Tommy John again or even to hear any more about him. But the college president, Dr. Alan Rankin, a man I deeply admired, unexpectedly took a hand in the affair one day when I met him on the campus.

"What's this I hear about your turning down a date with Tommy John?"

I was astounded. Did this man know *everything*?

"Who told you that?"

Doctor Rankin laughed.

"Oh, I just heard," said he. "But really, Sally, you don't need to be afraid of Tommy John. He's a really nice guy. I worked with him on the March of Dimes campaign and I can vouch for the fact that he's a thoroughly decent young man. He'll treat you like a lady. You can count on it."

This put a different face on things! He *was* handsome. When next I saw John Knox I told him that if Tommy John still wanted to meet me I would be happy to meet *him*.

"Too late!" said John. "Tommy's taken off for a golf tournament. You should have spoken sooner."

And that's the end of Tommy John! I said to myself. I was surprised at how let down I felt. Well, there'd be other young men, I supposed. But he *was* handsome, white shoes or no. And I put Tommy out of my mind—for good, I sincerely believed.

But I had reckoned without Tommy. That winter, during basketball season, when I served as a cheerleader, I sprained my ankle and had to give up cheerleading for a while. But I did not give up basketball. With my ankle in a cast, I hobbled to the game against Ball State in January, accompanied by my date, Craig Jackson, and sat in what was known as the "date section." John Knox, ushering at the game, was guarding the ropes at the entrance to the gym. Soon after we took our seats, John shouted to me, in a voice that could have drowned out the referee's whistle:

"Hey Space! Come down here and meet Tommy John!" I cringed at the sound and looked down at John Knox, but I was too mortified to make any reply. At John Knox's side stood the very man I had seen at the football game, unusually tall and straight, wearing a stylish black raincoat. Obviously embarrassed himself, he had turned away and seemed to be motioning John Knox to silence. But John would not be silent.

"Come on!" he persisted. "You wanted to meet Tommy

John! Here's your chance!" The kids all around us were laughing. Craig Jackson was squirming. He started to get up.

"Go ahead, if you want to," he said. "I'll sit somewhere else."

"No! You stay right here!" John Knox had come close enough now so I could speak to him. "I've *got* a date," I told him. "I don't want to meet Tommy John." (It's a wonder the words did not stick in my throat. I had had a clear view of Mr. Tommy John and I liked every bit of what I saw.) So John Knox gave up and when I dared look again at the entrance, where Tommy John had been standing, the tall striking figure was gone.

Meanwhile, my schoolmates all around me continued the chorus:

"Go meet him, Space! Hey! How about meeting Tommy John!"

They continued to tease me all through the game and afterwards. Meet Tommy John! Meet Tommy John! I thought I would scream if I heard it once more.

But I heard it again when I least expected it, at ten o'clock the very next morning, when I was jolted out of a deep sleep by the telephone. I scrambled out of bed, for I realized suddenly it was the day of the basketball game with Illinois State and I had to be ready to leave at noon. The voice on the telephone was unusually deep.

"Is this Sally Simmons?"

I tried to sound bright and wide awake.

"Yes!"

"This is Tommy John. . . ."

"Oh, come *on*!" I snapped. "Is this you, John Knox?"

"No. This is Tommy John."

I was just about to snarl, "Who is this, *really*?" but there was something about the way he spoke. Maybe . . .

"I want to apologize for what happened last night. I was just as embarrassed as you were. Would you like to come out for coffee?"

"Well, yes," said I, who had never tasted coffee in my life. "I'd love to!"

"I'll wait for you in the lobby."

"Ten minutes," I said, and hung up. I began at once to yell to the girls for help. I had to get dressed in my *best*. And do it in ten minutes. There were fifteen girls in the dorm and they all rushed about to help collect the garments I needed. Before I was all put together, some of the girls took turns idling through the lobby and they hurried back to report how he was dressed, how tall and handsome he was.

When I went down at last my stomach was fluttering so I was not sure I could speak. He *was* tall. Slender, too. Not all bulky like some athletes. But not skinny. Just strong looking. And his shoulders! The little wings that fluttered in my stomach simply would not be still. Tommy held the door open for me and even opened the *car* door—a practically forgotten courtesy in my circles. We went to The Big Wheel in Terre Haute and I was simply too flustered and too shy to ask for something different when he gave the order for coffee. I sat waiting for him to use sugar and cream, so I could follow his lead. But he drank the stuff black. So I drank the stuff black. Yuucck! It was *bitter*! I had to look down at the table to hide my dismay. How could anyone drink a cupful of this stuff? But Tommy was drinking his with relish. So I—very slowly—drank mine with relish. Had it been carbolic acid Tommy was drinking, I believe I'd have been able to get a portion of it down.

I was still all aflutter in the stomach to be with this man. He was so mature, so far removed from my world. Who *was* he anyway? A baseball player? I fumbled through my brain to find even a scrap of something intelligent to say about baseball, or some question to ask. All I could come up with was "Mickey Mantle." What did I know about him? Nothing.

But Tommy was not talking about baseball. He asked me about my home, about my family, about my studies, and I was able to offer sensible comments to everything he asked.

He told about his own family in Terre Haute, about his father especially, whom he seemed to love most dearly. The only baseball player he mentioned was Ken Boyer, whose name I had never heard before. He had been pheasant hunting with Ken Boyer and he told me funny stories about that. I had no need to grope for topics. And, for a change, I was not required to express amazement, or admiration at any of *his* great deeds. He was probably the first young man I ever had a date with who refrained from recounting, with imitation modesty, tales of his own prowess on the football field, the basketball court, the classroom, or the cocktail lounge. Telling the whole episode over to myself afterward, I think I was most impressed by his modesty, which was obviously part of his nature. Afterward, I really had not much more understanding of who or what he really was than I had before.

When I had sipped at my coffee until it was cold, I told Tommy I had to catch the team bus to Bloomington, Illinois.

"Well, come on," said he. "I'll drive you to the bus. Are you packed?"

"Oh, yes!" I lied. I was not about to neglect any *more* opportunities! We sped back to the dorm, where I raced upstairs and threw this and that and God knows what else into my bag. We made the bus easily enough. It was not until I went to change in the hotel at Bloomington that I discovered I had left out my tights and my tennis shoes. One of the other cheerleaders had an extra pair of tights that fit me and I finally borrowed tennis shoes from the cleaning lady at the hotel.

Before Tommy left me, he asked if I would like to come with him to a sports banquet in Worthington, Indiana, where he had to give a talk. Would I?! It was a struggle to conceal my excitement as I told him yes, I guess so! I was so high now that I could hardly feel the floor beneath my borrowed tennis shoes. Someone had told me that Kathy, our cheerleader captain, had dated Tommy the year before. She was, of course, older than I was. More sophisticated, too. I looked at her with different eyes now, wondering how she might look to Tommy John. Compared to me, for instance. But I never spoke to her about Tommy.

The Worthington banquet was a gathering of small boys and their fathers, who sat in a group to listen to Tommy speak. And I, in my second-best outfit (I had already worn my best the first time out), sat right up there beside him absorbing all those stares. I kept my eyes on Tommy, or tried to. I had no experience at being a "celebrity." Afterwards, the little boys (and some of the *big* boys) lined up to get Tommy's autograph—and, for Heaven's sake, they wanted *mine* as well! Tommy said, "Go ahead, sign your name!" My hand trembled as I signed all those out-thrust notebooks, and cards, and papers. Imagine Sally Simmons giving autographs like a movie star! Imagine Sally Simmons going out on a *date* with a star! What kind of banquet was this with no food!? I was starved. But I was too shy to say so.

Before Tommy called to pick me up that night, my father had given me a long solemn talk on the phone about ballplayers and their ways with girls. They were not to be trusted, even the best of them. "Here," he said to me, "Put a dime in your shoe and call me if he tries anything—if *anything* goes wrong!" Obediently, I tucked a dime inside my shoe.

But nothing went wrong—at least not until we were well on our way back home. Then Tommy, after some wry comments about banquets where no food was served, asked if I was hungry. I was famished! "Me too," he allowed. "Let's stop and eat somewhere."

The "somewhere" he chose, to my growing alarm, was the Albert Pick Motel, notorious in college circles as an ideal spot for one-night stands. A girl seen coming out of that place in the morning might as well carry a sign on her back. "Oh, no!" I told myself. "Not little Sally!" I felt suddenly sick to have my illusions destroyed so brutally. Then Dad was right about ballplayers!

I looked about me for some escape and noticed a freestanding pay phone booth outside the gas station nearby. As I climbed out of the car, I reached down into my shoe and drew out my dime. I can get to that phone booth before he can stop me, I told myself. And I'll shut myself in. Dad said he would come get me no matter where I was. I'll just stay inside until he comes. Tommy had headed for the motel entrance and I trailed him by several strides, hoping of course that I *might* be wrong about his intentions but more than half sure I was right. Inside the motel entrance, without even a glance, Tommy strode right past the registration desk, and turned toward the coffee shop. I could have cried out with relief. I scurried to catch up with him and we entered the coffee shop together. Oh, I was hungry! As I took my seat I looked down to find that warm dime still clutched tight in my hand. Tommy, I am sure, had no idea why I laughed so suddenly.

This silly episode wiped out my last doubt about Tommy. Of course, I still didn't know him well—or really know him at all. But I did know, just as my mother had told me I would, that I was in love with him. There wasn't any wondering or wavering. It just happened. And I knew it. I had already told myself, and told my friends, that if I didn't marry Tommy John I would never marry anyone. My mother was delighted with him when I took him home so Dad could check out "my ballplayer." And Dad, who had never really approved of any of my previous "dates," practically adopted him as soon as they met. "But," he warned me, "he's too *mature* for you!" Well, of course! I was a teenager and he was nearly six years older. And that's what I wanted. He was more experienced, wiser in the ways of the world, someone I could trust, and look up to, and lean on when I was in trouble. And he was the man I loved.

Our "dates" many times were just visits to his home for dinner, where I had a chance to observe at first hand his devotion to his parents, who did all the bragging about Tommy John that Tommy John had omitted. And I began to learn more and more about what Tommy was really like. Tommy would often pick me up right after class and we would go someplace to eat ice cream and popcorn, or sometimes we would lunch together. It was a quiet, steady romance, deepening day by day. As a matter of fact, I was playing it cool. Despite Tommy's attentiveness and the unfailing respect with which he treated me, I was never positive just where I stood with him. While I had no negative feelings about myself, nor any desire to own some other girl's glamour, or fame, or position in the world, I knew I was just a small-town girl, a college student, keeping company with a Big Name. I was aware that Tommy had dated many other girls—indeed still dated them from time to time, just as I went out with college boys I had been dating before Tommy and I met. But Tommy sometimes escorted really famous women, including TV star Kathy Garver when she came to Terre Haute. And I could not still the fear that one of these days he might tell me, "Well, I am going to marry Miss America. . . ." or someone of fame equal to his own. It seemed to me that Tommy could marry *anyone.* And I knew he had been out in the company of some real beauties, sophisticated girls who would be at home among stars in every profession. Who was I, really, to compete in such company? So I took great care to keep Tommy from knowing just how completely infatuated I was with Tommy John. More than once, when it seemed to me that we had spent an unusual amount of time together, I would ask the girls in the dorm to tell Tommy I was out on a date when he came calling for me—when I was really hiding in my room eating a small piece out of my heart.

But his company never failed to thrill me. Each date was almost a repetition of our first meeting, with my stomach still going all tingly at the sight of him. I would laugh at myself sometimes to think how I used to ask my mother how I could tell when I met the ONE man I would want to marry. I met so many boys that I liked, so many I thought might be perfectly acceptable lifetime companions. And then I met Tommy, and all doubts vanished.

In the spring of 1969, Tommy left for spring training and then came home again, with word that training had been postponed. Actually, the players had gone on strike, something I could not grasp. All it meant to me was that Tommy and I had more time together. It being standard practice in that day for college kids to flock to Florida in spring vacation, seven of us pooled what cash we had and made plans to drive down—day and night—to enjoy the sunshine. Tommy urged us to come to Sarasota, where the Chicago White Sox would be staying now that spring training had resumed. Three of my girlfriends and I headed to Florida, with bathing suits, one change of clothing, and little else—two in the front seat and two in back—stopping only for gas and scanty meals. Tommy reserved one double room for me and my girlfriends. Right then we were so excited, we could have been comfortable under a park bench. This baseball world seemed just one thrill after another—a world with a new sort of inhabitant, with new ways and new language. (I remember that when I got home from this trip and told my mother of Tommy's introducing my friends to a "hard-throwing right-hander" she looked at me as if I had spoken to her in Latin.)

Tommy introduced the girls to the ballplayers and everyone had a date every night. We all watched baseball every afternoon. Such food! Such swimming! Such friendly, happy people! One night Tommy took me to dinner at the home of a teammate—Gary Peters—whom I probably soon learned to describe as a "hard-throwing left-hander." I liked Gary's wife Jean at first sight. But I was taken aback at the first question she asked me: "Are you the American Airlines stewardess?"

"No, I'm just a student." The others laughed. Apparently Tommy had specialized for a long time in stewardesses. No one, however, made anything much of this. He was an attractive bachelor! And this was before he met *me*. Still, it reminded me to continue to play it cool. If my heart was going to be broken, it would not be broken in public.

When the baseball season began, Tommy was gone from

Terre Haute, and my thoughts were mainly on graduation. I had majored in physical education with a minor in English. The phys ed teachers wanted me to think about teaching. The English teachers assured me there was a career for me in writing. I think if I'd had a choice, I'd have chosen writing, but I really was enjoying sports. Tommy, indirectly, made the choice for me. He had enlisted in the Air National Guard and came home for drill one weekend every month, weekends when we spent all our spare hours together. Tommy was well known to the local TV people and he took me with him one day to meet his friend Paul Denehie, the WTHI-TV station general manager. The very thought of TV excited me. I liked the people, the atmosphere, the well-ordered hubbub, the air of enjoyment that pervaded every department, as if even the lowest paid were having the time of their lives. After talking to me awhile, Paul Denehie said suddenly: "You know, I think you'd be great in this business! Why don't you give it a try?"

I took a moment to catch my breath.

"But what could I do?"

"What do you like to do?"

"I like to write."

"Well, why not try writing TV commercials? Or promotion? We use writers."

Tommy was beaming. I looked from one to the other. What on earth could I say? For the moment there was no job in the world I would rather have. Paul Denehie was squinting at me, obviously turning over something in his head.

"You like animals?" he said.

"I love animals."

"Good. We have a Saturday show for kids that features animals. 'The Doctor Hopp Show.' The Doc needs someone attractive to give him a hand on camera. We tape it on Wednesdays. Want to give it a try?"

And that's how I became a short-time star on an animal show (no jokes, please!), eventually even advancing to cohost. And my biggest moment with Doctor Hopp I think was the day he handed me a large garter snake. With Tommy out front grinning at us, I took the snake in my hands and held it, holding it up for the invisible audience to see. Tommy laughed out loud. He had not realized that snakes never frightened me in the least. Now if it had been a *spider*! But we never had spiders on this show.

I loved that place. Before I had been there more than a few weeks, I had tried almost every aspect of the business. I did commercials for the local department store, making a special hit with one I cooked up to sell pantyhose. Instead of the mannequins with their legs in the air that they had been using, I recruited some long-legged sorority sisters from the University, outfitted them in miniskirts and pantyhose and sent them scampering across the park grass, while the cameraman crouched on the sod and focused on those flashing legs. That one sold a *ton* of pantyhose. Most of my suggestions for commercials were successful, as a matter of fact, because I was able to see them from the point of view of a shopper—and a large percentage of the shoppers were college girls. Tommy and I would do several together. One of my favorites was advertising CPO jackets and it won an Addy award.

I had my animal show and I even did a short spell as weather girl. I wrote short promotional bits for some of the network shows, on TV and radio too. Still my thirst for TV action was not completely slaked. The big opening, Tommy and I decided, was in sales, so I asked for a shot at that. Bob Larr, the sales manager, was a pleasant fellow, whom I sincerely admired. But his heart turned to stone when I applied for a job. Absolutely *not*! There were no women on the sales force and there would never *be* any while he was conscious.

"Besides," he said, "you're only part-time. You can't sell TV time and go to classes."

"Why not? I can do all the other things without cutting any classes." (I had too. I had been into every department in the station, from acting to production, and sales was the only department I had never tried.)

Bob studied me for a while and then apparently thought up a clever ploy. He picked up a list and showed it to me. On it were accounts the sales department had listed as "impossible." "Sell one of these and we might hire you," he said. I looked them over and my heart skipped a beat when I saw the name "Terre Haute Chrysler-Plymouth." That was Bob McClelland's business and Bob was one of Tommy's best friends. I had even heard Bob growl once that he would *never* spend a nickel with WTHI-TV. And because I had just started working there, I asked him why. "Oh," he said, "I had a run-in with one of the bigshots there and they are just off my list for good."

Well, I knew Bob too well to think any grudge like this would keep him from doing Tommy John a favor. Why, Bob had even supplied the car that took the gang to Sarasota that spring. So I asked Bob Larr in my most innocent voice: "What if I sell some time to Terre Haute Chrysler-Plymouth."

Bob Larr looked as if he was having a hard time to keep from laughing.

"Okay," he said. "Sell some time to that outfit and you've got a job."

I trotted out of his office directly to a telephone. Bob McClelland did not even stop to argue when I told him what I wanted.

"Sure," said he. "What have you got?"

"The moon landing," I told him. "For two thousand dollars."

"Great! Put me down for that!"

Back I trotted to see Bob Larr. "I would like a sales contract, please," I said. For a moment Bob sat there with his mouth slightly open.

"Don't tell me you *sold* that account!"

"Yes, I sold them the moon landing."

Bob muttered to himself that he would be darned, or something worse. Then he stood up and offered me his hand and his usual expansive smile.

"Welcome to the sales department!" he said.

This being my senior year in school, with graduation only about nine months away, it seemed to me that my immediate future was assured. I had done my practice teaching and had really loved it, almost as much as I had loved TV, so I had my pick of professions. I know it would have been natural for me to be thinking about marriage, but the strange truth was that I still felt that, deeply as I loved Tommy, I still did not really know him. Not really. Not the way you know a family member. When we were with the baseball people, the talk about celebrities and distant resorts and golf tournaments and air travel excited me. But sometimes it bewildered me, too. What was Sally Simmons from Plainfield doing in a world like this? And Tommy, God bless him, never talked about himself. Even when he told of his adventures he always concentrated on what he heard and saw and what other guys had done. So while my admiration for him deepened, my awe of him increased, and I even dared ask myself now and then: what did he see in a small-town girl like me? (As it turned out, we *were* distantly "related" in a way. His dad and my dad both worked—in different areas—for the same utility company.)

Tommy and I had been dating not even a whole year and there had been no talk of marriage and only vague dreams about it on my part. So I was honestly surprised when the subject first arose. And it arose without any warning, without any build-up, without any bluebirds fluttering about or any bells ringing. Tommy had picked me up at the dorm one October night and we were off to Illinois where he had a speaking engagement. As we drove along he talked of where he had been—the Professional Baseball Players Golf Tournament in California. The weather had been warm and bright. The course never played better. Not being a golfer, I was hardly equipped to grasp all the marvels of a tournament. All the same, I could feel again the excitement that had filled me when I visited Tommy in Sarasota and the air had been ripe with talk of famous places and famous people. Then Tommy, whose eyes had been fixed on the road (we were straining the speed limit), gave me a quick glance.

"Next October," he said, "you really should come with me. It would be twice as much fun with you there."

My reaction was instantaneous.

"But I *couldn't*! Next year Karen Barlow and I are hoping to go to Europe. And I'll have my job. . . ."

Tommy, with the car still trolleying along at top speed, put one arm around me and gave me a quick squeeze.

"Oh, you don't want to go in for that stuff. You ought to get married and come with me."

This took my breath away completely. To hear my dream come true in this almost offhand way! I tried to form some kind of sane reply, while my brain was spinning and I was dancing and shouting inside. At the same time, that little inner voice was warning me: "He may be just kidding! Watch it, Sally. Don't make a fool of yourself." After a second or two, I managed to form a few sentences in a slightly choked voice about "plans" and "Europe" and my teaching job. I think actually I was still a little afraid of Tommy. Not physically afraid of him, but scared, or rather overawed, by his maturity, his fame, his distance from my life. And scared perhaps of walking into a life too strange, too far above my head, where innocence and inexperience with the ways of that exotic world might undo me.

But Tommy just drove on and said no more about marriage. The butterflies that crowded my stomach continued their fluttering. Tommy had come back for Homecoming Weekend at Indiana State, just for my sake, he insisted, for he had no real taste for the festivities. But to me it was one of the biggest events of my college career and I was wound up heart and soul in the dances, the parties, the shows, and the sorority doings that crowded every hour. I was more than a little put out at Tommy for his failure to share my excitement. And I was shocked into disbelief when, after I explained to him excitedly that *Johnny Carson* was going to be the featured guest at the entertainment that night, Tommy frowned and said: "But we'll miss the *Alabama* game!" The Alabama game! What in the name of all that's good and holy did that matter on a day like this—perhaps the merriest day of my last college year! Tommy read my dismay at once and assured me that he would go with me anyway to all the receptions. Of course, he had seen Johnny Carson. He *knew* Johnny Carson. And he could not possibly share my own thrill at being close to a genuine TV star. I was grateful anyway that he had come to be with me and I think I understood—if not then, at least a little later—that all these carryings-on must have struck him as a bit immature. But did he *have* to keep asking—everywhere we went—"Have you heard the score of the Alabama game?"

Well, that was Tommy. And I was going to have to get used to it. Because there was no other man alive that I would even think about marrying. And I did think about marrying, going over in my mind again and again what he had said on that ride to Effingham, Illinois. What if he had been only kidding? I was not always able to tell when he was being serious. I was too busy, however, to waste much time on brooding over such matters. In my senior year it seemed I was into everything. There was so much studying to do, so many Chi Omega affairs to absorb my evenings. And there was my job at WTHI-TV to keep me running back and forth. Weeks seemed to evaporate. Fall turned into winter almost before I had a chance to notice that the foliage had turned from green to red and gold.

But the coming of winter meant one thing to me—Tommy would be back in December for the holidays. And, who knows? he might bring up that subject again. By this time, I was more than half-convinced that it *had* been just a joke, or certainly no more than half-serious. It just didn't stand to reason that my dreams should all come true so soon. Tommy did come home now and then all fall but he played in a lot of golf tournaments all over the nation, so his visits were always short, and my own schedule was forever filled with school and sorority dates and the requirements of the job. The moments we had entirely to ourselves were rare indeed. Often a date with Tommy meant just dinner with his folks or mine. And I had come to know his family about as well as my own, ever since we had all traveled the baseball circuit that summer, to Oakland, Anaheim, and Seattle, watching baseball games or sightseeing in a foursome. But this had not been anything like the spring training visit, for we had ourselves for company rather than the ballplayers, and I had felt completely at home wherever we went. Heaven knows, Tommy's folks were neither renowned nor rich. They were simple home-style people like my own father and mother and there was none of the other-worldly atmosphere of Sarasota in the spring. And Tommy's own private life still seemed like a story I might read in a book.

So when he came to pick me up at the dorm that December evening, I still retained that awe of him that was a little like fear. I climbed into the car beside him and for some reason he made no move to start the car. He dug into a pocket and drew out a small black box, no bigger than a biscuit.

"I have a present for you," he said. I took the box from his hand and tried to make out what it was, holding it up to get the light of the street lamp on it.

"Open it," said Tommy in a half-whisper. I opened it. Inside, sparkling with a fiery glow in the uncertain light was the biggest and most beautiful diamond I had ever held in my hand. I drew a deep breath and looked up at Tommy, trying to put my delight into words. He took a deep breath, too, and had trouble getting the next words out:

"Will—will you marry me?"

I had to turn away and get both my cheeks between my

teeth to keep from laughing out loud. He was so schoolboyish, so much the bashful young man in a storybook! And so far from the mature, sophisticated, urbane creature from another life he sometimes seemed. Then I got both my arms around his neck and told him in his ear:

"Of *course* I will!"

There were no words in my store, either then or now, to describe the joy I felt. I was dancing, singing, flying. And above all I wanted to shout my happiness to the world. But the first people to hear about it would have to be Tommy's parents, who were expecting us for dinner. The moment we arrived, we were informed, in good old Hoosier fashion: "Your dinner's getting cold!" It was not until we were settled that Tommy's mother said: "Well, did you ask her?" One look at my face was enough of an answer. She took me in her arms and kissed me. Tommy's father hugged me and kissed me and told me how happy he was. (Afterward, as I helped his mother with the dishes, I knew there was a little sadness in her eyes, too. Now her little boy was *really* grown up and ready for a home of his own.)

We had to sit down to the most amazing dinner I have ever seen on one table. There must have been, besides two kinds of meat, at least three salads and five kinds of vegetables. How could I possibly eat? My stomach had taken wings, along with my mind. Yet, Indiana-style, Tommy's parents kept urging me to stuff myself. "You haven't tried this salad yet!" "You haven't *touched* your meat!" "Don't you like the way I've fixed the potatoes?" "Would you like something different to drink?" I came to earth now and then, long enough to put a few bits in my mouth. And finally, when sufficient homage had been paid to the bounty, we had to leave. I was still a college girl and I had hours to keep—or there would be a penalty to pay. After more hugs and kisses we were back in the car and I told Tommy at once that I had to go to Plainfield to tell *my* parents, too.

"But that's sixty miles! You'll never make your hour!"

"I don't care. I *must* tell them!"

So off we sped, streaking through the night like a guided missile and grateful to whatever fates kept the cops by their firesides that evening.

My own mother and dad, if anything, were even more overjoyed than Tommy's parents had been. Of course they had no forewarning. My father seemed ready to explode with pride at having this fine young man in the family. My mother, naturally, cried while she told how happy she was. And once more, in good old Indiana style, they would take no refusal when they invited us to eat. So we sat down and had ice cream and cake. Then we jumped up, ran to the car and raced to beat the curfew at college. I got under the wire with a few seconds to spare.

According to the traditions of Chi Omega, I was not to reveal my secret except during a candlelight ceremony that had to be scheduled in advance. So I imparted the news privately to the chapter president and she made the announcement that a candlelight ceremony was in order.

The candlelight ceremony was the sorority way of announcing to the whole chapter that one member had been "pinned" or "lavaliered"—or, that ultimate ecstasy, engaged. (Accepting a young man's fraternity pin, or a pendant to dangle from your neck, were symbols just short of engagement.) The ceremony consisted of a sort of silent parade in a small circle of all the girls in the chapter, each passing around a lighted candle. Whenever the time seemed right, after going round and round a certain number of times, the happy girl who had received the ring, or the pin, or the lavaliere, would blow out the candle, and accept the congratulatory kisses of all the members. I don't know how many times we had marched in that silent circle, round and round, before I could hold it no longer—three times meant an engagement would be announced. Then with the utmost gravity, I held the candle before my face and blew. The explosion of joy was instant. Of course, there was no need to tell anyone who the young man was. But the ring! It was hard to believe that Tommy had picked it out himself. It was so stylish, so beautiful, so *rich*! The girls could not get enough of viewing it from every angle, on my finger and off, while the shrieks of excitement must have carried across the campus.

Of course the big question now was: "When?" June, I decided, was out. I could not handle graduation and marriage all at once with Tommy having to rush off to play ball. October, I thought, when school was back in session, near Homecoming, when everybody would be here. Baseball would be finished then and there would be time for a honeymoon. So we settled on October and tried hard to fit back into schoolwork—with time out every day, or even every hour, to admire my ring and let others goggle at it, too. What a perfect symbol for the realization of a dream!

It was my plan to fill the time when Tommy was off playing baseball, the summer before the wedding, with full-time work at the TV station, where I was making good on a brag Tommy had uttered one day when we were looking over the TV sales staff: "You can do better than *those* guys!" I don't know if I was really doing better but I was surely doing as well.

But Tommy, as I should have suspected, had a mind of his own and a way, occasionally, of laying down the law—as befits the older, wiser, and more experienced mind in any organization. He went along with the decision until almost graduation time and then told me quite flatly one day that he did not like it a bit.

"I'm not going to guarantee I can wait that long," he told me. "Why do we have to wait until after the baseball season? Let's get married at the All-Star break and then you can come on some road trips with me."

I have to confess that as graduation grew near the work at the TV station had begun to lose some of its gloss. Part of the time, instead of being new and exciting and glamorous, as it had seemed the first few weeks, it could fritter itself into a series of minor pains in the neck. Or it may have been that my mind was on marriage and on a life with Tommy while a TV career began to sound like a dressed-up name for a dull job. Anyway, Tommy wasn't asking me. He was telling me. It *had* to be July. And I accepted that without a pang.

I had never heard of a marriage being scheduled to fit the All-Star break. But there were many things about life in and around organized baseball that I still had to discover. So the date was set for July 13, which would allow us two whole days, almost, for a honeymoon. But I was sufficiently airborne at that time to have agreed to a marriage between halves of a doubleheader.

Tommy:

Talk about playing it cool. I was keeping my escape routes open, too. Having reached pretty near the age of twenty-seven without marriage, I had become well adjusted to a bachelor life. Of course I thought about marriage—thought about it almost continually, starting after I had known Sally only two weeks. But every time I would just about make up my mind to ask Sally, I would get a spell of the leeries and wonder why I would want to give up this perfectly pleasant way of living and commit myself to something I knew nothing about.

But then I would see Sally again and be overwhelmed once more with the feeling that *this* was the girl I wanted to spend my life with. Then I would pull back again and decide I needed more time. To prepare my retreat, I even told Sally at one time that I was planning a trip to Australia, to play some golf, see the strange land, and I don't know what else. I never had any such notion. Just playing it cool.

Come October, 1969, however, I decided I wanted Sally to be my wife. I even went to see a friend of mine in San

Francisco, Wally McWhirter, who was in the jewelry business, and ordered an engagement ring. But it took me until almost Christmas to get the words out. Even at that I picked a most unromantic spot for my proposal—the front seat of an automobile parked in front of the dormitory.

At first I went along with the October date. It seemed to make sense that we should wait until the baseball season was over and until after I had completed my two-week training in California with the Air Reserve. But the 1970 season was a series of minor horrors for me. The White Sox, three years earlier, without any twenty-game winners on the pitching staff and only one man on the roster batting over .250, had still stayed in contention for the league championship almost until the final gun—thanks to speed and spirit, much of it supplied by Tommie Agee in center field. But since that time, we had been sinking lower and lower. Tommie Agee was traded to the Mets. Eddie Stanky, perhaps the best manager I had ever played for—maybe even the best, next to Al Lopez—had been fired and the new management had been trying to build a batting order full of long-ball hitters. As a result the spirit was gone, the clubhouse seemed full of petty dissension, and the stands were nearly empty of spectators. In 1970, we hit bottom, getting ready to set a major-league record by losing 106 games in one season.

Fed up with the what-the-hell atmosphere of the clubhouse and the gloom that had settled over the ball park, I resolved I did not want to face a whole season without *someone* to cheer me. So I decided it would be a great idea to put the All-Star break to good use by getting married then.

I don't believe Sally's parents, who would naturally host the affair, had any hint of the size of the invasion that would take place once the invitations were out. The United Methodist Church in Plainfield, where the ceremony would be held, had not been built to hold even half the mob that showed up on that blistering Monday in July. The whole town of Plainfield held only 5000 residents and it seemed as if half of them had tried to crowd into the church that muggy evening. A clubhouse full of ballplayers came down from Chicago in a convoy of rented cars. And Sally and I had relatives flying and driving in from all over the area. I had to do some hustling to make it myself. I pitched seven innings in brutal Kansas City heat on Sunday and just barely made Plainfield in time for the rehearsal on Sunday night.

All day Monday, as you can imagine, with relatives parading in, gifts piling up, and clothes being fitted, Sally's house was jumping. It being the tradition that the groom was to keep his distance, I spent Monday afternoon on the golf course, taking part in a local tournament.

I wonder if there was ever a formal wedding in which something did not go wrong. I have known of times when the best man forgot the ring, when cufflinks were lost or someone stepped on the bride's train, when the preacher came up with a bad cough, a bridesmaid fainted, the bride snickered when the vows were recited, the groom at a Jewish wedding could not stamp hard enough to break the glass under his foot, or the honeymoon car wouldn't start. None of these petty disasters were visited on us. But we did have one major disaster and there were one or two aspects of the affair that might have struck some people as bizarre.

For one thing, after the church was filled to the doors and before any of us had taken our places, the air conditioning quietly gave up the ghost, leaving the entire dressed-up company to swelter. But I don't believe Sally or I paid too much mind to that. We were just too excited. No World Series start could ever have lifted my pulse like this. Maybe Sally and I both said a small prayer that the ceremony might not take too long, because the sighs and rustlings of discomfort from the guests behind us grew louder and louder as the rites progressed. But it was over finally, the minister made the pronouncement, and I held Sally in my arms for keeps.

Then there were hugs and kisses and handshakes and all sorts of greetings and good-byes as friends and relatives crowded around. We found open space enough to accept all the good wishes and gradually made our way to the doors where a shower of rice awaited us and a chorus of farewells. I dodged as much of the rice as I could and guided Sally quickly down the path to the curb. Only there wasn't any car! Whoever had taken on the job of seeing to the transportation, if indeed anybody had even been given the job, had really blown this one. Nothing to do now but stalk back into the church to find someone with whom we might hitch a ride. Sally's house was only two blocks away but to parade that distance in our wedding get-up along those steaming sidewalks was no way to begin a honeymoon. My best friend Bob McClelland, who operated the Chrysler agency in Terre Haute, came promptly to the rescue, apologizing at the same time that he "only had a station wagon." Only a station wagon! When we were ready to settle for a covered wagon and a horse.

With our hearts back in orbit, we accepted Bob's offer and zipped up to Sally's house—to a full scale reception that lasted well into the night. By the time we had changed clothes, said good-byes to everyone again, and after Sally, suddenly realizing I guess that she didn't live here anymore, that she wasn't Sally Simmons now but Mrs. Tommy John, had wept on her mother's shoulder for a while and done the same with sister and father, it was near midnight. Sally cheered up some by reminding herself that, after a road trip, she was going to come back here and commute to her job at the TV station for "at least until next year" (according to our current plans). Then we peeked at some of the presents, loaded everything into Bob's station wagon, and set off as gaily as when we had left the church. We were headed first for Chicago, where we would unload the presents at my apartment, then off to Lake Geneva, Wisconsin, to begin our two-day (or day-and-a-half) honeymoon at a resort called The Abbey.

I was letting the station wagon have its head along the empty highway, just inside the Chicago city limits, when I looked into the rear vision mirror and got a small jolt in my stomach: Here came a cop car, blue light flashing, and gaining on us every second.

"Cop's chasing us," I told Sally and she looked back in dismay. I slowed our pace quickly and instantly the cop was alongside. We could see the solemn face sizing us up as we kept pace for a few yards. It probably took him all of five seconds to size us up as bride and groom. Then he lifted his hand in a sort of "good luck" gesture and whizzed on past.

"He saw all that loot in back," Sally said, "and thought he had picked up a couple of robbers."

With the last of our cares (we thought) now lifted from our shoulders, we hastened to my place, unloaded all the "loot" and set out for Lake Geneva. The route was plain enough but now it was getting on toward morning and, beyond the headlights, the world was as dark as the inside of a stovepipe. We found Lake Geneva quickly. But I soon lost track of the route to The Abbey. We circled through empty streets, past dark houses and empty stores, and began to have visions of spending our wedding night in a station wagon. I was almost falling asleep at the wheel. Then I spotted a police cruiser standing in a parking lot, with exhaust faintly smoking. We pulled up beside the cruiser. But no one stirred. I leaned forward to look inside and saw the uniformed cop sound asleep behind the wheel. I got out and tapped on the window. The man inside went into a sort of spasm, yanked himself upright and pulled out his gun! I backed off and took care to keep both hands in his view.

"Who are *you*?" the cop growled. He climbed out of the car and aimed his flashlight at me, holding the gun steady. Then he opened his mouth in wild amazement.

"Hey! Aren't you Tommy John? From the White Sox?"

I pleaded guilty and he stood there grinning at me.

"Well, what the hell are you doing out here?"

I explained that we were here on our honeymoon, had lost our way and would like directions to The Abbey. By this time he had tucked his gun away and was laughing out loud.

"Why sure, Tommy," he said. "Easiest thing in the world! It's right up here a piece." Then he stepped forward and pointed out the route to me, going over the turns two or three times, so I would not miss. He looked at me closely once again. "Tommy John!" he said. "Imagine that!"

I took his name then and promised to leave two tickets for him at the next game. He stood and watched after us, waving happily as we drove away.

So we found The Abbey in a few minutes and pulled up to the dark entrance just as the eastern sky began to show a streak of light. I was just barely able to hold my eyes open now and had hardly strength enough to tote my bag. But when the yawning night clerk set the registration card in front of me, I took one deep happy breath and with the utmost care inscribed, for the first time in our lives, the names of those new teammates:

"Mr. and Mrs. Thomas E. John, Jr. Chicago."

FOUR

Tommy:

The first game I pitched after Travis's accident was a night game against the Chicago White Sox at Yankee Stadium. And the emotional strain, believe me, was greater than it had been at my first World Series game. There was little room in my head before the game for anything but Travis. TV and newspaper reporters were kept at a distance by the Yankee P.R. staff. But still the strain and thoughts of Travis kept my mind foggy. As a result, I walked to the mound without even half a minute's mental preparation. Usually I need an hour or so to get myself mentally and emotionally ready to pitch. It was my regular habit to go over the whole job in my mind, to picture each batter as well as I could and then to envision myself pitching to him under all sorts of circumstances. I would, for instance, imagine that there were two men on base, with one out and the enemy's long-ball hitter at bat. I would then try to picture exactly how I would work to him, seeing every pitch as perfect, and would complete the fantasy by forcing the batter to hit a ground ball into a double play, to send an easy roller to third, or pop one to the shortstop.

This time when I stood on the mound during the National Anthem I could think of nothing but Travis. I was aware of the whirr of the movie cameras aimed my way, as I was aware of the superhuman voice that seemed to be filling the stadium right to the rim. But I could not picture myself in the act of pitching, or even call up an image of a single Chicago batter. I could picture only a little boy entrapped in tubes and wires while his half-open eyes looked up at nothing.

Yet I did manage to pitch that game—although, to my mind, I did it poorly. The whole team behind me seemed distracted as if my own trouble had infected them. We lost the game and I plodded back to the clubhouse feeling even lower in my mind than I had when I walked in. But George Steinbrenner was there head of me and I think I braced myself for some sort of reaming out. But George, as he often does, completely disarmed me by revealing a side of his nature that has always made it impossible for me to think of him as an enemy.

"That was a hell of a gutsy performance you put on out there," he said. "You didn't *have* to do that, you know. It wasn't your fault we lost. You did a great job and I admire you for it."

Well, that was the sort of talk I needed to hear right then. I had come to the park at the urging of Dr. Epstein, who had insisted I needed some "outlet." But if it hadn't been for George Steinbrenner's obviously heartfelt comments, I might have told myself that I didn't need *this* sort of outlet and might have called off my season right then. I went back to the hospital feeling at least partially refreshed and ready to spell Sally at Travis's bedside.

It was almost like a club, there in the Pediatric Intensive Care Unit, a club with a cruel admittance requirement—a severe injury or illness that required major surgery for a child. We parents, all of us sharing the same hour-to-hour fears, took comfort in our companionship and came to know each other as if we had all been raised in the same neighborhood. We would take turns fetching food and drinks for each other, hauling ourselves to our feet when our turn came with identical weariness. After a while, there was no need to take orders. We each knew that this one took coffee black and that one tea with sugar and milk and that one always wanted diet soda. And each of us knew all the ups and downs in every child's condition, for we continually asked for reports from each other, and visited with the other children when we could spare time from our own. In a way, I think we were like immigrants in a strange country, bound together by our common predicament. And of course many of us had a stronger bond from all sharing the skills of Dr. Fred Epstein, who would discuss with all of us the cases he was dealing with, so every family knew the problems of all the others and could ask sensible questions about the progress.

And the problems! Really they would make your heart cry. Sweet little kids who would never walk or be able to play normally. Teenagers who might never live to adulthood. I think every one of us was filled to some extent with the same urge—to be *doing* something to cope with all this tragedy. And the kids themselves were so *tough* and resilient. Whatever the handicap, they would move and laugh and play and talk to each other as well as they could and even help each other over some of the obstacles. All the tears were shed by the parents. The kids accepted their lot and tried every day to make the most of whatever strength their ailment had not yet robbed them of. We all learned from those kids, as we learned from each other.

I know one lesson I learned was that ballplayers, or professional athletes of even modest fame, own a talent that many of them are not aware of. That is, the ability to make some kids extremely happy with hardly any effort. This came to me one day when Dr. Epstein told me about one of his patients, a young lad of about sixteen, named Kenny, who had been operated on for a brain tumor and was just beginning to regain full consciousness. Kenny was a Yankee fan and would stare transfixed at the TV when the Yankees were on, obviously involved in the game even though he had still not recovered fully from the anesthesia. Dr. Epstein, watching Kenny as he tried to keep his slightly befogged mind centered on the action, noticed that I was pitching in the game and told Kenny that I was going to come to the Intensive Care Unit next evening and Kenny would have a chance to meet me. According to Fred Epstein, Kenny seemed to leap right out of his fog to stare at the doctor in disbelief. Could he *really*? He sure could! The next evening I went into Kenny's cubicle, shook his hand and talked to him for ten minutes or more about the Yankees. Here this poor kid, only partly recovered from a dangerous operation with no assurance at all that he would ever be well, could still become almost speechless with joy at meeting a real live Yankee pitcher.

After Kenny was moved out onto the pediatric floor, I learned that he had taken a lot of ribbing from the other kids, who just did not believe he actually had met Tommy John. So I made a point after that, when I made my "rounds" of the kids in the Intensive Care Unit, to go see Kenny, too, and hail him by name, so the other kids could know we were indeed good pals. I think of Kenny often now and remember him best as I used to see him, after Travis had just started getting up from bed, plodding along the corridor with Travis by the hand, the big kid and the little kid, each moving a bit unsteadily, side by side, as they learned how to use their legs again.★

The satisfaction I got out of contributing, even in this minor way, to alleviating Kenny's troubles for a while just could not be measured. But I found other ways of involving myself that at least eased the restless urge all of us felt to be of *some* help to the suffering kids and the overworked staff. One of the first schemes I hit on that earned the greatest return for

★Kenny, incidentally, made a complete recovery and now leads a normal life, free of symptoms with—according to Dr. Epstein—a good chance of staying that way.

the least effort was to bring in a couple of hundred Yankee caps to pass among the patients. It was like Christmas! Better than Christmas to many of those half-pint Yankee fans, who had never dreamed of owning a real official grown-up cap exactly like those their heroes wore.

But around a place like the Pediatric Intensive Care Unit, there are always minor jobs that need doing, that the people deeply involved in keeping little bodies alive cannot always find time for. It gets so you are actually glad to discover a task that is within your competence when so much that is being done is almost more than you can understand. I think one of the most miraculous, most delicate and most difficult operations that Dr. Epstein performed while we were there was the removal of a spinal cord tumor from a teen-age Swiss girl who had been flown in from Switzerland just to have Fred Epstein try to save her. When the girl came in with her parents they were completely bewildered. None of them could speak English and no one on duty the night of their arrival could speak either French or German so they had extreme difficulty trying to get the girl admitted to the hospital. I watched these efforts for a while as the parents tried vainly to put together words or phrases that some could make sense out of and I imagined myself in a similar fix—in a Swiss or French hospital, perhaps, trying to tell someone what was wrong with my little boy. Of course I could not act as interpreter, but I thought of where an interpreter might be found and, on my own, I called up the German mission to the United Nations to ask if they could send someone over to help. Alas, it was after hours there and there was no one to send.

But I could at least try to make the people comfortable. They were standing there by the little girl's bed, obviously wretched, talking to each other in low voices and looking forlornly about. There was only one chair in the cubicle. Well, I could do something about that at least. I hustled off and found a chair that was not being used and brought it in so both could sit down. I could not understand the words they used to thank me but their gratitude was plain on their faces. Then I realized that they were out of their depth in every way, unable even to ask for directions to the lunchroom. I dredged up the few French words I had picked up when the Dodgers played in Montreal and I asked them: "Café? Thé?" They both beamed at me. "Café! Café!" they chorused. "Au lait?" said I using up the last driblets of my French vocabulary. "Ah oui! Oui! Oui!" That part I understood perfectly and I took myself down to the cafeteria and fetched each of them a cup of coffee and a piece of Danish. That may not have been much of a contribution to international understanding but it certainly gladdened the hearts of those two visitors.

The operation on the girl, incidentally, went well. Dr. Epstein spent some seven or eight hours, I believe, removing the strange tumor that had intertwined itself with the spinal cord from the base of her neck to her waist. Telling the differences between tumor and spinal cord tissue and separating them out was apparently rather like plucking gray thread from white thread when both are twisted together. A sample of the tumor had been sent out for biopsy at the very start. The results showed that the tumor was benign so it was just a matter of removing it. That meant microsurgery, a tiny fraction of an inch at a time, and I am sure when Fred Epstein had finished that job he was pretty nearly a stretcher case himself. But Dr. Fred was used to long hours of tedious work. I don't believe I ever in my life met a doctor more dedicated or more able to sympathize with and share the feelings of patients and parents. He stuck by Travis's side as if Travis was his own and he had the hospital telephone him every three hours through the night, when he was supposed to be sleeping, to report on Travis's condition.

But Sally and I were able on one occasion to ease Fred's own lot just a little. On that first Saturday in the hospital, Fred Epstein put in a really trying day, beginning at eight o'clock in the morning when he found on examination that

Travis still had some symptoms of deterioration such as he had displayed the night before. (Instead of flexing his arms and legs in response to painful stimulation, he was extending them, and this, Fred explained, might mean that there was some deep-seated swelling, or even delayed hemorrhage.) So another CAT scan was needed and this revealed that, while there was slight increase in swelling around the original injury, there was no hemorrhage. But still, because of the deterioration in Travis's condition, Fred decided an "intercranial pressure monitor" was needed. So, right there at bedside, he had to make a new incision in Travis's scalp and drill a tiny hole in the skull so that a little screw could be placed into the space between the brain and the protective membrane, in the space filled with spinal fluid, to register on an oscilloscope the pressure inside Travis's head, so it could be monitored continuously. It looked a little like one of those caps kids used to wear with tiny propellers on them, but it was a necessary instrument so the staff could start prompt emergency treatment if any pressure waves developed.

Of course, as Fred had previously explained to us, Travis was already receiving treatment to reduce and control brain pressure, including two medicines to shrink the brain and corticosteroids to reduce the swelling, along with a "hypothermia blanket" to keep his temperature, which had been elevated, at near-normal level. By this time, Travis was tethered to more tubes and wires than I could count, what with respirator, electroencephalograph, electrocardiograph, oscilloscope, breathing tube, IV tube and heaven knows what else. Several of us, Sally and I plus doctors and nurses, would be gathered by the bed watching and listening. But once, according to Fred's story, Fred heard a tiny whisper that did not reach any other ears but his own. It startled him and he looked around to discover that it had been Sally, standing right at his side, who had whispered: "Don't screw up!" Fred chuckled and vowed he would not.

Fred had planned, before Travis came into his life, to

spend most of this weekend in Fire Island, with his family, but he had abandoned that idea. Still, with Travis's condition remaining stable, he did feel he could afford a few hours off, to go home and attend a play in which his daughter Samara would play the leading part. Then he planned to charter a boat to get him back to the mainland for the drive to the hospital. Sally and I agreed to this idea, even urged him to go, and Sally came up with one of her really bright suggestions. We had received whole stacks of flowers addressed to Travis. Obviously Travis could not enjoy them, so Sally selected a great bunch of blooming yellow roses and urged Fred to take them along. They could be his tribute, Sally said, to his daughter's performance. Fred was delighted with this suggestion and he took off with his arms full of flowers. He told us later of the sensation he created. Fred's wife had been able to find just "some scrawny, beaten-up flowers" (Fred's words) to honor their leading lady, and she asked Fred to carry them to Samara. "No need," said Fred. "I wanted to recognize her triumph too, and I bought this enormous bunch of yellow roses to give to Samara myself." His wife, Kathy, was speechless at this hitherto unrecognized surge of parental pride, and Samara was really overwhelmed. Afterwards, still flabbergasted at Fred's ability to come up with such lovely flowers on a Saturday night in the short time he had after leaving the hospital, Kathy wanted to know where he had discovered them. "Oh," said Fred, "on my way out on Grand Central I saw this new florist's and I got them there. It's called John's Nursery."

Of course it was not just Travis's case that kept Fred tied to the hospital day and night. Children with acute neurological problems were brought to him from all over the nation, sometimes after other doctors had given up hope on them. Such a case was little Laura from Houston, Texas, who was brought to Dr. Epstein for a "second opinion" while we were there. Laura, one of the gentlest and brightest little girls who ever rode a tricycle, suffered from what seemed like a tragic ailment: the bones of her skull, instead of being "free-floating" as they are on most little ones for the first few years of life, had fused completely so, as the brain grew, the skull could not expand to accommodate it. As a result her little face had become grossly misshapen—her eyes bulging from their sockets, her mouth protruding as if she were making a face, her chin disappearing. The doctors at home had told her parents the condition could not be corrected and they had come to New York University Medical Center to see Dr. Epstein with no real hope at all. It was just that they felt a second opinion would ease their minds. They flew in with no more luggage than an overnight case and they had made no arrangements for staying more than a single night. They actually bedded down in the parents' waiting room where there were couches, a shower, and toilets, but no real accommodations for staying more than a few hours. And when Dr. Epstein, after examining the girl, came out and suggested that he operate at once and that there was every hope of alleviating Laura's condition, they had to make sudden (and happy) changes in their schedule. The father, who had taken just two days off from work to make the trip, had to hurry back to Houston. But I, as one of the old residents in the Intensive Care Unit, helped the mother find a room in a hotel nearby at a decent rate, so she could afford to stay by Laura throughout the ten days or more she would need for recovery.

The operation, Fred Epstein told us, went well. He actually cut apart the bones of the skull and sutured them with thread that would stretch as needed, so the brain could grow normally and her features would soon return to their proper places. After that, Fred assured the mother, a few easy cosmetic operations would correct every trace of disfigurement and Laura could grow into an attractive young lady. This pronouncement was greeted with joy by all of the parents, to whom Laura had become a pet. I can see her still, her little head shorn bald and crisscrossed by great stitches, as she pedaled her "hot-wheels" tricycle down the hospital corridor, scattering all the traffic. And I think I understood for the first time then the depth of the satisfaction Fred Epstein must find in his profession. What other job could provide so many opportunities, not just for restoring little ones to life, but for lifting the curses laid upon innocent kids, for making the lame walk and putting broken lives back together again? Surely God guides the hand that performs these miracles. Nor do we need to look into ancient volumes of fairy tales to learn about wonders.

Miracles, of course, do not always develop when sought after and there were some children in the unit who were never going to be made whole. One was the sweet young lady who sent Travis the balloon inscribed "I Love You, Travis." She was sixteen or seventeen and would never walk. I think Dr. Epstein had performed more than twenty operations on her spine to cope with a defect that would not be wholly cured. All the same, she was able to concern herself with kids who seemed worse off than she was and she had love and sympathy to spare even for those whose ailments would never be as devastating as her own. I think that in itself was another miracle—of the kind that happen all around us and never earn any headlines or draw any crowds.

Sally and I used to smile when we recalled my own "medical miracle"—the one that overcame what we innocently imagined was about the worst disaster that could ever overtake us, for it seemed to mean the absolute end of my baseball career. But we had no babies then (Tami was on the way when it happened) and we could think of few turns in our life more devastating than to have to give up the profession to which I had committed myself when I was not even old enough to vote.

There was a great doctor who played the major part in that miracle too—a doctor who first impressed his greatness on me when he frankly admitted to me that he did not know enough about my ailment to tackle it alone. That he would have to consult and study and learn before he was ready to deal with it.

The injury itself occurred without any pain and for that reason seemed sure to cure itself, as other troubles had. It did not begin to hurt as much as the shoulder separation had hurt, the one I collected in Detroit when I tried to tackle an angry batter to keep him from belting me in the face. That one was agonizing, right from the start. But it got well without an operation—no thanks to the team doctor, who had insisted on an operation at once.

The angry batter was Dick McAuliffe of the Detroit Tigers and our run-in happened in August of 1968, when I was with the White Sox and had never even heard of Sally Simmons. I didn't really try to brush Dick McAuliffe back with the pitch, or even set out to come close to him. The count was three and two for Pete's sake! But I lost my grip on the ball somehow and it sailed right over Dick's head. I believe if he had stopped to think for even a second he'd have known how ridiculous it was to think I would try to hit him. But he didn't think, he just came roaring out toward the mound ready to take me apart and put me together in some different way. I tackled him, for I knew by this time that the way to end a baseball fight is to get the other guy down and hold him until the crowd arrives to break up the battle. Then nobody gets hurt.

But my tackling form was suffering from lack of practice, I guess, for I took that battering knee on my shoulder and Dick went right on over me, leaving me writhing on the ground. And that did hurt! I just walked off to the clubhouse and let the doctor look at me.

After an examination, the doctor told me I would have to have the thing operated on to get the bones back into position so they would heal properly. Oh, no! I thought. I don't want anyone cutting up my pitching arm! I told him, very mildly, that I would like to get a second opinion. Well, he told me, you'll have to talk to Ed Short, the general manager, about that. And that is where I learned something about the position of a ballplayer in the eyes of his employer. For Mr. Short told me I could not have a second opinion. It was not permitted in my contract that I go to an outside doctor! (Thanks to Marvin Miller, the basic agreement today gives the ballplayer the right to choose his own doctor.) I went out, without permission, and looked for another orthopedist. Our attorney in Chicago, Bill Sampson, suggested Dr. Danny Levinthal, once the team doctor for the Chicago football Cardinals and now practicing in Los Angeles.

As I was headed for Los Angeles anyhow, to play in a golf tournament, I saw Danny out there. I took my X-ray pictures to Dr. Levinthal and he explained what had happened.

My left shoulder had been separated by the impact and the ligaments that held it in place had been torn. Nothing to do but let them heal and make sure meanwhile that the bones stayed in place. An operation would not hasten that process.

"Just take care to carry your golf bag on your right shoulder," said Danny. "Give those ligaments a chance and they'll heal themselves."

Of course Danny was right. The only "operation" I needed was the operation of natural healing process. I let nature take its course. After nearly two months' rest I went down to Sarasota, Florida, to join the White Sox team in the Instructional League. While I didn't pitch in any games down there, I worked out every day and tested my ailing shoulder without disaster. When next the White Sox club physician looked at me, he noted that the shoulder was completely well and strong as ever.

"A good thing I didn't operate," he commented, almost as if he had made that sage decision himself. My thoughts in response to that probably could not have been printed.

One funny follow-up to this event was its effect on Dick McAuliffe. Some of the players asked me, after the battle, if I was going to get even with McAufliffe by throwing at him next time.

"No," I said. "I won't throw at him next time. I'll square things in my own time and in my own way. I'll get him when he least expects it." Whether the threat ever got back to Dick, I don't know. I do know that he stayed very "loose" every time he faced me and never got another hit off me as long as I was in the league.

But all this was trifling compared to what happened to me when I was with the Los Angeles Dodgers in 1974, just before the All-Star break. I was still irritated then, from having been left off the All-Star team, even though I had the best pitching record in the league for that season—thirteen wins and three losses. I blamed the National League All-Star manager, Yogi Berra, for that oversight, but Yogi insisted it was none of his doing. I don't recall if I believed him or not. But all that had nothing to do with what happened to my arm. I was pitching against Montreal the night of July 17 and at the end of the third inning we had a 4 to 0 lead. To start the fourth inning, Willie Davis got to first on a drag bunt. Then I walked Bob Bailey. Actually I think I struck out Bob Bailey. I thought the 3–2 pitch was a strike. The umpire thought it was a ball. And in the world as it is now ordered, the umpire's opinion is the one that counts. Still, I didn't see anything much to worry about. If I could get the next batter to hit into a double play I felt sure I could get out of the inning with no more than one run. The next man up was Hal Bredeen, known as a good pull hitter. I told myself that if I could get him to hit a good sinker, thrown down and away, the chances were he would send a ground ball to shortstop or second base and we would be pretty near out of the inning.

I set out to feed him my sinker—a pitch that drops suddenly as it reaches the plate, causing most hitters to top the ball and beat it into the ground. It is usually thrown by loosening the grip of the index finger so that, even though you fire the ball with full strength, it lacks a little spin and so begins to drop earlier than a fast ball would. This time I put plenty of oomph into the pitch and just as I got the arm down into the throwing zone, where the arm reaches its full extension, and I let go of the ball, I had the strangest sensation I had ever known. A "nothing" sensation, as if the arm wasn't there. The ball just blooped up to the plate and the catcher took it well out of the strike zone.

What the heck was that? I wondered. I looked at my arm to make sure it was still hitched to my body. I moved it and it moved freely, without pain. Okay, let's try the sinker once more. I went into my stretch and tried again. The same thing! That "nothing" feeling from my arm, and a lazy bloop to the plate. This time, however, I felt, or heard, a sort of "thump!" in my forearm as I let the ball go. It still didn't hurt. But I knew I could not pitch. I asked the umpire for time and walked off the mound. Walt Alston, the Dodger manager, came trotting out to meet me. But I walked right past him.

"You'd better get somebody in there," I told him. "I've hurt my arm."

I grabbed up my jacket from the bench and headed straight for the clubhouse, where I hung up glove and jacket and started to change out of my uniform. But in seconds I was surrounded. Dr. Frank Jobe, who had been watching the game, was there, and a collection of front office folk, including the P.R. man, who had hastened down to make sure the right words were uttered. Bill Buhler, the trainer, hurried in, along with another doctor. And there were sports writers and TV reporters on their heels. Dr. Jobe took me into a side room and examined me but could make no definite decision. It could be just a muscle cramp. It could be something worse. But most ballplayers, especially pitchers, are subject to these occasional tightening-ups or spasms of a muscle that can usually be cured by shaking the arm or working it slowly for a while. Dr. Jobe told me to ice the arm and go home and keep an ice pack on it. Meanwhile, we could tell the press that it was a muscle spasm and that I would need a few days' rest. Then I could come to his office at two o'clock next afternoon and he would give it a thorough examination.

I iced it up in good style and fended off the reporters by telling them I had got a cramp or something and would be all right in short order. The arm had stiffened up a lot, as muscles will after a strain, but there was still no pain when I got home and I really had no inkling of permanent injury. I collected a supply of ice and kept the forearm thoroughly refrigerated. But next morning it was really sore. My arm hurt when I reached for anything or when I tried to turn a doorknob. But even so I was not much worried. I had had arm injuries before—including an operation to take a bone chip out of my arm. Of course this seemed to douse any hope of gathering twenty wins this season. But I had been going good. I never needed more than three or four runs for my side, then I could close the gate on the enemy. I figured I could pick up three or four more wins before the season was over, even with time out for recovery.

Early in the morning the telephone began to ring—reporters from everywhere wanting to learn the outlook on the arm. I didn't tell them that the arm was barely able to reach for the telephone. I stuck to the story—a muscle spasm that needed rest. But the telephone never stopped. This was a *big* story. The Dodgers were in first place. I was their best pitcher. What was happening?

I really did get griped at one story that came out on TV—that I had strained my arm by trying to throw too hard, just to prove to Yogi Berra that I should have been on the All-Star team. That was really an ignorant statement. No one who really knew me could have dreamed up that tale. I had been pitching long enough to know that you didn't win games by indulging in shenanigans of that sort. Any experienced pitcher knows that you have to pitch within your own capabilities and that overpitching is just a quick route to the showers.

When I reached Dr. Jobe's office that afternoon, the arm had really spasmed up and Frank Jobe noticed immediately. "Really is tight in there, isn't it?" he said. He took my left arm by the elbow and moved the forearm this way and that, like a semaphore. He looked at me very gravely.

"I'd like to take some X-rays of this."

They took seven or eight pictures and when Dr. Jobe had them in hand he studied them a long time and kept shaking his head.

"I don't want to be an alarmist," he said. "But I have to be realistic too. I think you've torn a ligament. I took a stress test in there, pulling it off to one side, and you can see the result here." He pointed out the picture. "You see, your elbow opens up about thirty degrees. And that's way beyond normal. Now I wish you'd go down and see another doctor. Take the X-rays with you and tell him to call me after he's looked you over."

The other doctor was Herb Stark, a sort of old country boy from Tennessee. He looked at my arm, checked over the pictures and shook his head. "Well, boy," he said, "you sure did it this time, didn't you? Yes, sir! You sure did a job on your arm!"

Well, he sure did a job on my self-assurance and I began to suspect that I was going to be a long, long time getting well.

"What do you think?" I asked him.

"Oh, I don't know, boy. I got some ideas. But I just better talk this over with Frank Jobe first. You just let me talk it over with old Frank."

I let him talk it over with old Frank and I took off for the ball park. Dr. Jobe showed up at the ball park himself after his office hours and we sat down for a conference. The result of the discussion with Herb Stark had been a decision that I had torn a ligament in my arm and that an operation would be unavoidable.

"But that's somewhere down the road," he said. "What we'd like to do now is just treat it with rest and home therapy, and if you're real lucky it could be that it's not as serious as it might be and you'll be pitching again in three weeks or so."

That sounded great to me and I went home feeling moderately cheerful. Nobody could have been more faithful in following the doctor's instructions than I was. I worked the stiff muscles out regularly in accordance with directions. After a week or so there was no more pain—just stiffness. I tried throwing then, just tossing the ball in my backyard to my neighbor, Ed Varvello. After a stretch of this, I decided it was time to rejoin the ball club and have a try at pitching batting practice. I could throw the ball now, as long as I did it in a careful manner, not putting my full effort into the throw. And I was eager to see if I could gradually get back into competitive shape.

I joined the ball club in New York and before pitching batting practice I threw on the side for about twenty minutes, determined to get real loose before I tried throwing to batters. But when I started pitching batting practice, I could not reach the plate, even throwing half-speed. My pitches flew in six different directions and my arm *hurt*. And there was that same "nothing" feeling, as if the forearm were not attached. I quit and went into the clubhouse to see Bill Buhler, our trainer. I thought that if he would tape the arm up snugly, the way he would a twisted ankle, I might be able to keep control of my pitches. We tried that and for a while I was cheered about the outlook. The tape did keep my forearm from wandering off its moorings, and I could make the ball go pretty close to where I wanted it to. The only trouble was, I soon discovered that I could propel it at just about three-fourths of my regular speed. And I wasn't going to get any batters out that way. I took my troubles to Walt Alston and told him I doubted if I could pitch again. Walt said that I knew best if I could pitch or not and that if I was sure I could not I should just put the 1974 season out of my mind and concentrate on getting the arm well.

We were in Atlanta then and I called Sally on the phone

and told her I was going to make one more try to use my arm and if it didn't work I was going to come home for the operation. She agreed that this was the sensible course. I gave it a try and the arm worked no better. It was Sunday, and I called Dr. Jobe at home and told him I wanted the operation—that I had tried throwing overhand, three-quarters and sidearm, and the arm just did not work.

Dr. Jobe and I had had some long discussions about this earlier and he had put it very strongly that I had to *want* the operation. He was not going to go into that arm, he said, if there were any doubts in my mind, for that would mean I would always hang onto a suspicion that if only I had skipped the operation (as I had done on my shoulder) the arm might have got well. Well, I knew by this time that I was at the end of my rope. The 1974 season was done for me. If I didn't have the operation right away I might miss out on the 1975 season. I still would not allow myself to think about giving up pitching together. That would be a total disaster.

Dr. Jobe had explained what he thought he might find when he went into the arm. If it was a slight tear of the ligament, then they could repair it and I would recuperate fairly soon and be ready to pitch. If the ligament had torn free of the bone, it would be a more difficult job but they could repair it and eventually I would be able to pitch again. Or it might be a rupture—a tear in the middle—and that would be unrepairable. I didn't want to hear any such word. Did he mean *nothing* could be done? Well, there was a ligament transplant operation that they had used on hand and wrist injuries. But it was a long and complicated process and even then the chances of recovering full use of the arm were doubtful indeed.

"I'd like to think that your arm will get well enough by resting," he said. "I really don't want to do this operation. It's extremely risky and extremely difficult. And even with the operation the chances of your pitching again are slim."

"Like what?"

Dr. Jobe chewed on that for a second.

"I'd say about one in a hundred. It might even be longer odds than that. But I'd say that would be a fair estimate."

"And what would my chances of pitching be if I did not have the operation?"

"Zero in a hundred."

Now, on the phone, I told him I was ready to run that risk.

"Well, I'm glad you're convinced," he said. "Because unless you really are one hundred percent sure, you would not work on your rehabilitation as you will have to. And it is going to be a long hard pull, with no assurance that you will ever make it."

"Okay, I'm ready."

Dr. Jobe told me then that he would schedule the operation at once, just as soon as he could find a date when both he and Herb Stark would be free.

"I'm not going to tackle this operation without Herb Stark there with me," he said. "And there are a few others I want in the operation room, too. This is a difficult operation and frankly, I'm not that good. I'm going to have to go back and read up all I can find in medical literature about this operation. And I need all the help I can get."

And that, as I said, is what convinced me that in Dr. Jobe I had a really great doctor and I headed into the operation with no qualms at all. I forgot to say that this particular time, September, 1974, had seemed destined to mark a climax in my life, both public and private. It was the year I felt sure of winning, for the first time, twenty ball games in a season, maybe even taking the Cy Young Award, given to the top pitcher in each league. It was the year the Dodgers seemed sure to take the league championship. And it was the year Sally and I were going to have our first baby—which nature seemed to have timed to coincide with the end of the baseball season.

Now it seemed time to mark the end of my career. Dr.

Jobe had been level with me from the start and I feel sure he felt he would never see me pitch again. But I felt I had a secret weapon. I had a very deep faith that nothing was impossible with God. And I also knew that whatever I had to do to get my arm back in shape again—no matter how tedious, how long, or how strewn with booby traps the path might be—I would stick to it until I reached the goal, or until the very last faint flicker of possibility was extinguished. Dr. Jobe had suggested that perhaps I should think about golf as a new career and I had some vague notions about getting into the automobile business with Bob McClelland. The Dodgers, Dr. Jobe told me, had agreed to pick up my contract for 1975, after he had told them it would take probably a whole year for me to recuperate. "But then," he warned me, "you'll be on your own and I think you should spend that year trying to get established in some other line of work to support this growing family." But I really wasn't ready to fret about that. Maybe he had given up hope. But I hadn't.

The operation was scheduled for September 25. I checked into the hospital the night before, near midnight, for Sally and her mother and I had gone to the ball game at Dodger Stadium after dinner. I told myself, as they ran the preliminary tests on me, that if I came to with a bandage on my right arm that would mean they had had to go in there to take a ligament for the transplant. And that would mean the worst had happened.

The operation next morning lasted more than three hours and they had to really slug me with anesthetic to keep me under. When I did come to, my foggy mind had clung to that idea that I must find out about the bandage on the right arm. After coughing loose the tube from my throat, I fumbled around dazedly for my arm. My left arm was swathed in bandage and it was hard to move. But I got my fingers over to my right forearm finally and, half-drugged as I was, I still knew a small chill of apprehension when I discovered the bandage. They *had* done a transplant. And I was in real trouble.

Sally and her mother came to visit me once I was back from the recovery room. But I was fading in and out of full awareness so we did not discuss the operation much. Sally, who had obviously been crying but was trying to act cheery, said she had been having pains in her back and I urged her to get on home, as the stork might well be on the wing. Next morning I was reasonably clearheaded and, surprisingly, not particularly downcast. Well, I didn't have time to be downcast, for my telephone rang at half-past six. It was Sally, and she felt sure she was in labor.

"See if Dr. Jobe will let you come home," she said. "I want you with me when the baby comes." I promptly called the operating room, for I knew Dr. Jobe had another operation scheduled at seven. I left word for him to call me. In about fifteen minutes, he came into my room and I told him about Sally's request.

"All right," he said. "I guess we can spring you for that. But you can't drive! You're still too weak and woozy to get behind the wheel of a car. And I want you back this afternoon so I can have a look under that cast."

I knew I could get Ed Varvello to come drive me home, so off I tottered, bandages, cast, and all, with the last few wisps of fog still clinging to my brain. Sally was timing her contractions when I got home and the doctor had told her she was still in the early stages of labor. We had time to pack up the clothes she would need, and get the wardrobe together for the new little John, and prepare a welcome. But by afternoon the pains came more frequently and it was obviously time to get started to the hospital. No kindly neighbor on hand this time to chauffeur the station wagon. I had to drive, regardless of my two disabled arms. We had warned the doctor we were on the way and he had promised to have a nurse and wheelchair at the entrance to whisk Sally in. Sure enough, as we pulled up to the entrance, there was the welcoming party. I climbed out of the car first, adorned with a three-day beard, dressed in pajama top, rumpled trousers and sneakers, with enormous wrappings on both arms. I turned to help Sally, who was bright and blooming as usual, dressed for the day, her face alight with that lustrous smile. So naturally the nurse, her face furrowed with concern, rushed the wheelchair over, shoved it behind me, and set a hand on my shoulder to guide me tenderly into the chair.

"No! No!" I told her. "It's my wife, Sally. She's in labor! We just phoned the doctor."

"Then you're Tommy John! Oh yes!" She chose the right passenger then and wheeled her through the doors. I came along, looking like the survivor of a head-on collision, and tried to make the proper entries on the admission form. I had to shove the pen in between the protruding fingertips of my left hand. But, having managed that, I could not write a word or scratch a number. The nurse had to put down all my answers and then I had to provide an uneven scraggle to represent my signature.

I was escorted to the labor room where Sally lay, already in the hospital gown and waiting for the doctor. When he came, he examined her quickly and allowed that the moment was at hand. They wheeled Sally into the delivery room, then outfitted me with a white gown and let me come in and position myself behind Sally, where I could watch our first child being born.

Talk about miracles! To see a complete and conscious, perfectly fashioned little human being emerge from its mother's body was like being present at the Creation. I don't know what I had expected. But to see how perfect this creature was, with little grasping, doll-size fingers, and each finger equipped with a complete fingernail, no bigger than a snowflake! In school they used to read to us about the Immortal Hand that made the tiger. I wonder about the Immortal Fingers that can fashion such dainty imitations of even the tiniest fragment of a full-grown human body. The thrill of watching that ancient-looking little face squint and grimace and gasp—already alive and looking for its place in the living world! The sight left me dizzy!

"You've got a beautiful little girl," said the doctor. For half a second I thought they might hand her to me to hold. Then I noticed my arms. My Lord! I had forgotten my operation completely! I think if anyone had come up behind me suddenly at that moment and asked me if I was ever going to pitch again I might have answered: "I don't give a hoot if I do or not!"

There's just no reckoning what the arrival of that little girl did for me, not just then but for weeks afterward. For I had some real bad times coming. And I might easily have taken to brooding on my lot, had I had nothing else to fasten my heart on. Because very soon after the operation I found the little finger on my left hand had gone completely dead, without warmth or feeling or movement. Dr. Jobe looked at it and assured me it was not an unexpected development. Nerves did not always regenerate 100 percent and regeneration took time. He explained that the ulnar nerve had taken something of a beating and ought to get back to normal in two to three weeks. That would be pretty near the end of October. That time came and I still had no feeling or movement in that finger. Four weeks, five weeks, six weeks went by and still no change. Now what?

Nothing for it, said Dr. Jobe, but to go back in again and try to fix it. Before winter set in I was scheduled for another arm operation. But this was a relatively short one and I was up and about the same afternoon. Dr. Jobe explained what they had done and why. Apparently, in pushing and pulling the ulnar nerve about and trying afterward to get it back into its proper channel, they had put a tiny twist in it, like the kink in a garden hose, that had prevented any sensation from reaching my little finger. Also, they found that scar tissue had overlaid the nerve at the point of the operation and that, too, had helped cut off sensation. They had put the nerve in a completely new channel, on the inside of my elbow and down through fatty tissue where there would be no scarring. Now, said Dr. Jobe, all we could do was wait and pray for that nerve to regenerate. It's usually a slow process, just a few centimeters at a time.

"But I want to explain something to you about these operations," he went on. "If the first one does not work out, you'll never pitch again. But if this second one does not succeed, you're going to have a crippled hand, just a sort of claw."

Well, I had a sort of claw sticking out from the cast right then. And when we went back to Indiana for Christmas, I would have been a candidate for pity if it hadn't been for Tami, our new little girl. The relatives who gathered to welcome us would all have been giving me the "poor Tommy" routine, which was not something I needed right then. But Tami absorbed all the attention and, whatever the relatives may have been thinking, they were too busy adoring the baby to say any of it. And believe me she was adorable—just perfect in every way, bright, happy, and beautiful, like her mother. With two useful little hands, which was more than her daddy could display.

They took the cast off in late January and Doctor Stark, after looking at my arm, said that if I could throw a ball from the mound to home plate by summertime, he would count the operation a complete success.

"I'll be doing that in two weeks," I assured him. He laughed and warned me not to get too ambitious. Incidentally, I had already thrown a baseball at Dodger Stadium, for I had been invited to throw out the first ball for the first playoff game in 1974. But I threw that with my right hand.

Dr. Jobe then gave me some exercises to do, to work the arm back into shape. They included a lot of easy throwing, which I performed in my backyard with Sally as my catcher. Throwing to Sally, I was not likely to forget myself and try to uncork an old-fashioned fast ball. I also threw to my neighbor's wife, Lil Varvello, for a while and I suppose, had I never recovered, I might have earned a full-time spot in the Ladies' League.

Understand, though, that I still could not use my fingers to grab up the baseball. I had to take the ball in my right hand and shove it into my left, which had frozen into its claw shape, with the first two fingers spread apart and slightly bent, the last two fingers folded right against my palm, and my thumb also curled back. But the arm felt good, although of course I made no effort to test it with full-strength throws. I was planning to begin that when I got down to spring training.

Spring training, however, was by no means a sure thing right then. At the end of the 1974 season, when the Dodgers had won the play-offs (and lost the World Series to Oakland), I had a call from Peter O'Malley, president of the Dodgers. He just wanted me to thank me, he said, for what I had contributed to the season. Without that fine work from you in the first half, he told me, we would probably never have made the play-offs.

"Just wanted you to know how much we appreciated it!" he told me.

But that "appreciation" was not evident when my contract reached me, offering the exact same salary I had drawn in 1974. I sent the contract right back and noted that if they were really grateful for what I had done, they ought to have indicated it in the numbers showing on the contract. I was not after a big raise, just some sort of token to indicate that my efforts had been satisfactory.

Well, you might have thought I had mailed the boss an obscene letter. Al Campanis, Dodger vice-president, promptly called me at home and wondered loudly what had got into me. "Why, you're not even going to be able to pitch this year!" he cried.

Quite so. But baseball contracts were always based, not on what a player was going to do, but on what he had done the year before. And Peter O'Malley had already told me how much my efforts had meant to the club. Now I wanted some concrete evidence of that. If I was going to stay with the club, then I should be working under a better contract. But this seemed dire ingratitude to Al. Here they were ready to pay me my full salary and I wasn't even grateful enough to sign a new contract without a raise. Well, I had been told that *they* were grateful to *me*. Now I wanted to see a modest acknowledgment of that fact. Of course if they had no plans for keeping me on after my arm got well, they should simply let me go now—give me my release and let me shop elsewhere.

This contract, Al said, is not based on what you did last year. Then what is it based on? I wondered. It's based on what you're going to do next year! What if I were able to pitch next year, what would you go by? Then we'd negotiate on last year's contract! That means that year after next, I'll be negotiating on the *previous* year's contract. So you pick the year that is most convenient for you? I guess that's right.

It's not right for me, I told him. If you guys didn't really believe I was instrumental in getting you into the play-offs, why did you call me up and say so? And if you did believe it, then why not act on that belief? Not a fat raise. Just a nominal adjustment.

No answer to that one. And I did not sign the contract. And I did not go down to early spring training. The only thing the Dodgers could do then was invoke the option clause under the old reserve rule. That meant I *had* to go down to spring training, so Sally and I took off.

When I reached camp (to give you an idea of the childishness that often pervades employer-employee relationships in professional baseball) the front-office people acted as if I had a communicable disease. Secretaries and mail-room workers and the like would glance at me sideways as if they were afraid they might be accused of being friendly with a traitor or they would see me coming and get quickly out of my way.

Here was the guy who tried to start a mutiny on the Good Ship Lollipop!

Walter Alston called me into his office and gave me a fatherly greeting. How was I doing? How was the arm?

I was throwing, I told him. I was feeling good.

"Now, listen," he said. "I don't want to get involved in any contract discussion, but do you know what you're doing?"

And in my impudent way, I replied: "If you didn't want to get into a contract discussion, Walt, why did you call me in here?"

"I just wanted to be sure you knew what you were getting into. Do you want to get released?"

"Not particularly. I like it here and I hope to stay. But they can release me at any time, whether I can pitch or whether I can't. I'm sure if they had any notion that I would never pitch again, they'd let me go without thinking twice. But I can tell you one thing. If they release me, I'll be in Cincinnati in a minute, signing with the Reds."

"I just wanted to give you some advice. You can only push these people so far and then they're going to let you go."

"If that's the way it's going to be, that's what it will be," I told him. "Baseball has to end for me sometime and I suppose this might as well be the time." I thanked him then for his advice and walked out.

Immediately after that, Peter O'Malley called me in for another fatherly talk just to see "what you're up to." I repeated to him what I had said to Campanis, that I thought the proper way for them to show the gratitude they had expressed was to give me a raise. Peter looked as if he had started to choke on a chili pepper. A raise! And you won't even be pitching!

"Look," I said, "I know I can't pitch. But I'll do anything you ask me. Scout other ball clubs. Work with the young pitchers. Anything! I'll be traveling with the club."

"How do you know you'll be traveling with the club?

That'll just mean you'll be collecting meal money that we could be saving!"

"I thought you'd want me working out with the trainers, throwing under the pitching coach's direction. But if you want me to stay home, fine! I'll work out in my backyard. That way if anything happens to my arm, my wife can take care of me, or my neighbors."

Peter choked for another few seconds and finally we called the discussion off. After that, from time to time Al Campanis or someone would open the discussion again. And again I would repeat all that I had said before, winding up with the suggestion that if they did not mean to treat me as if I was going to stay on the roster, then they should give me my release. At last it came to a full-scale conference, with all the brass and me. And they announced, with great condescension, that they had finally decided that they would grant me a raise on my 1975 contract. How much?

"Three thousand dollars!" said Al Campanis. "How's that strike you?"

"I was thinking of something more like five thousand."

This time the stuff really hit the fan. Of all the ungrateful ill-mannered oafs! They didn't *have* to give me anything! They were just trying to grant me an extra favor. They could have held me to my contract if they wanted to. And so on. I finally told them I'd take the three thousand. I wanted no hard feelings and no hard words. I just wanted to get my arm well now and win a lot more games for the Dodgers.

Getting my arm well was tedious. But I expected that. I worked on it all my waking hours. Meanwhile, of course, I was on the lookout for ideas about another profession. But I just could not get my heart into the search. What I really had my heart in was getting so I could pitch again. I worked out every day, not throwing real hard, but throwing, it seemed to me, just a little better each time.

Meanwhile, with my contract argument over, the chill in the front office disappeared, as if I had been suddenly cured of my leprosy. There were big smiles and hearty greetings again, now that I was an acknowledged good guy. Of course, my teammates had never been anything but cordial. It was always, basically, us against the management anyway, when it came to money matters. But almost everyone on the club was secretly convinced, I think, that I was not going to make it. I could tell by the way they used to ask me how my arm was, as if they were not going to believe my answer anyway.

But one guy was different. Ben Wade, chief of scouts for the Dodgers, and once a big right-handed pitcher for the Dodgers when they were in Brooklyn, watched me throwing one day and asked me how my arm felt. It felt good. And I thought I was throwing a little bit better each day. Not hard yet but just improving bit by bit. Ben watched me a while longer and asked me:

"Your arm doesn't hurt? You're not lying?"

"Why would I lie? What would I gain by that?"

"Then, if that's the truth I'm going to tell you something. You're going to make it! If you've come this far in such a short time and you're still improving and you have no pain in your arm, I can see you pitching again within a year. Maybe I'm the only one that thinks so. But I could guarantee it."

As you can imagine, this lifted my spirits about fifty degrees and I went back to my exercises with some real zest. I had a whole series of forearm exercises, using a one-pound weight. And I regularly followed the hot-and-cold routine Dr. Jobe had given me at the start—first an ice pack, then water about as hot as I could stand it, alternating. Then ultrasound treatment and massage from Jack Homel, one of our trainers. Bill Buhler, our head trainer, stayed right on top of this regimen all through training. Had it not been for Bill and Jack, both of whom pushed me hard, I might never have pitched again.

When they broke camp in April, Walt Alston asked me to stay behind so I could continue to work out in warm weather, without interruption. Throughout training, I had followed all the regular routine with the rest of the guys—bending, stretching, running, playing pepper—until it came time to bat. Then I would go over and throw against a concrete wall, grabbing the ball up when it bounced back and throwing it again. I didn't see any point in asking a catcher to waste his time when I could not yet throw well enough to sting a kid's fingers. And I knew I could get along without comments or advice or even encouragement. I just threw and threw and threw.

I joined the club when they got to Los Angeles, where I continued to drill with the team in all the preliminaries, and would then go to my forearm exercise and massage and all the rest of the routine. I had got hold of a big egg of Silly Putty and I carried that with me everywhere, squeezing it as well as I could into all sorts of shapes, trying hard to get my fingers working again. I thought for a while that I might be able to pitch if I taped my first two fingers together. That was the only way I could keep them from spreading out. But that didn't work.

One day I was driving home and got that feeling you get sometimes of wanting to get your hand off the wheel and stretch the cramp out of your hand. I did that, absently, and behold! my little finger popped out straight! It was alive! I felt like yelling the news to all the drivers on the road. Instead, I sped happily home and when I came into the house I put both hands behind my back.

"Close your eyes," I told Sally. "I've got a surprise for you."

Sally gave me a kind of squinty half-smile as if she knew that I had a frog or a plastic spider or some other squirrely thing behind me, then she obediently closed her eyes. I took my left hand out, fingers folded, and told her she could look. Then I slowly stretched that little finger out full-length. Sally let out a scream. Then we hugged each other and started dancing around. This was sure IT! This meant that little by little I could get all the fingers back. And that's the way it went. I worked that Silly Putty into a thousand different shapes, squeezing it whenever I had my left hand free. And gradually the other fingers began to come around. Dr. Jobe told me to cut off the shaft of a golf club and keep the grip in my hand, squeezing it, squeezing it, squeezing it, morning, afternoon and night. He urged me also to play golf as often as I could. Tough medicine, eh?

At that time we were living right on the golf course in Yorba Linda, so I would be out there before breakfast to swing a club, run a mile, take a swim, eat breakfast, then get back to the golf course to practice chipping and putting. In late afternoon I would go to the ball park and resume my workouts and therapy, full of confidence now that I would soon be back on the pitching mound firing that ball full-strength again.

Immediately after that the club left on a road trip, to Pittsburgh and St. Louis, and I went along to continue my workouts and therapy with the trainers. Nowadays I was doing my throwing to a catcher, although I was not getting full power into the throw yet. Indeed, my pitches seemed to kind of flump into the catcher's glove, even though I thought I was letting go with a good share of strength. But one really humid night in Pittsburgh, after throwing for a few minutes, I grew a little irritated at the failure of my throws to pop into that glove in the old style. I reared back a bit more and made a conscious effort to get that ball off with more steam.

"Hey!" Mark Cresse, the catcher, yelled. "That one really jumped at the end!"

I tried again and the catcher stood up after the pitch and shook the ball in the air. "You're popping them!" he called. I realized then that I had finally overcome the last barrier, the psychological barrier, the fear of hearing the forearm go thump again that had kept me from getting all my strength into my throws. I kept on pouring them in for about forty minutes. When I was finished the catcher told me: "That's the best you've thrown since I've been here."

For three straight days then I threw the ball hard. When we went to St. Louis, I started throwing batting practice to the pitchers, then I would take myself to the bullpen and throw some more. Altogether I think I must have been throwing nearly an hour every day—without a twinge or a strain—three or four hundred pitches, not all full-strength but building up gradually to where I was pitching just as hard as I could. After that, I started trying my breaking pitches, putting spin on the ball and seeing it break in good style. My exercises and my therapy continued, of course, and my fingers started loosening up until I could do everything I wanted with them.

In September the club wanted me to go down to the Instructional League, with the idea that I was to throw no more than fifty or sixty pitches in game conditions. Or three innings. If I used up my quota of pitches before the end of three innings, I was to quit. My first game was against the Angels. The first two pitches I threw were "ball one, ball two." I could practically hear the coaches telling each other: "Well, he just hasn't got it anymore." Then on the third pitch, our catcher Brad Gulden called for a curve. I thought that was a peculiar pitch to call for when I was behind the batter 2 and 0 (a curve being more likely to miss the strike zone than a fast ball would). But what the heck, I told myself, I've got nothing to lose. Let's try it. I tried it and it went for a strike. I got that batter out. I got the next guy out. I got the next guy out. Just fast balls and curves. I went three innings without giving a hit or a run. And I struck out four. Four strikeouts in three innings. For me, that was close to sensational! I had thrown just thirty-nine pitches. That was great! I wanted to work another inning, but nothing doing. Three was my limit. Next time they upped the pitches by ten, to either sixty or seventy. Then I went four innings. Then five. Then seven. And I pitched well. I wasn't pitching in the major leagues but I was satisfied that I had pitched well. The coaches agreed that I would be ready to take my turn in 1976.

The 1976 season, however, was the season the owners locked us out, in the foolish hope that they were going to put an end to Marvin Miller's leadership. They might as well have tried to overthrow the British monarchy. Marvin was there to stay and eventually the owners realized it. But the lockout was tough on the pitchers, especially me, for if anyone needed spring training that year, I was the guy. Pitching against recent high school and college graduates in the Instructional League was no substitute for pitching against the Cincinnati Reds or the Phillies or the Pirates. Of course, I had kept up my workouts all winter, and I was in pretty good shape. I had only three games in the abbreviated spring training, and I came into the season without a great deal of immediate experience behind me. I actually did fairly well, I thought. But the coaches were concerned about my fast ball.

"Better work on that," they told me, "because we've been timing you with the radar gun and the fast ball isn't there."

"Listen," I said, "if you wanted Sandy Koufax you're kind of late. He retired in 1966. You never had a Koufax in me to begin with and I'll never be a Koufax."

"All right. We just wanted you to know that's what we're worried about."

The season started and I pitched my first game against Atlanta, giving up five runs, two or three of them earned, in five innings. Next day Walt Alston came to me and said: "We're going to give you one more shot. And if you haven't got it then, we might have to move you into the bullpen." (The bullpen, in case anyone doesn't know, is where the pitchers wait who are going to be used in case a starting pitcher falters.)

"What for?" I said. "I've only pitched five innings. What kind of a trial is that when I've been out a year and a half? Just let me find out if I can pitch. If I can't, okay. But you have to give me a better chance than this." Even Red Adams, our pitching coach, agreed with me on that.

"Well, I have to think of the team," said Walt. It seemed to me then that they had all been conditioned to the idea that I wasn't going to come back and what they had been looking for was anything that would confirm their decision.

"Let Fergy catch me," I said (Joe Ferguson, a big catcher, had been with the Dodgers for six seasons and had been playing a lot of outfield as well as catching. He had been in right field against Atlanta and had noticed something I was doing wrong.) "I think Fergy can help me."

"Okay. We'll give it a try."

I started against Houston. You know how things go when you are in the showcase and have to make good in one try. Something is bound to go wrong. The first batter hit a ground ball that bounced high over my head and that the shortstop could not get to. Then on the hit-and-run, when the second baseman moved over to cover second base, the batter sent a single through the hole he vacated. Now we had men on first and third and nobody out. Caesar Cedeño, up next, hit a ground ball and we turned it into a crazy double play. Guys were running all over the field like a Chinese fire drill. I know we got one out at home and one out someplace else and we wound up with a runner on third and two out. I then got three balls on Bob Watson. Right away, Walt Alston had someone get up in the bullpen and start throwing. Here I had allowed two ground-ball hits, had two outs and one runner still on base and Walt was already preparing to lift me; not just lift me, but consign me to near-obscurity. At this point, Fergy asked for time and came out to talk to me:

"Listen, if Walt is going to yank you after two ground-ball hits, then let's go out in a blaze of glory. Just rear back and let me have three of your best fast balls."

I agreed. I reached way back and fired in a fast ball that I knew Watson would let go by. Strike one. Another full-speed pitch. Watson fouled it off. Strike two. Now I dug right down to the bottom of my guts and gave the next one all I owned. Watson swung and missed. Strike three. The side was out and I was saved for a better fate.

I went on then for six more innings and did not give up a run. But we hadn't scored a run either, for J. R. Richard was pitching against us and he wasn't giving anything away. That was the year he won twenty games and struck out 214 batters. In the eighth inning they sent in a hitter for me, and I retired to the clubhouse without having given up a run and having earned myself at least one or two more tries before the axe fell.

Back in Los Angeles after the road trip, I was to start my first game in Dodger Stadium since my injury two years before. It was promoted as a major event in the press and on the air: "Tommy John Comes Back!" "Come See the Comeback of Tommy John!" That went on for a whole week before the game. It was like a World Series opener—not only in fan response but in the effect it had on me. I was charged up like a seltzer bottle. Sally too. I bought seats for Sally so that she could not be picked out in the "ballplayers' wives" section and need not feel "on stage."

The game, against the Pittsburgh Pirates, was a good one for the team and for me. We hit the Pirate pitchers from inning one and I was working with a lead almost from the start. I had a shutout going into the ninth and the crowd was cheering every out. In the ninth I wobbled a bit. Two doubles, back to back, brought in a Pirate run and Alston decided I had had enough. I did not disagree. Mike Marshall came in to save my first win in fifteen months and I walked cheerfully to the dugout. I had taken only the first step when the whole crowd—a full forty thousand of them—stood up and began to applaud—clapping, yelling, screaming, whistling, calling my name. What a welcome! "Great game, Tommy!" "Welcome back Tommy!" I could feel the chill run down my spine and I held up my hat in a fervent thank you.

Now that I had proven I could pitch again, my attorney, Bob Cohen, a good friend whom Sally and I had known since he and Sally had both been patients of Dr. Jobe in 1972, thought it was time to talk about a new contract. My own inept efforts to "sell" myself to general managers by reciting all my virtues and accomplishments had convinced me by this time that I needed someone to represent me—someone who would be able to speak objectively about my pitching ability and who would not take the belittling of a player's value, a normal part of the bargaining process, as a personal insult. Bob was an excellent talker and a man not easily upset. His first meetings with Al Campanis, the Dodger general manager, were pleasant and productive. Al agreed at once that I deserved a raise in salary. Just how much was a matter for discussion. My salary at that point was $78,000. But Al cast some doubt on the permanence of my recovery. He suggested a salary structure based on the number of wins. Twenty wins, so much more money. Bob resisted this. But of course it was a starting point for bargaining. Al suggested then that the increase be based on the number of innings pitched, or the number of complete games. But that, Bob pointed out, would leave it up to the manager or the club to decide whether or not I would reach the goal. They settled at last on the number of games started. If I could hold a place in the regular rotation, then I would certainly have "come back." That then was the final agreement—an extra $20,000 if I started twenty games, and an extra $38,000 if I started thirty games. I was pleased with the deal and started off my season with a high heart.

But there was one near-hitch in the deal about the time of the All-Star break when a Los Angeles sports writer reported in print that the Dodgers were going to a four-man rotation and that Tommy John therefore would be dropped from the starting list. My temper came to an immediate boil. A move like that could cost me my entire bonus—the money I already had a lock on. I hurried to Walt Alston's office and demanded an explanation.

Walt seemed as surprised as I had been. But he refused to grow excited. As long as I'm managing this club, he told me calmly, you are going to be a starter. Don't pay attention to these off-the-wall news stories. I cooled off promptly, thanked Walt, and went back to work. My thirtieth start—my bonus game—came against the Atlanta Braves. After the catcher took my first pitch, I asked for time, retrieved the ball, and tossed it into the dugout to be held for me. What was this? my teammates wanted to know. Some kind of record? Nope. Just a $38,000 milestone. (Actually I started thirty-one games that season, one above the requirement.)

My record in 1976 was ten wins and ten losses—a pretty good "comeback" mark I thought—and I finished the year with a real flourish: a 9–0 victory over the Cincinnati Reds. Then, just to ice the cake a little, I went out the next day to play in the Kings Island Open Pro-Am tournament and teamed with George Burns to win first prize. After that, awards piled in like Christmas cards: the Fred Hutchinson Award, the St. Louis Sportswriters Comeback Player of the Year Award, the National League Comeback Player of the Year Award, The Chicago Sportswriters Comeback Player of the Year Award. These were just a few of the plaques and trophies that came my way. I look at them, there on my wall, from time to time and I think—not just of the long weary stretch of hard work and prayer—but of the gratitude I still feel for the fans and the writers, and above all of my gratitude to God, who must surely have some sort of plan for Tommy John, some plan that will keep me strong enough to work many years more for God's greater glory.

I faced the 1977 season pleased with my comeback and especially about the new manager the Dodgers had chosen. Walt Alston, after twenty-three years, had yielded at last to the call of golf, hunting, and fishing and decided he deserved relief from the rigors of running a baseball team. In his place the Dodgers named Tommy Lasorda and Tommy, I felt, was a manager I could count on to let me finish a few more games. He had been a pitcher himself (with Brooklyn and Kansas City) and was perhaps more likely than Alston was to understand a pitcher's problems.

Also I felt that Tommy was better equipped to bring peace to the locker room. Under Alston there had been more than the normal amount of bickering among the younger players over who ought to be in the lineup and who ought to be riding the bench. Tommy Lasorda, I thought, was diplomat enough to quiet some of those arguments. He had raised most of these kids in the minors and they all looked up to him. And while I had always respected Alston for baseball knowledge, I was convinced he had decided I was never going to be able to pitch a complete game again. If I gave up a hit or two, or even if I gave up a hit and a walk in the seventh inning, when Alston was in charge, I would unfailingly see a man get up in the bullpen to make ready to relieve me. Tommy Lasorda, by contrast, came to me immediately after he was appointed manager and told me I was going to be one of his five starters.

"Tommy," he said. "I *need* you to help us win. You *are* going to pitch and you *are* going to win for us!" His straight-from-the-heart assurance put new life into my heart and into my arm. I wanted the season to start *right then.* In all my career I had never had a coach or manager express such confidence in me. What a simple thing it is to really inspire an athlete with a solid pat on the back like this, rather than to try to scare or bully him into performing. I was ready after that to pitch a twenty-six inning game for Tommy Lasorda.

Tommy is, by the way, just about the most lovable guy anyone ever worked for—full of fun, full of sympathy and understanding, full of enthusiasm. And occasionally given to some of the wildest practical jokes any ballplayer ever cooked up. I'll never forget the complex hazing he gave some of us one Sunday.

There were a number of us on the club who lived in the Orange County area and we used to form a car pool to drive to the park together. On the way we would usually pick up Tommy Lasorda, because Tommy, even though he had four or five cars in his driveway, never seemed to be able to get one to work for him. (He couldn't pat *cars* on the back and make them perform.) But on this particular day Tommy amazed us by calling to say he was going to pick *us* up—Billy Russell, Joe Ferguson, Burt Hooton, Charlie Hough, and me. Believe me, knowing Tommy's way with automobiles, we were all a little nervous about being late to the park. But Tommy showed up at my house in plenty of time and quickly accepted an invitation from Sally to come in for coffee and a chat while the rest of us stood around, just waiting. As soon as Tommy came in he caught sight of little Tami and picked her up and swung her around. "You love your Uncle Tommy, don't you?" he asked her. "Uncle Tommy loves you!" This went on for a few minutes, then there were two cups of coffee at a very leisurely pace. Billy and Fergy and Burt and Charlie and I meanwhile were straining at the bit. It was getting *late*! Practice would be starting!

Finally Tommy bade a fond good-bye to Sally, hugged Tami once more, and we started off. But on the way, we came to our favorite snack stop, a local doughnut house, and Tommy stopped to pick up a little something to stave off starvation while we rode on. When we reached the Stadium, batting practice had already begun. We all scrambled to get into our uniforms and get out on the field. Tommy, who had headed straight for his office, came out, stared at us as if he was seeing us for the first time, and announced: "You guys are fined fifty dollars each for being late for practice!" I think we must all have looked at him with exactly the same expression of shocked surprise and all uttered the same protest at the same time: "But you *drove* us here!"

Tommy's expression of stern disapproval never changed.

"Never trust the person driving to get you to the park on time!" he declared. "It's up to *you* to leave in plenty of time to avoid being late!" With that he turned away, then looked back to add: "AND that's fifty bucks a man, fellas!" The fine stood too.

Tommy was also a great motivator. Once he had a player

who came down with a sick stomach on the day of a play-off game and told Tommy he wanted to stay in the hotel for fear he was going to vomit.

"Well, listen," said Tommy. "Why not come down to the clubhouse and stretch out on the trainer's table? Then if you do get sick to your stomach the trainer will be there to take care of you."

"Good idea," said the player, and off they went to the park. Once they were there, Tommy urged him: "Take off those tight-fitting street clothes and get into your uniform. You'll feel better in loose clothes."

"You're probably right," said the player and promptly changed into uniform. When he had his suit on, Tommy invited him to come out and take a seat on the end of the bench. "The fresh air will help you," he explained. "And the game might take your mind off your stomach." The player agreed and took his seat at the very end of the bench. When the game began, Tommy came and looked the man over.

"You really don't look too bad." said Tommy. "I think you look well enough to play. I've got you slated as D.H. (designated hitter) in the fourth slot. Now go up there and get a hit." The man did. He played the whole game. And he got three hits in four times at bat. Tommy told me this story himself and I believe it. I believe anything Tommy tells me. And if need be, I'd give him the shirt off my back. It wouldn't fit him. But he can have it any time. Indeed, when Tommy came to the Dodgers I told myself I was going to stay with this club just as long as they wanted me.

But my education in the wiles and ways of baseball executives was very far from complete. I had worked the season of 1976 on the usual one-year contract. But the Andy Messersmith-Dave McNally court decision had been issued in 1976, tossing the infamous "reserve rule" into the wastebasket. (Old Kenesaw Mountain Landis, baseball commissioner before I was born, had warned the club owners years before that they should get rid of that rule because "someday it will destroy you!" Now a court had saved them the trouble.) No longer could a ball club "sign" a player by simply invoking the option clause in the standard contract. The baseball magnates had always held that the option clause itself, like the other contract terms, could be renewed automatically, thus effectively binding a ballplayer to the same club in perpetuity, inasmuch as the option clause along with the other provisions could be renewed at management's discretion, without the ballplayer's ever signing another contract. (It used to be possible to look over baseball records and read the names of players long forgotten, even long past playing age, who remained the "property" of the club that first signed them.) The Messersmith-McNally decision, which held that a one-year contract expired at the end of one year, in all respects meant that when I had completed my 1977 contract I could become a free agent. But I had no such plan. I loved Los Angeles, I loved the ball club, I was devoted to Tommy Lasorda. Still, I wanted the assurance of a longer contract when this one ran out.

Bob Cohen was already engaged in negotiations with Al Campanis for a new contract that would take me past 1978. But the talks began to take some peculiar turns. When I was winning ball games, Campanis could never find time to negotiate. But when I had pitched some bad games—and I did pitch two horrible ones, against Philadelphia and Montreal—interest in negotiations would suddenly re-ignite. Then it was: "How can we give your man that much money when he's doing so badly? He's given up thirty-two hits in the last thirty-eight innings!" (The Yankees, incidentally, operated in the same way when they were trying to ease me out, talking about "twenty runs in twenty-eight innings" and refusing to discuss the four or five good games I had pitched earlier. "They don't count," they would say. "We go on current stats.") After I had pitched nine innings against the Mets in May of 1977 and had given them only one run, we settled on a very good two-year contract to take me through 1978. The new contract relieved Sally of worry over security too. (Our second baby, Thomas Edward John III, was born on August 31, 1977.) Sally survived a frightful delivery and I, having survived my own ordeal, was pitching as well as I had ever pitched in my life. This, we both agreed, was going to be *our* year.

It was too, for I went on to complete the best season of my career so far—twenty victories and an earned-run average of 2.78. Still, satisfying as the new contract was, I retained a slightly bad taste in my mouth because of the length of what struck me as often unfair negotiations. I simply had never got adjusted to the "business is business" attitude and was still inclined to take any depreciation of my ability as a personal insult. I know I should know better and I have learned since that the Dodger people were truly good friends of mine. But I guess I'll just never be a negotiator.

I give Tom Lasorda most of the credit for my great year. His confidence in me pulled me through many a tough inning and his willingness to stay with me when I was having a bad moment or two just added to my own confidence—the quality no pitcher can do without. Tom boosted that confidence sky high when he chose me to pitch the first game in the league play-offs, the first time I had ever reached the play-offs—and to be the starting pitcher too! While I failed to get the victory in game number one I came back in game four, the deciding game, and pitched one of the best games of my career—certainly the most exciting as well as the most important, for it put us in the World Series. I went the full nine innings in the pouring rain to beat the Phillies, 4 to 1, giving me a total of thirteen play-off innings, with eleven strikeouts, an exceptionally high mark for me. There was a party at Lasorda's restaurant afterward to celebrate our winning the pennant. There was champagne flowing but I needed none of it to render me high as the stadium flag. I could not recall ever having been happier. And one of my best laughs came when Roland Hemond told the people that they should thank him for my present state. After all, he was the one who had traded me from the White Sox! Tom Lasorda's telephone rang almost without let-up. Frank Sinatra called. Don Rickles called. And after they spoke to Tom they wanted to talk to *me*. I think that thrilled Sally as much as the victory. We went home on a cloud and spent most of the rest of the night just telling each other over again all the joyous and unbelievable things that had happened on that rainy day in October, 1977.

In the 1977 World Series against the Yankees—my first—Tom Lasorda pitched me in the third game. I wish I could say that I won that game for him but I did not. We lost it (as we lost the series) largely because of pesky Mickey Rivers who picked our pockets for two doubles and a single. Nevertheless, I was entirely pleased with what I had done that year. I had even pitched eleven complete games—thanks to Tommy Lasorda's willinginess to go the extra mile with me—the most games I had finished in the previous five seasons.

In the spring of 1978, it was negotiation time again and the routine was the same—what had I done *recently*? I would be a free agent at the end of this season and again I had no desire to take advantage of the privilege.

In our contract talks this year management began to bear down on my "ingratitude" for all their goodness and loving kindness. They were offering me a two-year package totalling $500,000 to be divided any way I chose. But, I wanted *three* years. I felt I had earned that and was adamant about it.

But look at all we have done for you, they would repeat. Don't we deserve *some* gratitude? Some of the sports writers took this up and made it sound as if the Dodgers had invested thousands gratuitously in my hospitalization and rehabilitation, had carried me for a whole season at a big-league salary when all I did was hold the radar gun in the stands to time the pitchers.

What you did for me, I told them, was only what you had to do. It was based entirely on business considerations. You paid for my operation because you were obligated to do so under the Basic Agreement. Even at that, my expenses for the operation were all covered by your insurance policy. You signed me for 1976 because that was the only way you could hold an option on my services. The only choices you had were sign me or release me. If you hadn't signed me for 1975, some other club would have. And that was not speculation. It was a fact. This is business with you and it is business with me. I want the security of a three-year contract.

Peter O'Malley finally admitted that I was quite right about their having been moved by business considerations entirely. Before it ended, the discussions became fairly unpleasant, with much talk centered around my lack of common gratitude. Echoes of all this continued in the press. But I hung tough and so did the Dodgers. They had appraised my value with great care, they said, and could not see how a man my age, with the chance that my injury might recur, could command any more than they had offered. But my arm, I told them, and Dr. Jobe told them, is just as sound as any other arm on your whole staff. And the chances of re-injury diminish month by month. Actually my chances of being injured in the same way were exactly the same for me as they were for every other pitcher on the club.

It is true, I did hurt my leg fielding a topped ball over by the first-base line and I had to leave the game with a pulled tendon. I had to lay off for seventeen days—ten days of rest and seven days of light work. But I came back and pitched three shut-out innings against Cincinnati. Then I pitched six more shut-out innings against San Diego and beat them. All the time my leg was taped up from knee to ankle to provide support. I finished that season with seventeen wins and ten losses and an ERA of 3.66.

The 1978 season was a difficult one emotionally for both Sally and me. I don't like to think what might have happened if we had not had Tom Lasorda to comfort, encourage, and even distract me when need be. Sally was pregnant with our third baby and the seemingly endless bickering over the contract interfered with my concentration. But Tommy Lasorda made it clear that he was on my side at all times. He called me frequently to ask if there was anything he could do to facilitate the contract talks. "Don't worry about it," he would assure me. "It will work out. Just go out there and pitch your best and everything will come out in good shape. You'll see."

One night before the game began Tommy called me away from batting practice to come see him in his office. Now what? I wondered. Did I say something wrong to Al Campanis? I tried to recall what went on at the last discussion.

"Close the door," said Tommy, when I came in. "Sit down."

Well, I thought, here it comes! If I could just remember what I *said* to Campanis! But Tommy had turned away and was pulling plastic containers out of a drawer. Six or seven of them, all fragrant with a fine aroma. Chinese food!

"Let's wait for Fergy," he said. In a moment Fergy came in and the three of us merrily tucked away a six-course Chinese dinner! Ever since that moment I have loved Tommy like a brother. What a man! What a manager!

Lasorda pitched me second in the play-offs. I pitched against the Phillies and shut them out 4–0. In the 1978 World Series, Tommy had me start the first game because he hoped to have me pitch three times if the Series went seven games. I worked seven plus innings against the Yankees in the first game and we beat them badly. In my second start, in the fourth game, I pitched seven innings again and gave up only two runs before being relieved. We lost that game in the tenth inning. Reggie Jackson, having murdered us in the 1977 World Series with his three successive home runs in the sixth game, got two home runs in this series and the Yankees beat us again.

In August 1978, the Dodgers had made me a firm offer, with the stipulation that if I did not accept it within twenty-four hours they would "take the offer off the table." I gave it much hard thought. I talked it over with Sally. We decided together that, considering the current conditions of the free-agent market, it was just not good enough. I told Bob Cohen to turn it down. The Dodgers were incredulous. They asked Bob: "Does he know what he's doing? This is the Dodgers!"

On the last day of the World Series, the Dodgers gave me a "final" offer that was very little different from the one before. Now it was too late. The battle lines had been drawn. I had decided that, much as I loved Tom Lasorda, regardless of the fun I had had with the Dodgers, and regardless of my respect for Peter O'Malley and Al Campanis, it was time to move on.

Then, on the night before the free-agent draft, Al Campanis called Bob Cohen and told him the Dodgers would retain their rights to draft me if I would simply call him on the telephone and say out loud that I would like to stay with the Dodgers. Bob passed this message on to me. But I felt that the real question was, did the Dodgers want me? If they did, then they could have signed me. But I was already sniffing the breeze from the free-agent draft and I was eager to see what might lie beyond the horizon. I told Bob I would not make that call.

FIVE

Sally:

Waiting for Travis to awaken from his coma was like watching, in the middle of a black winter night, for some faint hint of the coming of dawn. Almost every hour it seemed one or the other of us would try to coax a response from that tiny frail body. We would tell him of home, of the Muppets, of our love for him, and we would sing him songs he used to ask for. We had brought his favorite playthings from home, hoping they might stir some flicker of understanding in his eyes. We used to move our hands before his face in the hope that his eyes might focus and follow them.

But the first voluntary movements came in the strangest and most unexpected ways. The first move was such a natural one and so seemingly insignificant that we almost missed it. One day, while Tommy and I were both watching Travis, one little hand moved very slowly and a little shakily up toward his face and, for the tiniest part of a second, the small fist brushed at his eye, the way a child will do when waking from sleep. I screamed with the thrill of hope. We hardly believed what we had seen. We looked at each other to make sure we both had noticed it. We told ourselves, I think, that it could have been merely a sort of spasm or a meaningless involuntary movement such as occasionally caused his arms and legs to flex. But the doctor had told us to watch for a "purposeful" movement and this might have been described that way.

We tried then to wheedle another sign from him—a movement of his eyes, a flicker of recognition at a name or a sound or the sight of something he had been fond of. But that was all, just a faint imitation of a sleepy little boy rubbing one eye. The brain, the doctor told us, is just beginning to awaken. It will not wake up all at once, just little by little, as the impulses are able to trickle down the reviving nerves. And there is no sure way of predicting how soon, or even how completely, he will recover all his faculties. He will be like a new baby again and may have to learn all over again how to talk, how to walk, how to feed himself.

How difficult it was to be patient after two whole weeks of waiting! And how dismaying when that first little sign was not repeated but seemed to be followed by a sinking back into a dreamless sleep! Well, Travis would have his peaks and valleys, the doctors had warned us. Now we had to wait for another "peak."

That came in a strange way, too. We had brought from home Travis's favorite blanket, a well-worn little coverlet such as babies sometimes grow attached to. This blanket had a small hole in it, where Travis had picked the threads loose and had thrust one tiny index finger through. Often, lying in his bed at night, he would send one small hand searching for the spot where he had made an opening. We put the little blanket over him as he lay there tethered to that array of machines and I really did not notice when the movement began. But suddenly I realized that Travis's right hand was creeping across the blanket ever so slowly and without special direction, like a small animal looking for a way out. Then his hand found that hole and he poked the finger through, just as he used to do when he was well. It was as if he had taken hold of a friendly hand. The searching stopped and he lay content. And I knew that *this* time that small brain knew what it was doing and the message had traveled clearly down the sleepy nerves. He *was* waking up.

After that, even though Travis continued alternately to sink into sleep and come partly awake again, the advance was more regular. Of course I continued to fret over just how much brain function he would recover. And we both would weep with joy at every small sign of recovery. Would he ever laugh again? Would he talk? Would he have to crawl like a baby? So even the minor indications of the recovery of one function or another were occasions for rejoicing.

Certainly one of the happiest moments in the long train was the visit of Reggie Jackson. Reggie had to come to the hospital at the behest of George Steinbrenner, who had decided that there must be some physical ailment behind Reggie's failure to produce mighty home runs at the rate of earlier seasons. He sent Reggie to have his eyes examined, his blood count taken, his insides probed, even his bone structure appraised. And in between times, Reggie would stop to visit Travis. Reggie seemed to own a special affinity for our kids. His face would simply glow in their presence. And every time he visited the hospital he would make a point of coming up to visit us. This was really unusual, for ordinarily baseball players do not involve themselves in the off-diamond woes of their teammates. But I don't believe Reggie could ever walk by a child in trouble.

On this visit Reggie noticed the collection of hand-puppets among the toys we had brought in for Travis—and which, of course, he could not play with. Reggie fitted one of the Muppets—I think it was Animal—over his hand and got right down on his knees beside Travis's bed.

"Hello, Travis!" he said, in a gruff voice that sounded not much like a pro ballplayer, and less like George Steinbrenner. "I'm George Steinbrenner, I came to see you. I want to tell you about this guy Reggie Jackson. I think he's really wacko, Travis! He's always doing something crazy! And he's trying to drive me crazy! Don't you think he's wacko, Travis? I think I'll have to send him to get his head examined!" And so on and on, until he had all of us—nurses, doctors, and parents—snickering or laughing out loud, not so much at the wild things he was saying as at the sight of this husky athlete down on all fours making fun of himself to amuse an ailing baby. But Travis still lay there, unmoving, his eyes not seeming to be focused on anything, until Reggie, out of breath, got up and flopped in a chair. "I think maybe I *am* crazy," he laughed. And suddenly on Travis's face the very beginnings of a smile began to grow—not a full smile, just the gradual curling up of one corner of his mouth, the way Tommy's own smile begins (and the way Tommy's father's smile begins, too). I don't know whether we gasped, or laughed, or cried. I know I must have cried a little from joy. So he *could* hear! And he *could* see! And he could understand as well! I think Reggie was as surprised and as enraptured as we were, and I am sure that he thought—as we did—that he had performed a miracle. Travis finally smiled.

After that, there were continual small signs that Travis was coming awake. I think the next one, too, involved baseball. Tommy was playing in Chicago one evening and all of us, Carol and I, and at least one of the doctors, were watching him on television. Sometime early in the game one of the umpires called a "balk" on Tommy. Immediately Tommy left the mound and started toward the umpire. The crowd howled. Tommy strode so purposefully, I thought he might be about to challenge the man to a fight. Without thinking, I got out of my chair and screamed at the TV: "No! Tommy! Stay away from him! He'll throw you out of the game!" Tommy did stay away, or at least did not come much closer to the umpire than talking distance. I learned from Tommy later (Tommy would always fly right back to the hospital after he had pitched a game) that he had no murderous intentions at all, that he had simply walked over to ask the umpire to explain what he had done wrong, for he had not been aware of any incorrect move. The crowd had roared and the TV camera had moved for a tight shot on Tommy's face. And Tommy, as he walked back from exchanging words with the umpire, was laughing out loud. There was his laughing face, big as life, on the TV screen. Travis, who had been facing the TV, looked straight at Tommy's face. Suddenly his eyes widened and a full smile grew. That was his *daddy* there!

Reggie Jackson played a part in that drama, too. He hit a home run in the game and afterward he was interviewed on radio. First he asked the entire audience to join him in turning their minds and their prayers to a little boy in a hospital in New York—Tommy's son Travis! Then he declared that his home run that night had been dedicated to Travis. That was not something that Travis could grasp but all the rest of us in that small audience did. And I am sure we all vowed, as I did, that even if Reggie never hit another home run or caught another fly, he would hold a place in our private Hall of Fame forever.

I don't want you to think that these small episodes brought our worries to an end. On the contrary, I think the sudden raising of hopes that these small signs created simply accentuated the fears that returned when there was a subsequent slide back into coma. We actually lived in a state of mild terror throughout this period, fearful, of course, that the sign we had received might simply have marked the final high mark of his recovery. In some ways, it seemed the better he became, the worse I became, for I also dreaded the day when I would have to leave this haven, where there were doctors and nurses and every sort of facility for saving him if he should suffer a reverse. So, while we rejoiced in every hint of returning consciousness, we still watched fearfully for signs of deepening coma.

We had received, since coming to the hospital, almost a trunkful of letters from people who had family experience of comas of varying depth and length, so many that we actually numbered the letters: Coma Story number 1, Coma Story number 2, up to Coma Story number 200 or something.

Some of the letters were encouraging and all were marked by degrees of sympathy and love. But there was one that really frightened me. It was from a mother whose little boy, just about Travis's age, had also suffered a fall and lay for a long time in a coma. He had come out of it finally. But he was brain-damaged and crippled. The mother enclosed a picture of the child: face as innocent as Travis's own, but the tiny limbs twisted grotesquely as if they had been frozen in a seizure. This was exactly the fate I feared most for Travis and the sight of the picture set me to weeping. Tommy finally took the picture and tore it up. But it was many days before I was able to erase that scary image from my mind.

There were other letters too, not all of them sympathetic. One mother wrote me a bitter complaint against the fortune that had kept Travis alive, while her own little girl, who had fallen only two stories, had died. Why had God chosen to favor me? She too was a Christian and she had led a Christian life, faithful to her duties. Why was I any different? What medicine had kept Travis alive? Who was the doctor who had worked the miracle? And how could she retain any faith in a God who had dealt so unjustly? I did not know how to answer this, for I had had my own faith sorely tried and I had no heart for attempting to persuade her now that God knows best. I recalled how I had urged in my own prayers that *my* will, not God's, should be done. And I was barely beginning to learn about the goodness that might grow out of tragedy. So I put that letter from me too, although I could never put it from my mind.

Every one of the letters finally was answered, with this little verse written by a very dear friend, Maureen Brennan.

TO MY FRIENDS

Memories of your thoughtfulness
    Will live with me each day
Remembering how you showed you cared
    In a very special way.
I needed your constant prayers

And into your hearts you dug
So in return I hope you'll accept
A special Travis hug.

Love, Travis

(For a long time afterward, we kept meeting people who had kept this letter and showed it to us when we met.)

I think it is probably commonplace that heights of joy, fostering the notion that happy days are here for keeps, are followed after a setback by even deeper plunges into gloom. But the ups and downs Tommy and I experienced as Travis slowly found his way back to health nearly shattered us emotionally. The doctors had tried to prepare us for this by warning us continually that Travis was not going to leap back to normal but would creep back over many months. We probably never had accepted that in our hearts, however. Privately, we kept looking for the moment when our little boy would come wide awake and be his lively and mischievous self again. So to us the recovery period was like climbing out of a well, finally grasping the rim—and then suddenly losing our grip and slipping back into the depths. Both of us, despite a number of happy moments, like the experience with Reggie Jackson, knew some of our blackest hours when the dawn was really close. We were plunged so many times into despair after a few moments of joy that Tommy and I hardly dared be happy. Instead, we began to look upon each sign of recovery as an omen and took care not to rejoice too much—like pagans who feared to tempt the gods by exhibiting an unseemly happiness.

We did have moral support, however, from every quarter. Many of Tommy's teammates came often to the hospital to cheer us. Travis's plight seemed to transcend all tradition and these hulking men came in, sometimes two at a time, to show that they held him in their hearts and in their prayers. Some of them, however, simply could not bear to look at that inert little body with the shaven head, the burr-holes in his skull, the manifold tubes and wires attached to his body, and the weird machine, like a tiny propeller perched atop his scalp. They would studiously avert their eyes as they assured us they *knew* he was getting better.

There was one man who gave us this assurance in a far more convincing way. That was Cardinal Cooke, who walked in on us unannounced one day, to our open-mouthed surprise. He knew, of course, that we were not of his faith and he came simply to comfort us and lend us his advice. Our love for each other, he told us, was visible on our faces, and in our support for each other. Now he wanted us to pour that love upon Travis. "I am sure he can hear you," he told us, "regardless of his present state. Tell him of your love for him! Keep telling him! He will hear it and take strength from it. And he *will* get well. I *know* it. He *will* get well."

It is amazing how these solemn and positive words from this holy man strengthened and cheered us. We urged him to come with us to visit the parents of another little boy, just the age of Travis, who was suffering from a malignant brain tumor. The boy's father, Matthew Ercolano, himself a devout Catholic, was nearly overwhelmed at the sight of Cardinal Cooke, right at his side, blessing his son. Matthew's eyes started from his head as if God in the flesh had appeared before him. Jerry, the policeman, who also had a child there in the hospital, was equally astounded at the living presence of the cardinal and he too stared at His Eminence with bulging eyes.

Bucky Dent did not cause quite such a stir, although I observed that some of the nurses found extra errands in our direction when Bucky visited. Bucky, however, came at our invitation, for he was a patient in the hospital himself, having had an operation on his hand. Knowing that he had no one to keep him company during his stay, I had left word for him to come see us when he could. He came and brought a big sack of candy to Travis.

Letters of course continued to pour in by the cartonful, some forwarded from home, many from the Yankee office but most sent in care of the hospital itself—not just letters from Nixon and Ford and Reagan, which I have already mentioned, and from other celebrities, but from acquaintances, dear friends, and plain folk we had never met but whose good wishes and prayers were as dear to us as were those of the VIPs.

This period of ups and downs seemed like half a lifetime to us, but actually it lasted only a little more than a week. It seemed there were countless times when I held the pillow against Travis's feet and urged him to push against it and almost wept to see how those wasted and trembling legs tried to obey my commands. And I could not number the many times I had held up a brightly colored ball and told Travis that he could not reach it, tempting him of course to prove me wrong—which he did again and again, painfully and slowly, but with a ferocity worthy of his father, reaching and reaching until he finally grasped it in his fingers.

Finally, Travis began to improve, no longer by inches, as the doctors had predicted, but by sudden giant leaps, as if his spirit had suddenly been electrified into forcing his body ahead. We had already learned that bright colors would attract him, so Tommy had brought in a box of golf balls colored a bright yellow-green, a sort of chartreuse shade, and these were what I had used to persuade him to reach out and take hold. One day, after taking hold of the ball, he moved his arm, with that same painful slowness, into throwing position. He was not quite ready to perform a motion as complex as that, but it was clear that he knew what a ball was made for.

After that, Carol Schaefer and I began lifting Travis to his feet, letting him "stand" on his bed with one of us holding him on either side under the shoulder. His body seemed so wasted now that he weighed no more than a Christmas stocking and his legs seemed to have withered to the size of sticks. By moving him a little back and forth with his feet on the bed, we felt we might evoke his muscles to the task of walking again. At first he was limp as a rag doll and his feet would simply drag across the bedcovers. But we knew now that he had started to get well, and we were ready to walk him back and forth for weeks if need be, until his muscles began to respond.

Tommy was often with us at these times, for even though, with Travis getting better, Tommy had started to travel with the Yankees on road trips, he would always fly back after taking his turn pitching and would not have to join the club until his turn came around again. So we still had long hours to sit and live over again the moments in our lives together that we had been holding in our hearts—funny moments, scary times, excitements, and all the rest.

I liked most to relive the very early part of my married life, when I began to get used to being a new and different person—and discovered that in most ways I was just the same person with a slightly different name. Being a ballplayer's wife, I had been told again and again, was like being married to a sailor. There would be long spells of loneliness, and dark doubts about girls in other ports and, when the player was home, hasty early dinners, evenings either at the ball park or by myself, and sometimes "extra innings" that would start new doubts abrooding. But I had no doubts about Tommy. And besides, Tommy and I had already been on the road together and I would accompany him again and again. Baseball life still stirred me, enthralled me, and even exalted me in a way, for it still felt to me like living on some higher plane, as if I had been transported to a land populated by the famous, the young, and the beautiful. But then, I was young myself, hardly old enough to vote, and still thought of famous folk as beings made of some special clay.

There was, however, one very dark moment in my early married life that had nothing to do with baseball. This came in Rosemont, a Chicago suburb where Tommy, with the aid of his friend the Rosemont mayor, had found us a beautiful apartment. I had been there just about long enough to find my way around and still got a kick out of visiting the supermarket, two miles away, to shop for the John "family." One bright morning, when Tommy was on a road trip to Detroit, I started my shopping almost as soon as the grocery was open, about 9 A.M., and was proudly trundling my cartful of groceries out to the parking lot, when I became aware that someone had followed me out the door and was coming along close behind. How nice! I thought. Someone is going to help me load the stuff into the station wagon. I glanced back and had a brief glimpse of a youngish man in blue jacket and jeans who was staring at me with the intensity of a madman. And to my utter horror I saw he was deliberately exposing himself. I started on the dead run, the cart flying before me, threw the bags into the car seat and sped off without a backward glance. I went straight to the office of a lady who owned the restaurant where we often took meals—an older woman, Tommy's friend, who had urged me to bring to her any problems that might assail me when Tommy was away. I was almost hysterical when I reached her and it took me more than a few seconds to get my sobs under complete control. But she heard my story quite calmly.

"Well," she said, "that's Rosemont for you. You really have to watch yourself all the time when you're alone. There are a lot of weird characters around here all the time. Stay away from the park. Don't go *near* the woods! Don't go out alone."

That was hardly the comfort I was seeking. She acted as if sex deviates were as commonplace as cats. And it simply reinforced my growing suspicion that Rosemont was the pits. It was close to O'Hare Airport and naturally had become a haven for "swinging singles," attracted I suppose by the presence of so many attractive stewardesses and the easy availability of accommodations for transients. There seemed to be a drunken party in progress at every hour and the foot traffic seemed almost as steady in the apartment corridors as it was during rush hours at the supermarket. As a girl fresh out of small-town Indiana, I had already been shaken by the free-and-easy sex manners of some of Tommy's teammates—men I knew to be married—but he had simply urged me not to judge them, indeed to ignore what I saw. But this latest horror was something I could not ignore. I was getting out of here!

I spent hardly more than a half-hour packing up whatever clothing and toilet gear I would really need. I called my mother and told her I was coming home. And home I sped, never to see Rosemont again. (Tommy was, as always, understanding and sympathetic and made no effort to talk me into coming back there to live. Instead, we set about looking for a spot where we could settle for good.)

It may seem strange that the freakish and uneasy moments of my early married life stand out so in my memory. But that, I think, is simply because the happy days were so much like each other, one following another as gently and regularly as the summer sun. There were plane trips—not always with Tommy, for I often had to take a regularly scheduled plane and then wait for the ball club charter plane to come in—that were almost pure joy. And long blissful evenings at the ball park—when I finished a lot of knitting and enjoyed watching the fans as much as I did watching the play on the field.

And there was the joy, too, of finding our new home in Scottsdale, Arizona, a spot I had picked out as being about as close to the realization of a dream as I was ever to find in this world. But before we lived there, and before I had been married a month, I got myself arrested as a spy. Well, almost arrested. How it ever happened is something even the United States Government could not quite figure out. The White Sox were playing in Washington and I was there, with Tommy of course, for my very first visit to this postcard capital where all the statues and buildings stand that had adorned my schoolbooks. I had my camera with me, naturally, and I had almost filled the first roll of film with shots of all the sights that moved me. Then Tommy had to go to the ball park and I had a whole afternoon to search for new sights by myself. Our congressman, John Myers, who was going away for a vacation, offered us the use of his "extra" car for my excursion and I accepted the keys, picked up the car in the Congressional parking lot, took Tommy to the ball park and he directed me to the Beltway that runs right around the capital. Anyone who has ever driven there probably knows how easy it is to become disoriented. For a small-town girl in the Capital for the first time, I guess it was inevitable. Anyway, I took one wrong turn after another, looking for familiar signs and sure I was headed in the right direction, when I wound up in a wide, wide empty space that looked, I thought, almost like an airfield. Indeed it *was* an airfield. But I did not realize that at once. I had come to an apparent end of the pavement and saw a wide, level, grassy stretch between me and a wide, straight highway. I negotiated the grassy stretch without trouble and set out down the "highway" at a good clip, looking for signs. There were markers of some sort along the way but no signs. Then I saw *airplanes*! This was a runway! I looked frantically about for a way to get out of here. There were buildings in the distance and I headed for them as fast as the car would move. As I passed the planes I noticed that they were not passenger planes at all—just two-passenger jobs with military markings. Startled men in uniforms gaped at me as I flew by. And there, glory be, was a gate! I headed straight for that, pulled up next to the man who seemed to be standing guard at the gate and asked him the way back to the Beltway.

He must have stared at me silently for about ten seconds before he replied.

"How'd you get *in* here?" he demanded. "You never came through the gate."

"I just turned off the Beltway and came in back there somewhere." I had already lost track of the route I had followed.

"You never came in there," said the soldier. "You'd have had to knock down a barbed-wire fence! Get out of your car, please."

I got out and found myself the center of a group of very tough-looking soldiers. Could I identify myself? Oh, yes, indeed. I started to fish in my pocketbook for my license but the man nearest to me took the whole pocketbook away. A military policeman lifted the keys out of the ignition and set out to open the trunk. Two others looked under the floor carpet and felt around the floorboard. What are they *doing*? I wanted to know. No answer. Two of the military policemen gently marched me into the nearest building, where a solemn young officer awaited me.

"How did you *really* get in here?" he demanded. So I told the whole story of what I was doing in Washington, of my troubles with the Beltway and my innocent discovery that I was on an airport runway. The officer obviously did not believe me. He looked at the license as if it were a counterfeit five-dollar bill. I had given my name as Sally John but my license said Sally Simmons.

"What are you doing with a congressman's car?" he asked suddenly. I did not know that the officer had already checked with John Meyers's office and had learned that the congressman would be out of town for three weeks. Nor did I realize that, in the light of this information, the officer had reported John Myers's car stolen. So I was an obvious car thief, a probable spy, and a young lady using a false name, offering a very silly-sounding story about being a visiting ballplayer's wife who had got into Bolling Air Force Base through some entrance that did not exist. My having a camera was as incriminating as if I had held a Russian passport. The soldiers opened my camera and methodically exposed the film. I stood there with tears streaking my face and watched the fruit of a whole day's sightseeing go blank before me.

Unless I changed my story and told them the "truth," my captors warned me, it would go very hard with me indeed.

Sally, (*second from right*), as high school cheerleader *(Frederick Barker Studio)*

Tommy with the Cleveland Indians

Sally and Tommy, now with the Chicago White Sox, shortly before their marriage *(J.D. McCarthy)*

On their marriage day: July 13, 1970
(Bob Harker)

Sally and Tommy after his trade to the Los Angeles Dodgers

Rehabilitation device made by Dodger trainer Bill Buhler to strengthen Tommy's grip after the injury that almost ended his career *(Dodgers photo by Mark Malone)*

A multiple-exposure shot of Tommy in action for the Dodgers *(Dodgers photo by Mark Malone)*

Tommy, now a New York Yankee, with the late Thurman Munson
(Louis Requena)

With California Angel owner Gene Autry

Tommy with David Hartmann and Dodger manager Tommy Lasorda (*far right*)

Avid golfer John with sports personality Joe Garagiola

With the Rev. Robert Schuler in the Glass Cathedral

Tommy, along with fellow honoree Edmund Pratt, board chairman of Pfizer, accepts Gil Hodges Sportsmanship Award from Bishop Francis J. Mugavero and N.Y. Mayor Edward Koch. *(Bob Mitchell Photography)*

Sally and Tommy with President Gerald Ford

Sally with Howard Cosell *(Carol Schaefer)*

The Johns today *(Will McIntyre)*

Whether this meant the firing squad or merely a day in the guardhouse, I did not know. In my current state neither verdict would have surprised me. I cannot help thinking now that had the interrogators been women instead of gung-ho young males, at least one of them would have observed that I could hardly have come barreling through a barbed-wire fence without marking the car nor would I have arrived in a congressman's car and asked directions of an MP if I had really been bent on stealing military secrets. And they would have known that young brides often have their maiden names on their licenses. But these boys were obviously relishing their unmasking of a cleverly disguised foreign agent. Happily, a teaspoonful of common sense trickled into the proceedings when an older officer, newly come into the room, noted that the White Sox were indeed playing in Washington and that they had a pitcher named Tommy John. I suspect that the youngster in charge may have been a bit let down by this indication that he might not have collared a spy after all. But he dutifully checked with the ball park, learned that Tommy John was there, that he had a new wife named Sally and that John Meyers had indeed lent them his car. I was offered sweet apologies, all the articles dumped from my purse were replaced, and I was given back keys, license and camera. But nothing, alas, would replace all those treasured snapshots. By this time, however, I was so relieved to have escaped prosecution that I counted them well lost and I hastened back to the Beltway, with a military escort! Before the MPs left me, they laid out for me in full detail the route to Kennedy Stadium. I arrived there when there were two innings to go.

I was growing uneasy at some aspects of baseball life—the long days alone, the off-center days when night games were scheduled, and the extra innings that make it necessary to keep dinner hot for Lord only could predict how long.

My first lesson in *this* discipline came most inappropriately when I was preparing for Tommy and two ballplayers, Bobby Knoop and Joe Horlen, a dinner of fried chicken, gravy, mashed potatoes and asparagus. Like an idiot, or an inexperienced bride, I accepted as gospel the time Tommy "guessed" he would be home—seven o'clock. I had never heard much about extra innings, nor dreamed that they would concern me. By seven o'clock I had the table all set, the chicken all fried, the potatoes mashed, and the asparagus ready to go on the table. But no Tommy. The minutes stretched into an hour. After watching the food grow cold, I called my mother in Plainfield. How do I keep things hot? Well, you put the chicken in the oven. But the mashed potatoes? Well, you'll have to mix them with cheese and make a new "dish" which you can cook in the oven in a few minutes. I did as I was told, and suffered as the chicken turned dry and hard and the potatoes made a vain attempt to absorb the cheese. It was nearly ten o'clock when Tommy and company arrived, and I was in a state of total panic. But Tommy and the two ballplayers valiantly chomped at the splintery chicken and tried to pretend they enjoyed the gross lumps of cheese embalmed in potato. I sat there listening to their dry chicken crackle and swallowed my tears. Bobby Knoop and Joe Horlen have never let me forget that "great meal."

Baseball was notorious too for the sudden breaking-up of friendships, when a close friend was traded to some far-off team and there was only a dim prospect of ever seeing him or his wife again. I wanted to settle someplace where we could stay, and where we might have friends who did *not* play baseball. So Arizona was my idea of forever. But first Tommy had to put in his stretch with the Air Reserve in California, so we found temporary quarters near George Air Force Base in Victorville, California, at Roy Rogers Apple Valley Inn. Well, I don't know how they kept the apples on the trees, the way the wind blew there—not just in occasional strong gusts from one direction or another as it did at home, but almost gale-strength, steadily, from the same quarter always. Sometimes it would seem about to lift the screen door off our apartment and carry it back to Indiana.

Not that I fretted much about that. But the wind took me unawares one day and put me into a fix that I first feared I might not escape from with my life. It was one of those foolish accidents that you tell yourself never could have or should have happened. I had started to load our luggage into the trunk of our car and became impatient with my inability to reach all the way into that deep deep trunk to gather up Tommy's golf gear—golf balls, shoes, and what-not-else—that had been tumbled in there days earlier. Finally, I decided I would have to get right inside and pick the stuff up in my fingers. So in I crawled and as I did, the wind, like a naughty kid brother, slammed the trunk lid shut and trapped me in darkness. For a few seconds I thought of stories I had heard of children smothering inside such traps as this and I shoved frantically at the lid to force it open. Of course I had not nearly strength enough. But as I struggled I did observe that there were cracks where light and, of course, fresh air could come through so my panic diminished a little. I would just shout for someone to come let me out. So I shouted. I pounded. I shouted some more. "Help! Help! Help!" I was not even sure my shouts could be heard. Certainly they brought no response. I grew tired of yelling then and decided that if I sang a song good and loud someone was sure to come close enough to find out what was afoot. For no reason I can think of, I chose "Puff, the Magic Dragon" and sang those silly lyrics over and over and over again until my voice cracked. Wasn't anyone *alive* out there? Tommy wasn't due home until four-thirty and it was now not even noon. I took a deep breath and went on in a voice that grew scratchier and scratchier: "Puff, the Magic Dragon lived by the sea! . . ." Maybe some music lover would come hurrying up to put a stop to this!

But I went on apparently unheard for about two hours

and had even begun to consider just curling up to sleep when the lid suddenly popped open and a very short man looked in at me, wide-eyed.

"For Heaven's sake, little girl!" he exclaimed. "Don't you know better? . . ." Then he stopped and gaped when he saw that I was not a little girl at all, but a grown lady who certainly *should* have known better. We were both able to laugh a little when I told him what had happened and we decided that there should be inside latches on all car trunks, so children would not be caught inside, nor kidnap victims too easily imprisoned, and to keep demons for neatness from falling victim to their own frenzy.

I think that Tommy and I enjoyed living over again all petty "tragedies" of this sort, and even some real tragedies, because we could afford to smile at them now when we realized at last how trifling they were in comparison to the deep and shattering tragedies we saw all around us here in the Intensive Care Unit.

I did, however, before I had been married too long, skirt the edges of a very real tragedy, one that scared us both, kept us scared for a long time and that only now we were able to talk about quite calmly. This misadventure befell me at the birth of our second child, Tommy John III, and of course a long time after Tommy had recovered from his own most serious accident. When it happened, I felt sure I was looking death in the face and believe me I faced the possibility of my own death far more calmly than I had been facing the possibility that Travis might die.

But I was scared! Scared probably as much of being paralyzed as I was of dying. The last words I recall hearing before things began to get dark that afternoon were the doctor's order to the nurse: "Prepare her for the epidural." That was the spinal injection that would numb my lower body sufficiently so I could, along with Tommy, watch our second baby arrive. But this time I felt a searing pain—like a hot iron (or a giant icicle!) searing my spine from my hips to my neck.

I could see the room about me. I watched my arms and legs fall free, as if they did not belong to me. But I could not speak. I could not even breathe! It was like a nightmare, when you will your muscles to move and they will not. I tried to gasp in air and nothing came. I heard the doctor cry out for "Oxygen! Stat!" And I felt sure I was dying. Life seemed to be slipping from me, gently as a garment falling off my shoulders. Oh God, I thought, let them save my baby! Then the whole floor beneath turned so dark and deep that I sank into it, down and down, almost gratefully.

I returned, with no consciousness of time passing, to a world full of golden light, light that shone directly down into my eyes. Then I opened my eyes to the face of the anesthesiologist, so close to my own I could count every whisker in his beard.

"You're going to be all right, Sally," he told me. "You're going to be all right." For a moment I was almost angry at having been dragged back from those blissful depths. But then panic began to grow as I realized I could not move. I could not breathe either! There was a respirator enclosing my chest. Nurses were moving my head and I felt no more sensation than if they had been taking off my hat. What *is* this? Am I to be paralyzed for life!? What about my baby!? But I had no chance to form that question when the doctor, still leaning close, told me:

"You've had a beautiful boy, Sally! Healthy as can be!"

Then in a moment Tommy's dear face replaced the doctor's. I wanted to reach up and touch it but I could not. I could only blink.

"Don't worry, sweetheart," he was saying. "You're going to be okay. It'll take a little while for the anesthetic to wear off, then you'll be okay. The baby's beautiful! Perfect!"

I managed to make some sort of noise in my throat. Tears flooded my eyes so I could barely make out Tommy's face. I wanted to see my baby! Tommy bent close and touched my cheek.

"Don't try to talk," he whispered. "Just rest."

But I really could not rest. Gradually movement came back to my arms and fingers. After a time I could talk, or could try to talk. I sounded like a drunk and Tommy poked fun at me, all the while stroking me and telling me how beautiful our little son was. They moved me into the recovery room and brought me the baby to admire. I smiled at that tiny red face, all squished up like a little boxing glove, and I cried too, when I saw how lovely he was. And then the headache began. Lord have mercy! I had never known anything like this. It was as if there were an iron ball of pain trying to force its way out through my skull. The doctor ordered sedation and warned me that I would have some difficult hours ahead. I would have to remain flat on my back all night. Have you ever tried, when wide awake, to lie flat on your back all night? It is as close to torture as I ever hope to experience. But I lay there, more than half-awake, not just all night but all the next day.

Happily, I had a roommate who could not sleep either and we managed to distract each other with conversation until, together, we watched the sun come up. But then my right arm and shoulder began to hurt as if someone were attempting an amputation without anesthetic. Doctors hesitated to give me strong pain relievers for fear of what it might do to my little nursing baby. But heat packs and massage gave no relief. It was impossible for me to lift my arm or even to hold my little one. These pains were worse than the pains of childbirth and they were unremitting. By the third day, Saturday, the pain began to ease, although I was still unable to use my arm properly. Now I wanted to go home and I let everyone know it. The doctors said nothing doing and so I was still in the hospital that Sunday, watching the TV broadcast of the Dodger game, which Tommy pitched and won. It was his seventeenth win of the season and in the postgame interview I heard him dedicate the win to our new little boy, Thomas Edward John, III. After that, they let me go home, still with a tremendous headache and a very sore and weak right arm.

The aftermath of this was unpleasant, dragged-out, and frustrating. I think it began after we received the hospital bill and observed that we had been charged for oxygen and emergency procedures that the doctors denied they had performed. And for a *three-hour* operation that should have been complete in an hour at most.

I immediately visited the Scripps Institute in La Jolla for an evaluation and learned that I had actually suffered a whiplash when I was being hurriedly moved into position to have the oxygen tube placed in my throat. And the paralysis had been caused when the needle for injection of the anesthesia penetrated just a breath too far into the spinal column sending the anesthesia coursing upward to my head instead of downward to my hips. I did recall now that the anesthesiologist had apologized to me soon after I had been brought into the recovery room. "This never happened to me before!" he told me. But I was not sure then exactly what *had* happened. At the Scripps Institute I found out. I also received there from Dr. Otis, their kind and thoughtful neurologist, a therapy regimen to help restore the function to my right arm, for the nerve that fed the muscle supporting my right shoulder blade had been destroyed. (By some strange stroke of fate this nerve was the counterpart of the very one that had been damaged in Tommy's accident to his left arm.) Medication and therapy helped put my arm—not back to normal, for it never will be normal—but back into working order. My right shoulder blade, however, will always stick out like a partly folded wing. And we did, after considerable unpleasantness, receive a settlement from the hospital that assuaged but will never eradicate my hurt.

Tommy:

I know it is a strange thing to say, and even strange to recall now, but once Travis started to improve I actually used to look forward to my return to the hospital. Every time I came back—to the place that seemed like home now, for my family and friends were there—Travis seemed to have made another leap forward toward complete recovery. For instance, there was his progress in throwing. I left one day to go take my turn pitching and before I left I gave Travis a collection of little balls made of sponge rubber. He had played with the bright green-yellow PGA golf balls and had taken hold of some yellow tennis balls that Wilson Sporting Goods had sent him. But with the little "nerf" balls I gave him he and I were *almost* able to play catch. That is, he was able to take a full grip on the ball, lift his arm and feebly propel the ball three or four inches in my direction.

I was gone, I think, three days altogether. I used to go out the day before my turn on the mound and come back the morning after. It was the third day that I came in and invited Travis to play catch with me again. I stood right close to him, ready to seize the ball as it trickled from his hand. But Travis, after lifting his arm in proper fashion, actually fogged the thing at me. A good thing it was soft. I was so delighted, I know I yelled out loud.

It was the same way with his walking. Sally and Carol at the start had been satisfied just to hold him in a standing position on the bed. Then they began to "walk" him along the floor, holding him between them with his feet solidly on the floor and then moving him forward so that his feet kind of flop-flopped involuntarily along. Dr. Zimmerman, watching this effort one day, warned Sally that it might be four or five months before Travis could really walk, because his system had progressed to only about the crawling stage. It was less than a week later, I think, when, as they put Travis through this exercise, his feet seemed to find themselves and he took three deliberate steps. Sally and Carol could just about contain themselves. And next time they tried, Travis took *five* steps, obviously moving his feet on his own. This time Sally could not hold in her happiness.

"Sol!" she cried. And Dr. Zimmerman hustled in, probably expecting to discover some new emergency. "Watch this!" said Sally, as she held Travis erect. Dr. Zimmerman crouched down and held his hands out a few inches in front of Travis, and slowly pulled them back as Travis lurched forward. One. Two. Three. Four. *Five* full steps. Then Travis toppled into Dr. Zimmerman's arms and clutched him about the neck. Dr. Zimmerman was about as cool and unemotional a customer as I had ever dealt with. Otherwise I doubt if he could have gotten through a day in that unit without an emotional crack-up. But this time, as Travis held him tightly by the neck, Sally swears she saw tears fill his eyes. I know they filled mine. But nobody ever said I was unemotional.

When Dr. Epstein saw the performance he said simply: "I don't believe it! I really don't believe it."

Not long after that, Travis provided another unbelievable experience to Fred Epstein. The good doctor was strolling past Travis's bed and observed that Travis was toying with a bright-colored golf ball. He nodded to Travis and kept on going. Whereupon Travis fired the golf ball in an overhand motion and caught the good doctor right about in the kidney. Fred jumped. Then he laughed.

"Never had a wallop in the back that felt better than that one!" he declared.

To avoid a more serious incident, we then built a baseball for Travis out of crumpled newspaper wrapped with tape and provided a bat for him in the form of a tightly rolled newspaper. After that it was baseball every day in the pediatric unit, with Travis at bat and usually one of the guards at the bedroom door as pitcher. I know that Travis knocked the first pitch right back into the guard's face. The nurses who passed through the unit after that used to stay on the alert for a flying ball and would laugh when they had to dodge one.

Come to think of it the whole recovery process had an unbelievable quality. And its effect on the rest of us was slightly incredible, too. For instance, it gave me a whole new slant on baseball training methods. I had always had many of my own private ways of getting myself ready to pitch and keeping myself in shape. But I was still subject, through most of my career, to the standard regimen both in spring training and in work-outs during the season. But when I was committed to staying close by Travis's side, I would be with the club only on the days I was scheduled to pitch, and I skipped a good deal of the routine—the pepper games, the shagging of flies, the fielding practice and all the "limbering up" stuff that was supposed to keep you fit to play baseball everyday. Instead, I got far away from baseball three and four days at a time. And when Travis began to get better, these off days were happy ones, as well as distracting in the sense that they filled my mind with matters that had nothing to do with getting batters out but instead were concerned with cheering up youngsters, rejoicing in the improvement Travis was showing, and lending a hand wherever I could to the other parents whose kids were being treated there. In that way, I truly think these off days made me into a better person, showed me how God sometimes uses suffering to broaden you, to enlarge your understanding, and to help you see the true meaning of loving thy neighbor as thyself. For there in the Intensive Care Unit we were all neighbors in the very best sense. And the experience actually made me a better baseball player by teaching me that it was good to get my mind off baseball at times, to rest myself mentally as well as physically. And I do believe that this method of frequent breaks from the routine of the game might help batters and fielders as well as pitchers.

The standard routines for spring training have been in place since before you and I were born. In the very beginning of the leagues, I suppose, the trips to Hot Springs and similar spas were sometimes useful in boiling the winter fat out of the systems of some of those old ballplayers who helped give professional baseball a bad name. A great deal of the training regimen is just superstition—employed because "we always did it that way." Of course ballplayers, like all athletes, have to work out to keep the muscles toned, the weight under control, and the mind alert. But, to do that, do they have to spend hours "shagging" in the hot sun, when part of the time is spent just goofing off? Or learning over and over again moves and methods that have become second nature? I'm a great believer in good practice—good concentrated practice. But I think this business of going through the motions just to be true to John McGraw's traditions can breed mental fatigue that is fatal to the kind of intensity you need to play ball on a professional level.

I know that when I got back to the ball club after my days at the hospital, I was refreshed, eager for action, and mentally prepared for that cat-and-mouse game to begin. And I am sure that other ballplayers would feel the same way. Pitchers certainly would, for most of them, like me, have their own methods for staying in shape and don't need to spend a half-hour or more loping around the outfield after fungoes. (Fungoes. That's a word heard nowhere but in baseball circles and I don't think one ballplayer or sports writer in a hundred can tell you what the word means or where it originated, or if they do tell you, can tell you correctly. Let me take time out to tell about it here, because I made a point of asking someone who knew. Fungo, or fung-o, was a game played by kids in Scotland centuries ago. "Fung" was a dialect word meaning to snap or toss into the air. And fung-o was just tossing a ball into the air and hitting it for someone to retrieve. And that's just what it is today.)

Should I ever have the running of a baseball club, and I often look forward to the day when I can do just that, my training regimen will have very little flavor of John McGraw or even Connie Mack. Instead, it will be based on the theory that a certain amount of healthy relaxation is as valuable as hours of hard work with bat, ball, and glove.

My system would be a set number of hours each day of warm-up, mostly running, for pitchers anyway need strong legs. Shagging flies would be for outfielders. There would be batting practice, of course, for no one gets enough hitting just playing in games. But I would want the fundamentals—hitting the cut-off man, backing up bases, fielding bunts, holding runners on base, double plays—all practiced under game conditions as far as possible. And I would give the players a day off every week to do just as they pleased whether it was playing golf or taking the kids to the movies—just a chance to get the mind off baseball long enough for it to refresh itself. I have known some coaches who think that if players gripe at the tedium of practice and groan at endless repetition, then the practice is doing them good. I don't feel that way at all. I would like my players to come to the park every Monday morning eager to play ball again, not wishing the whole business was over.

Paul Brown, one of the greatest football coaches who ever lived, used to speak unfavorably of coaches who would, as he called it, "slaughterize" their players on the theory that they were thus toughening them for the conflict. And there are, as far as I know, still football coaches who believe that a lot of contact work during the week makes the player more "physical" (that is, violent) on game day. But I think there are more and more coaches who have discovered that, once the squad is in peak condition, contact should be as light as possible—not just to avoid injury but to help sustain in the players an appetite for the game. And, while baseball players don't go in much for physical contact, I know that in my case at least, a short stretch of R and R brings me back to the ball field with a strong appetite for competition. Pitchers, of course, work as hard as anyone else on the team, except catchers, and so can no doubt profit more from off days. But in spring training, certainly even outfielders need occasional days when they can recover their zest for plucking fly balls off the fences and hitting a thrown baseball.

There was, as a matter of fact, one baseball manager who handled his squad pretty nearly as I would handle my own.

That was Al Lopez, who, as I may have said, was one of the best managers I have known. Al would never keep his charges moping about the ball park just to satisfy some puritanical notion that it was wrong to stop work while there was still light enough to work in. If you completed your running, throwing, batting, stretching, bending, fielding and play-studying at noon, then you could shower and take off. But Al did have one rule that he insisted on. No one was to go to the golf course before three o'clock. I think this was Al's one concession to the Calvinists in the game who thought it was sinful for hired hands to have whole afternoons off when they were being paid for a full day's work.

Al was extremely considerate of pitchers. No pitcher could throw for more than five minutes when he first came to spring training unless he had been playing winter ball—all the others, veterans and newcomers, were limited to five minutes throwing. And *no* throwing in the outfield. An outfield throw is not a pitch but an overhand heave and Al was convinced that the difference in mechanics between the two throws would get your pitching mechanics out of whack. Al would gradually increase the throwing time for his pitchers until finally they were all ready to pitch in an exhibition game. No sore arms in Al's camp. But a lot of time to yourself once you completed your workout. Although Walter Alston ran a pretty laid-back camp, with few rigid rules and lots of relaxing time, I never knew anyone who ran as comfortable a camp as Al did.

By contrast, the camp the Cleveland Indians ran in 1962 was like a jail sentence, or a stretch in a reform school. You *ran* everywhere. Have to go to the men's room? Then run. Time for batting practice? *Run* to the cage! Time to shag flies? *Run* to the outfield! In the Cleveland camp not a single walking step was permitted on the practice field.

Al did go deeply into pitching fundamentals. He would never allow you to throw more than two bad pitches in a row. You could get by with one bad pitch. But if you threw another you would hear a piercing whistle from either Lopez or Ray Berres, the pitching coach, and they would be right on you to warn you—you were dropping your elbow; you were not staying back long enough; and you were rushing your motion. Lopez would spend a lot of time too on regular baseball fundamentals—hitting behind the runner, bunting, leading off first. In those days, pitchers were hitters too and Al just believed that, inasmuch as you were likely to come to bat in a game when one of those maneuvers was called for, there was no reason why you should not learn how it was done.

When Ed Stanky took over, the atmosphere changed. As loose a ship as Al ran, Eddie ran a tight one. He was a bug on physical condition. He had brought in a physical education instructor from West Point and that guy put us through drills that would sweat a soldier—stretching, bending, straddle-hopping, running in place. There was none of the Mickey Mouse stuff we suffered from in Cleveland. But there was plenty of hard conditioning. No doubt it did me good, although I don't believe I became a better pitcher because of it.

Still, I liked Eddie and rate him as one of the best men I ever worked for. He was as tough as everybody said he was. But he was fair, never played favorites, and was, I think, especially good at evaluating ballplayers. He had one rule that I enjoyed. If a pitcher, under Eddie's regime, made the enemy hit more than twenty ground balls while he was pitching nine full innings to victory, Eddie would buy the man a suit of clothes—a real fine suit too, of Park Avenue quality. I won two of those. The one I was proudest to own was the one I earned in Fenway Park, where they are supposed to have the heads of left-handed pitchers impaled on pikes to mark Red Sox victories. It was 1967, the year the Red Sox won the pennant, and I beat them 5 to 0 and collected about twenty-four ground balls. It didn't matter to Eddie if they were hits, outs, or errors. He wanted his pitchers to force ground balls. My "Red Sox" suit is one I will always remember, for it was a golden brown color, like an autumn leaf, and may have been the best fitting one I ever owned. It was made by Petrocelli, or some other Italian genius, and it cost $225.00—about three times what I was used to paying for suits in that day.

That year, incidentally, was the year Carl Yastrzemski was the toughest out in the league, for me at least, and for most other pitchers as well. He hit 44 home runs that year and drove in over 120 runs. He probably won't attain those numbers again but fifteen seasons later he is still a tough out.

That was also the last good year the White Sox were going to see for a long spell. And by the time three seasons had passed, my pitching seemed to go completely to pot. I could have blamed Johnny Sain, the pitching coach, for my troubles or Chuck Tanner, the manager. But actually I have to blame myself because I can look back now and realize that I probably learned more from Johnny Sain than from any coach I ever had, at least as far as pitching philosophy is concerned, for I use much of Johnny's philosophy today.

At that time, however, it seemed to me he was trying to persuade me to throw pitches I just could not throw—and indeed he was. But the real lesson he was trying to impart, and the lesson I was not experienced enough to absorb, was that there are always more ways than one to get a batter out—that a pitcher should not fret too much about mechanics but should just throw the pitch—whatever pitch happens to work best, whether it be a blooper pitch, a slider, a slow curve—because the sole aim is to get the batter out and sometimes the job is easier than it seems. But what he tried first with me was to get me to throw the slider—the "short curve" he called it—the pitch that Early Wynn had tried to teach me in Cleveland and that Johnny Lipon in Seattle had promptly talked me out of. I tried that slider, at Johnny Sain's urging, for twelve dismal weeks and saw myself deteriorate so fast, as a pitcher, that I really could not pitch five decent innings. As a matter of fact, had you seen me on the mound in the first part of that season, 1971, you would have walked away thinking you had seen some high school prospect who was never going to pitch big-league ball, or had seen some tired old has-been trying to make himself believe he could still get batters out. I could not throw two pitches in a row over the plate. Thank God I had married Sally Simmons the year before, because Sally's commonsense advice really saved my pitching career.

All she did was suggest I call Ray Berres, my old pitching coach, and ask him if he would watch me and see what I was doing wrong. Ray, in retirement in Wisconsin, was not at all surprised to hear from me. "I was wondering when you would call," he told me. He had, he revealed, been watching me on TV right along and had some ideas of what might be done. I told him what I was *trying* to do—throw sliders. Ray Berres was not exactly a man of few words. But he still made all his words count.

"Why don't you just take that slider and stick it?" he suggested. "Go back to fast ball and curve. It's obvious that damn slider has ruined your other pitches. You're down on the side now, throwing low three-quarters instead of a high three-quarter delivery." Ray gave me some exercises and some mechanics to work on and I worked. But nothing seemed to happen. Johnny Sain was sympathetic but he had never been what would be called in this age a great communicator.

"Don't you know how to throw your sinker?" he asked me. Well, yes, I did. But it was not a matter of mechanics with me, as a curve ball is. That is, it was not turning your hand over, pulling down hard to put spin on the ball. It was a natural pitch. I just flipped my hand right through the ball, without an extra thought.

Now I was giving it thought. That is, I was trying to get away from that "low three-quarters" motion and get back on top. But I still wasn't doing it. I just had no idea where the ball was going. My teammate, Joe Horlen, was amazed at my inability to get balls over the plate. I had always had excellent control before. Now I was wilder than I had ever been in class

D. But just as I hit my lowest point, an ex-teammate came to my rescue. I was strictly a bullpen pitcher at that time and I had had very little work because so far there had not been many games in which we were so far behind that the club could afford to put me in to start flinging baseballs around like popcorn.

We were in Kansas City and I was working out on the side before the game, while the Kansas City club took early batting practice. Gail Hopkins, who had been a first baseman and catcher on our club for the three previous seasons, came over to watch me work. I tried four or five pitches and Gail shook his head.

"Gosh," he said, "that ball has a funny spin on it. It doesn't spin like a sinker at all. What's wrong?"

"You tell me, Hoppy," I said. "I'm trying."

Hoppy watched for another minute or two until it was his turn to bat.

"Hold it," he told me. "I'll be right back."

He came back and stood on the side another few minutes and then punched his fist at the air.

"I've found it!" he exclaimed. "I saw it! You know when you throw you look like you're trying to cut your fast ball, to make it sail."

"Well, I've been practicing this slider for a long time and now I'm trying to get my fast ball back."

"Let me show you. Look. Your hand is on the *side* of the ball when it should be behind it. Then, as you throw it, you're cutting over the ball and down and putting kind of a football spiral on it." (A screwball incidentally is sometimes called a reverse curve because you do put reverse spin on it by turning the hand in the opposite direction from the motion you use to put spin on a curve.)

"Okay," I said. "Watch this." I gripped the ball tight and tried to throw a screwball.

"That wasn't bad spin," Gail said. "Keep that up."

For the next three days then, every time I threw a ball I

would try to throw a screwball, getting my hand back of the ball and deliberately trying to get that reverse spin. Then I had a short layoff while Sally and I went down to Phoenix to look for a house. We found what we wanted in Scottsdale, and we put a down payment on it. Then I took off for Anaheim and caught up with the club there. I hadn't touched a baseball for two days now. When I reached the ball park, batting practice had started, so I put on my uniform and hiked out to the bullpen to throw. I started at once to use that screwball motion and suddenly the ball began to show some good down action, the way it had when I was going strong. Johnny Sain was watching me closely. His face brightened.

"Hey! Your ball is really starting to move good! Now let me see you throw that same kind of ball, only with that little control curve, that slider."

Oh no, I said to myself. Not again. No more sliders. What I did throw was a regular curve ball, just throwing it down on the side a little harder, to shorten the break.

"That's it!" John cried. "That's that little slider."

I said nothing. It was not my nature to buck the system but I couldn't try sliders again. All I wanted to do was to get my pitching back up to par. But I followed Ray Berres's advice, though not literally of course. I just put the slider out of my life forever.

As it turned out, I got a chance to pitch a couple of innings almost right away, in Anaheim, and I was pleased with myself. I gave up a couple of runs but I pitched better than I had in a month. At least I was getting my pitches low and the ball was moving better. They used me once more in relief and then they started me, against Baltimore, on a Sunday afternoon. The first batter up was Paul Blair. He drilled a pitch inside third base, a good clean single. But Paul wanted to make it into a double. Rick Reichardt, the left fielder, picked the ball up swiftly, however, and made a really startling throw to second—hard, straight, precisely on target—so that the ball was waiting there in Mike Andrews's glove for Paul to slide into. That was a hit. But it was also out number one. I had really made a bad pitch and had been rescued by Rick Reichardt's throw. I think for the rest of the game I gave out but two hits—and no runs at all—in nine innings.

For the rest of that year I felt like my old—or my previous—self again. What I enjoyed most about that year, I think, was Johnny Sain's decision to pitch me every third day. That was in accord with Johnny's philosophy, which was "Go with the hot pitcher." On the basis of my nine-inning shutout in Baltimore and a couple of other good outings, I was hot, and he asked me if I thought I could go with only two days' rest. Sure, said I, who probably at that point would have agreed to a half-hour's rest and pitched a doubleheader. I really felt strong, confident, hungry for competition. With Johnny's encouragement, I think I pitched five straight times with two-day intervals and won three games—and this with a club that wound up twenty-two games out of first place. Johnny was as pleased as I was to see his theory verified. People just get in the habit of hearing that a pitcher has to rest three or four days and they believe it, he explained. It's ingrained in kids so when they get up here they are mentally unable to go without that rest. But unless you're one of those guys like Koufax or Nolan Ryan or Tom Seaver, who just air out every pitch, you really don't need it.

Well, at least at that stage of my career I didn't need it. All I needed was advance notice to get myself mentally prepared.

But the White Sox that year, 1971, were not destined for any glory greater than a rather loose grip on third place in the Western Division. The team that Eddie Stanky had, without any hitting, kept in first place until almost the final series in 1967 had been nibbled to pieces by inept trades; the "pitcher's ball park" had been landscaped into a pitcher's nightmare with the implanting of Astroturf in the infield. What we had at Comiskey Park in 1971 was an infield through which grounders would scoot like balls on a billiard table, while fielders attuned to a standard "turtle" infield could not do much more than goggle at them in disbelief. And those supposedly mighty hitters for whose contracts we had traded off all our speed and high spirits would have needed siege guns to reach those far-off fences with any consistency. So I can't pretend I was thoroughly happy with the White Sox that season. It would be a long time before the Sox were back on top. And I began to get strong indications that they were a bit less than happy with me. Not that there were any hard words or hard feelings or even complaints—just an almost imperceptible change in attitudes.

And finally there came a very strong sign that Tommy John as a *persona* was not quite so *grata* as he had been in 1970. In 1970, when it came time for me to take off for California to pay my annual homage to the Air Reserve at George AFB, the club not only underwrote my air fare both ways but made me an allowance for my housing and a per diem grant for my keep—a total of about $1500, a rather plump pocketful in that preinflation era. In 1971, they gave me my air fare. Nothing else. When I asked if they intended to give me the same as last year, they answered that they lost too much money. Not that I asked for more or even felt entitled to more. Still, it was a signal that I found easy to interpret. So when I had cleaned out my locker, I took pains to say formal good-byes to everyone, to all my teammates, to Chuck Tanner, the manager, to Johnny Sain and all the coaches. And after I shook hands with the general manager, Roland Hemond, I took a ten-cent piece out of my pocket and set it carefully on his desk.

"What's that supposed to be for?" he asked me.

"Well," I said, as airily as I could manage, "I'm living in Scottsdale, same town now where the winter meetings will be held, so it will be just a local call. When you trade me you can just drop the dime to let me know where to report."

Roland laughed.

"Oh, no! No!" he protested. "You're definitely part of our

plans for next season. We're not going to trade *you*! Don't even think about such a thing!"

And just to show you how dangerous it is to wager much more than half a day's wages on the assurances you may receive from some baseball executives, Roland Hemond did drop a dime that December to express his sorrow at having had to trade me. For whom? Why, for Richie Allen of the Dodgers. The Dodgers! That was a dream come true. I had had myself convinced it was going to be Pittsburgh or Atlanta. The Dodgers! A contending team! A first-class operation! And just a few short jumps from home. I found myself assuring Roland that he had made a great trade. Richie Allen was just the hitter the club needed! (It needed a lot more, but I was not on the verge of saying so.)

It was with the Dodgers of course that I ran into what I, at that time, imagined was the greatest tragedy that could befall a pitcher. But it was with the Dodgers that I became a full-fledged pitcher again, and I thank coach Dwight "Red" Adams for that. When I joined the club, I was still convinced that I had only a mediocre fast ball and that I was going to have to depend chiefly on my breaking pitches to win ball games. But Red disagreed with me, emphatically.

"You've got a good fast ball," Red told me. "Not overpowering but a good one, with a lot of movement. You'll get plenty of batters out with that."

When I refused to be convinced, he and Chris Cannizzaro, the veteran catcher (Chris is just five years older than I am) set out to prove it to me when we played an exhibition game against the Chicago Cubs in Albuquerque. The game was played on a chilly, windy day—a bad day for curve balls anyway—and the altitude of Albuquerque made it difficult to get a proper break on a curve, which depends on air resistance to move it sharply down and away. I threw exactly three curve balls that day, against a club that was notorious for breaking the hearts of fast-ball pitchers, with men like Billy Williams, Jim Hickman, and Ron Santo all lying in wait. And I beat them by throwing all fast balls. From that day to this I have never lost faith in my fast ball. It does not have Goose Gossage's smoke. But it has *something*.

I had my differences with the Dodgers ultimately. But I never lost my respect for the club. In every way they are big league—big league in their spring training site, in their personnel, in the manner in which they publicize and sell the game of baseball. And big league certainly in their concern for their ballplayers and the families of the players. I had never known a training camp since the days of Al Lopez that had a more grown-up atmosphere, where the players were left to decide for themselves what sort of work they needed most and how much they needed. And where there was no sense of "teacher" checking to make sure you were on time and did not duck out too early. If you finished your work at half past twelve, you went home. If you wanted to put in extra throwing, you did so. And if you were going to be late for practice, you had only to telephone and say why. The Dodgers, too, remember, had, until recently, a private jet for their players and their wives, the only one in the leagues.

The contrast between Chicago and Los Angeles lay in more things than weather. To me, the greatest satisfaction came from playing before enough fans to make you feel as if you were earning your keep. A small crowd in Los Angeles would be 30,000. (A bad year in attendance would be anything less than two and a half million.) Yet I can recall a day in Chicago when Tony Cuccinello, our third-base coach, counted the house while he stood on the field and came within twenty-five of getting the correct total. "I'd have got those," he said, "but they were probably down in the rest rooms."

My real trouble with the Dodgers began, I think, when I accepted the first terms they offered, which were exactly the same as I was getting at Chicago. I thought I might have been offered a few thousand extra to make me feel welcome, or to indicate their pleasure at having me on board. But I wanted to keep the atmosphere friendly and not be classified as an ungrateful player, so I took what Al Campanis suggested. Ballplayers, especially young ballplayers, are at a real disadvantage in dealing directly with management. There should be an agent or a lawyer to stand in the middle and be the one for management to get mad at, and to address hard words to. A few of my exchanges with the Dodger brass led to words and attitudes that were hard to forgive. But as the saying goes—"time heals all wounds"—and I think the Dodgers and Tommy John are complete friends now.

Those negotiations, however, were boy-scout stuff compared to what I got into when I signed with the Yankees. Fortunately, in those dealings I had a lawyer to absorb much of the punishment—and besides, the deal was good enough to persuade us to shrug off some of George Steinbrenner's eccentricities. But it was hard to get used to the idea that a promise from George was often just a trial balloon and a signed agreement was merely a rough draft. Altogether we had three agreements put into "final" form and actually signed by George before we concocted one that stood.

In reading baseball history, I once came across a remark by Charles Comiskey, founder of the Chicago White Sox and a former first baseman, to the effect that he would always trust a ballplayer before he would trust a banker. Fortunately, in most of our first face-to-face negotiations with the Yankee organization we dealt with a ballplayer—Al Rosen, formerly a great third baseman and a good low-ball hitter, and always a gracious and honorable businessman. Usually, we would arrive at a satisfactory deal with Al, George would approve and sign it, and we would all go home happy. Then there would be a call from George—perhaps to my attorney Bob Cohen. This would have to be changed, George would say. This clause or that clause has got to come out. It made no difference that it had been signed. George's favorite ploy was to say: "That's not the way I understood it when we talked about it. I remember it *this* way." "This way" was usually some phrasing that had never even entered the conversation. But it was always take it or leave it, as far as George was concerned.

Our major hangup was a clause covering payment during a strike. George wanted the agreement to say that I would not be paid in the event of a strike. My attorney said that would be fine if we could have a balancing clause to the effect that I *would* be paid during an owner's lockout. Everybody agreed that was fair. The agreement went to George for signature. The signed document was instantly duplicated and copies simultaneously transmitted to all parties. Then Al Rosen called. The lockout clause had to be removed! Al said George was foaming at the mouth over that clause, complaining that I would have the only contract in baseball with such language in it. "All right," said Bob, "and we'll also remove the strike clause." After four or five days of negotiating, Bob and Al agreed on new language. The document was rephrased, signed, duplicated and "Quipped" to all parties.

Then George was back on the telephone. The agreement was off! Signature or no signature, it was not the way he remembered. I suppose I might have balked at this point and looked for a deal with Kansas City or one of the other clubs that had drawn me in the free-agent draft. But for many reasons, I really liked New York. And Sally liked New York. I was in favor of trying to reason with George. There were five of us in on a conference call—Al Rosen, George, Bob Cohen, one of the Yankee attorneys named Peter Alkalay, and me. Rosen had been roused from a vacation in the Virgin Islands. George, long after signing the contract, had looked it over once more, noticed there was no mention of my not being paid during a strike and, according to observers, grew "livid with rage." Rosen was tucked away on an island that had only one telephone. George found out the number—only George and his evil spirit know how—and called Al back to the fray. I had suggested to Bob Cohen that there was one area we might give a little on—the matter of the paid-up life insurance policy that was to be mine on signing—so Bob was ready to negotiate on that. But first he simply countered George with the perfectly reasonable argument that if we gave up the lockout clause, then he should be prepared to give up the "no pay during strike" clause.

"Goddammit," George cried. "That's not the way I remember our conversation! I remember we agreed to drop the lockout clause and to make the insurance policy paid up in ten years."

None of us could remember talking about the insurance policy with George at all. But I was ready to compromise. All right, Bob said. But you have to drop the strike clause.

Nothing doing! Every player on the roster had that clause and he'd be damned if I was going to be any different! If I wouldn't agree to that, then the deal was off! Definitely!

"Okay," said Bob. "If the deal is off, I suggest you call a press conference and announce you have backed out of the contract and that Tommy will negotiate with other clubs."

There was silence supreme. Then George snapped: "All right! You win! Put it on paper and I'll sign it! No lockout clause, no strike clause."

The conference ended. Al Rosen and the attorney hung up. But George had one more thing to say:

"Listen, Cohen! You should be working for me! You're a goddam sight better than any of the bunch I've got now!"

Bob just laughed. But I think I could read his thoughts: *I wouldn't put up with that guff for a half-million dollars a year!*

SIX

Sally:

The hospital cafeteria was our haven. It was by no means a cozy, comfortable place. It was as sterile as the hospital itself—all stainless steel and white enamel, clean, clattery, brightly lighted, full of busy people. But it was a friendly, almost a family place to us, because we knew all the faces there, were always made welcome by the people behind the counter, and felt as much at home as if it were our private club. Carol and I would come in there sometimes when we were almost too tired to eat and just go through the motions of picking our food, then would slump into those straight-backed chairs, lean wearily on the table edge, and nod in exhaustion, grateful for this respite from the blip-blipping of the monitors and the ominous coma noises that had borne in upon us for seemingly endless hours. I recall one time when we came to the cafeteria both so utterly deflated that we had barely the strength needed to lift a tray. I never came there out of hunger, but just to find the nourishment I knew I owed to the baby I was carrying. I made my choices, not by what tempted me, but simply on the basis of whether or not they might make me throw up. Salads, Cokes, crackers—whatever was light and inoffensive. This time I took Jell-O and chocolate milk. Carol chose broccoli and iced tea. In a weary procession of two, we plodded to a vacant table, set our trays down, stared at each other, and sighed. It was a full minute before we could make an effort to eat. Then Carol looked about her tray for utensils, saw none, and almost absently picked a broccoli stalk up in her fingers and fed it into her mouth. Thus prompted, I stared down at my little cubes of Jell-O. I looked for a spoon, saw that I had forgotten to bring any, and I too used my fingers to corral a blob of Jell-O, found that it held together and poked it into my mouth. We sat there, too fagged to talk, and fumbled at our food until suddenly we looked at each other and realized what a spectacle we made—grown-up women messing about in our plates like two-year-olds. Instantly we both began to laugh—to laugh and laugh and laugh, until cashier, counterladies, busboys, all stared at us and started to snicker too. There was nothing in our lives to laugh at then, and so we laughed at nothing, and kept laughing until the tears ran down. And our friends all around us laughed to see us laughing. I am sure it did us good.

There came a day finally when I did have good cause to smile. On August 31, Travis was moved out of the Intensive Care Unit and given his own little room on the pediatric floor, where he was able to walk about, to play with toys, even to sit on the floor with hundreds of letters around him, opening envelope after envelope, to find sometimes not just notes of cheer but lollipops, even dollar bills. (Dr. Irving Fish, the neurologist on Travis's case, would stop at Travis's door almost everyday and sneak him a candy bar.) So I was able to walk into the cafeteria with a smile on my face and at least remember to pick up spoons and forks when I picked up my tray.

There was a sweet black lady behind the steam tables there who saw me smiling and laughed out loud.

"Well," she said, "I certainly can tell that that little Travis is getting *better* 'cause you got a *smile* on your *face*! Been a long time since I seen you smile!"

It was that way all over the hospital, with doormen, security officers, police, cleaners, attendants as well as nurses and doctors, all keeping up to date on Travis's condition, as if he were their own little nephew. And that was one reason why, as Travis came closer and closer to the time when he would be discharged, I grew more and more uneasy. What would I do without all this family of helpful and competent and knowledgeable people to turn to if there was an emergency? Would I be able to get him back here soon enough if he had a seizure, for instance? The very thought of seizures filled me with dread. I had been reading, for weeks now, everything I could find printed about brain damage, spinal injuries, falls, etc., in the medical journals I could find and in the newsweeklies that carried a "Medicine" department. And naturally I had a whole calendar of symptoms that I felt I must be on the watch for. But what if the seizure came at night, when Tommy and I were sleeping? Where could I turn? Where was there even a doctor I could trust who lived near enough to come in an emergency?

These fears, which had been long in the back of my mind, now seemed to afflict most of my waking hours, so that, as Travis progressed, I seemed to grow worse. I bedeviled the doctors everyday with questions now, as I tried to fortify myself with information on every conceivable condition. What if he bumped into the corner of a table and bruised his head? What about those burr-holes in his skull, where the bone had not grown together? What if he should trip and fall? What if he should swallow his tongue in a seizure and there was no nurse there to save him?

On August 30, Dr. Zimmerman came to give Travis a final blood test and it very nearly finished me. Those little veins were so shrunken that they actually had to dig to find one. Dr. Zimmerman had taken him into a separate room and I could hear the doctor soothing him and making him ready for the pain which, he assured Travis, would be over in a second. Then Travis screamed, and I very nearly perished. I could feel that scream searing every blood vessel in my body. I had dedicated myself to keeping him from all pain forever! And now . . . But Travis came back in the room in a moment. The tears had dried on his face and he was smiling. "I was a *good* boy, Mommy!" he told me proudly. And I held him tight and assured him that he was.

But I was not going to take him out of the hospital, I vowed, until Dr. Epstein, who was my stay and my comfort, had checked him over and had answered my questions. Fred Epstein had been away for three days but he was due back that evening to check his patients. It would be late, however, so we would not be taking Travis home until the following day. When Dr. Epstein came in, he looked ghastly—as if he had just seen a friend fall down an elevator shaft.

"What on earth is wrong?" I asked him.

"Oh, I just don't feel too well," he said. "But I'll check Travis." So in his wonted way—gentle, painstaking, deliberate, and deft—he investigated all of Travis's vital signs and declared him in fine condition.

"But what if he should bump into the corner of a table? Or fall down?"

(I really think I was grasping desperately for reasons to hold on to Dr. Epstein just a little longer.)

Dr. Epstein laughed.

"What if Tami or Tommy bumped into a table or fell down?"

"Why *they'd* be all right."

"And Travis will be all right. Really Sally, he's *fine*. He's well. You'll have to watch him of course, and it will take time to get him reoriented. But there's nothing in his condition to worry about."

I asked about seizures and he smiled. He won't have seizures, he assured me. But he told me what signs to watch for and insisted again that I need have no fear.

"I know you've looked death in the face," he said. "And of course you're worried. But he'll be fine. I wouldn't send him home if I had the slightest doubt."

"But what about those burr-holes in his skull? They're still open."

"The protective tissue has closed over them and it will keep getting stronger. Nothing short of an icepick can break through there."

"Well, can I call you if anything goes wrong?"

"Of course. But nothing will."

So that was it. At half-past eleven, Tommy came back from the ball park and together we collected all Travis's gear and made ready for the move. At midnight, we kissed Travis good night (he was deep asleep) and returned to the hotel to pack up. Carol had gone back to New Jersey to get our car and bring it in for the morning.

But before we even started to move Travis out of the hospital, there came a new threat to his safety. Several of the news services had called seeking permission to come into Travis's room to take pictures. I wouldn't have it! No one was going to invade this little fortress where I was keeping my little boy from all harm. I would not have cameras pushed into his face, and flashes going off to frighten him into a fit of some sort. I called the New York Yankees office and told them that no one from the press or TV or any of the media was to come into the hospital to see him. I knew for one thing that there were reporters who felt sure something was permanently wrong with Travis and they were thirsting for proof. The Yankee office passed the word to all the media. But I must give total credit to the inspired work of the public relations staff of the New York University hospital. They managed the swelling mob of reporters, photographers, well-wishers, thrill-seekers, and just gawkers with consummate diplomacy, courtesy, firmness, and tenacity, so that not a single unpleasant incident developed.

I was in the hospital at half-past six the next morning, intent on seeing Dr. Zimmerman. I wanted to be sure he looked at Travis before we took him home, for my fears had by no means been quieted. I had lain awake for hours fretting over the return to that big house, with its three stories, its bridge across the living room. Would it be strange to Travis? Would he know his way around? Did we dare let him even walk across the corridor by himself? And I needed one final assurance that Travis was completely well.

Dr. Zimmerman checked him and found he had a temperature of 100 degrees rectally. Nothing significant at all, he assured me. But I was not so easily comforted. If there was one thing I had dreaded from the very beginning it was meningitis, so often fatal after brain injuries. They had told me that, in the blood that trickled from Travis's ear after the fall, they had found traces of spinal fluid and I had a real terror of infection. I had had encephalitis when I was eleven years old and so I was aware of the seriousness of any sort of infection in the spinal fluid. So the report of even a slight rise in temperature simply terrified me.

"But what if he should be getting meningitis?" I said.

Dr. Zimmerman eyed me very patiently. But I feel sure he thought I was getting hysterical. What he wanted to say, I am sure, was "Sally, we are the professionals. We would know of the danger of meningitis if anybody did. We would not be discharging him if we thought there was the slightest danger." But all he really said was what Dr. Epstein had said—that Travis was fine and there was no reason to worry.

So we went about then saying good-bye to patients and parents and nurses and residents, to the policemen who had guarded the door. It was a happy parting in a way but it was sad as well, and I shed more than a tear or two. These were, and still are, among my dearest friends.

And there was some feeling of guilt too—guilt that our child was well and others here never would get well. Guilt at leaving these people who had shared our own terrors and who now must live with their own. Yet I know that all my life I shall be thankful that I had a chance to know this world and to learn to sort out the important from the unimportant in life, to learn a little about the mysterious ways in which God works to perform so many of His wonders.

As I brought Travis down in the elevator that final morning, my knees were buckling from fear. Lord only knew what awaited Travis when we reached the ground. He might scream with fear at the crowd, or cry and beg to be taken back. But what really happened I could never have dreamed of. The elevator door opened and there stood what seemed like the entire staff of the hospital gathered to bid their little boy good-bye. And their little boy put his shoulders back, turned on his broadest and happiest smile and lifted his hand to greet them. The doctors, the nurses, the attendants, the policemen, the doormen, the cafeteria workers all clapped and cheered at his appearance.

"Hi, Travis! Hurray for Travis! Good-bye Travis!"

I burst into tears. But Travis, turning this way and that, like a pint-size politician on the campaign trail, waved to them all and shouted, "Hi! Hi! Hi!" As we marched on, with me walking close beside Travis, holding one hand, the crowd fell back on either side. I felt as if I were part of a royal procession, with all the cheers, the haste to make way for us, the glad faces turned toward us, and a retinue—Carol and the nurses—following.

Outside the scene was even more unworldly. It was not merely reporters and sensation-seekers. It was like half a small town full of cheering people. But nothing fazed our little hero. Proudly flaunting his Yankee T-shirt and his baseball cap, he busily returned their welcomes. I turned back to wave a last good-bye to all the hospital people. "Come back and see us!" some of the nurses called. And I saw them wiping tears away, just as I was doing. Because of the crowd, I could not get close to Doctors Epstein and Zimmerman, so I could do no more than offer them a special wave. Then I turned back to guide Travis toward the car.

"Could you blow the people a kiss?" I asked him.

Dutifully, he placed his hand to his mouth and deposited a kiss there, then weakly "blew" it toward his audience. The result was a concerted yell of delight. A half a dozen cameras were pointed his way—the picture of that farewell kiss was published across the country. Betsy Leesman and Joe D'Ambrosia, from the Yankee public relations office, had come down to help keep the reporters and cameramen from pressing too close. (I was really terrified that someone might shove too hard and Travis would be knocked over.) They, and the wonderful people from the hospital P.R. department, opened a clear pathway for us to the waiting car. It did take us a little while to make room for a gigantic toy tiger that Rusty Staub and Lee Mazzilli had sent to Travis. This five-foot beast, which Travis had named "Dena" after one of his beloved nurses, was Travis's favorite trophy and he refused to leave without it.

The tiger had to ride in the front seat with Tommy for he needed a whole seat to himself. Once we were inside, and I had collapsed into the back seat, restraints seemed to let go and the press people surged around. Cameras were shoved right against the glass of the window. Desperately, I tried to make some show of calm, so my anxiety would not be transferred to Travis. I picked a Mother Goose book off the car floor and started to read. Meanwhile, the cameras clicked around us as more and more photographers elbowed their way into position and I was trembling so I could hardly mouth the words of the rhymes.

Finally Tommy completed his own farewells and hopped into the car and we started to move, making our way slowly out of the mob to the avenue. Tommy had to stop at the hotel for a few moments to pick up the bundles we had left there, and as Travis and I sat in the car with Carol, two men, attracted by the sight of the stuffed tiger ensconced in the front seat, looked in and saw Travis.

"Is that *Travis John*?" one of them cried. "Hey Travis! How you doing, boy? Hey, you look great!" Travis beamed at them and waved a greeting. This unexpected show of love and concern just set the tears to streaming down my cheeks again. In what sudden and strange ways God's love shows itself! For a time anyway, the whole visible world was our neighbor.

I think some people think of God's love as a sort of mystic vapor that may envelop and uplift them in private moments. But to me it is a living phenomenon expressed in the love people feel for one another, and that sometimes overrides prejudice and petty dislikes and embarrassment and fear. Just recalling that outpouring of joy and love that greeted us both inside and outside the hospital and on the streets still brings tears to my eyes. Even as we drove to the river, a car passing us slowed down and the two people inside waved and called to Travis.

Tommy put Travis's favorite song, "The Rainbow Connection"—the Muppet song—on the tape deck and we played it continuously and sang the words—and I cried and cried, with joy at having our baby back, at the beautiful sunshiny day, at the love that had greeted and enfolded us. For a short time at least my forebodings were washed away, and I put aside my worries over how Travis might adjust to seeing his home after his long absence and his long sleep, when he had been, as the Muppet song put it, on "the other side of the rainbow." That song, incidentally, must have been played a hundred times on a tape recorder Rick Cerone had sent us so that we could play "The Rainbow Connection" right at Travis's bedside. The doctors had told us that anything to which he had been devoted in the past would aid him in his therapy by helping to rouse his sleeping memory. And nothing in the world had been dearer to Travis than "The Muppet Show," the tape of which we had at home so Travis could lie and watch it by the hour, pretending he was Kermit the Frog, strumming an imaginary guitar. (Jim Henson, creator of the Muppets, sent Travis a whole box full of Muppet characters and books while he was in the hospital and even sent along a movie that could be shown to all the kids in the hospital.)

The closer we got to home the more apprehensive I became. Would he even know his house? Could his memory have been wiped out? Should we have found some way to lead him back more gradually?

That spring I had planted many dozen impatiens along our driveway and when we had left the house a month before, they were just tiny green sprouts on both sides of the drive. As we drove up the long hill toward our house, I thought the trees that crowded the road and crowned the hilltop ahead of us had never looked so green nor had the foliage smelled so sweet. Then we topped the rise and turned into our own drive. I gasped at the sight. The impatiens had grown three feet tall, making a flaming garland all the way to our door. Travis sat up straight when he saw them:

"Pretty flowers!" he cried. I hugged him close and told him: "You're home, Travvy! This is home!"

But his eyes were not for the house but for the garage. He pointed at it and cried out: "My bicycle!" He meant his tricycle but it didn't matter what he called it. He remembered! And once more I cried.

In the house, there was a great stillness—for two or three minutes. Then the telephone began to ring. There were calls from all over the land. But I think the one that meant the most to Tommy and me was from Al Campanis of the Dodgers. The mending of Tommy's difference with this old friend was just one more of the compensating blessings that Travis's dread accident brought us. Of course I had *always* been devoted to the Dodgers and if I have time later I'll tell you why.

My first task was to get Travis settled. There was no question now about his memory. He had already called out a greeting to "My house!" the moment he came indoors. He was far too weak to manage the stairs by himself so I carried him to his room. Tommy went out to bring groceries and the telephone rang and rang. Then the doorbell sounded and the New York *Post* was at the door, seeking an interview and a picture of Travis. I think that paper must have an editor who would have assigned a reporter to ask Mrs. Lincoln how she enjoyed the play. When Tommy told them that we would prefer to have these first moments alone with our little boy they assured me—as if this gave them special license—that the New York Yankees had told them they could come talk to us. This was a falsehood. They must have followed our car home. So I bade them good-bye and closed the door.

I managed finally to put Travis down for a nap. But it was more than I could do to stay away from him. Every two minutes I had to peek in at him and make sure he was breathing. I turned the intercom up to its highest volume so I could hear any noise from his room all over the house. I put bells on his doorknob, bells on the gate at the head of the stairs, and I invented things to do in the rooms next to Travis. It was almost impossible to be separated from him now, so sure was I that something dreadful might befall him if he was out of my sight.

Then Tami came home from school for a truly joyful reunion. She had seen Travis in the hospital about a week before, when he was almost well. But this was different. Her baby brother was safe home! It would be their first dinner together for a month. Dinner was cooked by Mary Nagelvoort, one of our blessed friends without whose help in baby-sitting I might not have survived, and we sat down as a family for the first time and turned on the TV. The news was on, and of all things, there was a picture of Travis leaving the hospital.

"That's me!" Travis shouted, waving at himself. He

watched himself for a few seconds and then went back to eating. He had been eating solid food for not much more than a week and he had an appetite like his father's. Dinner was more important than TV, no matter who was on.

Next day the callers started coming—neighbors, some people we hardly knew, kids who had played with our kids—all wanting to see Travis and to hear all about it. "How did *that happen*?" "Why that must have been *terrible*!" I simply could not find the strength to cope with such questions. For some reason, the whole business seemed to hit me harder now than it had all during the ordeal. It was like the delayed reaction from a terrible fright. Suddenly all the ghastly possibilities and the sheer awfulness of the accident came back to me with extraordinary vividness. On the first night home we had to have Travis with us. Not just in the room but right with us, where we could keep our hands on him. Tommy and I hardly slept at all that night, listening to our little boy breathe, feeling his little body warm beneath our hands. If he would so much as twitch, I would sit up and watch him. Even if I had dozed off, the slightest movement of his body would bring me awake in an instant.

Then, about half-past four in the morning, when there was already pale light in the window, Travis suddenly sat up and started vomiting, all over everything, almost every twenty minutes. One of the burr-holes in Travis's head seemed to expand sometimes, and we had an elastic over it to minimize the swelling. Now the force of his vomiting seemed as if it might put impossible pressure on that scar, with terrifying results. Or could this signify that most dreadful of possibilities—meningitis! It was now half-past five. I told Tommy I was going to call Doctor Epstein.

"But it's half-past *five*!"

About this moment Travis vomited again.

"That does it!" I said. "I don't care what time it is."

So I called him. And Dr. Epstein was his usual patient self.

"You're not going to believe this," I told him. "But Travis has been vomiting regularly. It just won't stop. And he has a temperature of a hundred and two! I want to bring him right back."

"No, Sally," Dr. Epstein told me, in that gentle voice. "There's no reason for that. Just watch him. See if other symptoms develop. If he does not calm down in three or four hours, then call me again."

"But this must have something to do with his injury!"

"No. That's impossible. He may just have plain stomach flu. I am just getting over a siege of that myself."

So that was why he looked so pale and drawn that night he came in to check Travis!

"Then Travis got it from you!"

Dr. Epstein laughed mildly.

"No. As a matter of fact I think I contracted it from him." And to this day Dr. Epstein won't have it otherwise. I'm no doctor, of course. But my reasoning is that if Dr. Epstein had it first. . . . Anyway, this did not exactly reassure us. Instead, it scared the daylights out of us and we both sat up and watched him until the sun was high. Then I called Dr. Zimmerman, who comforted us in the same way. Just watch, he told us. Watch his temperature. Give him liquids—weak tea, whatever he can tolerate. Then, knowing how distraught I was, Dr. Zimmerman called me every three hours all through the day, to learn how Travis was progressing. Well, he was terribly pale, and weak, and shaky. But he got no worse.

I was grateful then that little Tommy was still with my sister and his grandparents in Indiana, for Travis needed me with him every moment. But there was no trouble with Tami. She was so happy to have her little brother with her, still alive, that she begrudged him nothing. Even to this day, Travis is the only person in the world who can dismantle Tami's dollhouse and not earn an immediate whack on the ear. Tami helped me attend him, took turns watching him, fetched and carried and never voiced a complaint. She was a perfect little nurse. She had really grown up through this ordeal.

I just could not leave Travis in his crib, for I knew he could climb out of it, or could before he went to the hospital, and the vision of his tumbling four feet to the floor gave me the shivers. So Tommy and I kept him right between us at night, where he could not possibly fall out, and felt his presence, listened to his breathing, and woke up fully at times throughout the night just to keep watch on him.

The flu lasted only twenty-four hours and then Travis began a swift recovery. It would be weeks, the doctors had told us, before he would have the strength to climb stairs. Travis began that a few days after he came home. Those pale little legs, thin and straight as pencils, began to fill out with muscle again. Each day he looked sturdier and found new deeds he could perform. Tami and Tommy and I spent nearly every waking minute working with him to get him entirely well. Tami would roll the ball to him, for him to roll back, for an hour at a time. She would toss it to him then and he would bounce it back. When he wanted to watch his beloved *Muppet Movie*, she would sit there and play the movie four or five times in a row, apparently as engrossed as he was in the antics of Kermit and Miss Piggy and the rest of the company. I knew there were a half-dozen other things she would rather watch. But she deferred to him in everything. And so, I think, did we all. We are all so delighted to have him with us, we could never grow sated with his company, nor fail to grant him whatever he desired. Carol and Chuck Schaefer dropped by daily to see their little friend. Carol and Larry Haggerty, some very dear friends who have a child who is ill, brought Travis a beautiful furry blanket with a little bear on it. He snuggles with it every day! Both Dr. Zimmerman and Dr. Epstein laughed at the way we were "spoiling" him. He'd grant me six months, Dr. Zimmerman said, before I'd give

Travis his first spanking. He was wrong about that, too. It was eight months.

But the burden of guilt and fear from his first accident never left me. To this day I find myself moving things, picking up things, closing windows, trying to foresee every possible mishap. All sharp things I put out of his reach. All heavy things that might topple I take out of his way. All hot things I move back from the edge of the table or stove. And for several weeks I took him everywhere with me, to the beauty parlor, to the grocery store—even to my obstetrician's during my pregnancy. (At this time I was almost in my final month of pregnancy. My fourth child, Taylor, would arrive in six weeks.) I bought new furniture for the basement playroom, with rounded corners that could not dig into a little head. I took up the indoor-outdoor carpeting from the basement playroom floor and put in double padding covered with thick plush carpeting that you could even sleep comfortably on.

I really thought I had always been extra concerned about the safety of my children. But I *had* overlooked that window! I would never forgive that in myself. And now I became doubly concerned, not just with their safety but with their comfort and happiness. Tommy too has noticed this in himself. He had always been a man who put his family first. But after that accident he simply put his family more than just first. He put it foremost—twenty games ahead of baseball. And we find now that this attitude has rewards we had never measured. If something annoys or depresses us—some Steinbrennerism, some newspaper story that distorts the details of some baseball development we know about—we can put it right out of our minds when we are with the kids, when Travis come up with one of his amazing observations, when Tami rejoices in her dancing, when little Tommy brings a thrilling story home from school, when little Taylor adds another word to his vocabulary.

Baseball itself puts a strain on a family, as no one knows better than Tommy and I. We postponed having children, for we were both troubled about what the strange hours, the constant travel, the long absences of the father might do to the kids, to say nothing of the frequent moves, meaning new schools and new friends. And while Tommy never decided on signing with one team or another strictly on the basis of the family's convenience, I was always strongly influenced by the attitude of the baseball management to the very existence of the ballplayer's family. I know there are some club owners and general managers who look on wives as a sort of necessary nuisance, something to be appeased, kept away from the clubhouse, and useful only on some P.R. photo opportunity. But the Los Angeles Dodgers and the California Angels are different.

My own love affair with the Dodgers began on the very day Tommy signed his first contract with that club. That day will always retain a spot in my imaginary memory book because of two or three far-out adventures that marked it. We drove to the ball park where Tommy was to sign and he left me outside in the car. This is my chance, I decided, to get a look at Hollywood! I took the car down the most inviting avenue to a nearby crossing. Sunset Boulevard, the sign said. *This* was Sunset Boulevard? It looked like Terre Haute. Where were the beautiful women, the swaggering stars, the spectacular studios, the hordes of extras, the block-long limousines? Of course I was at the wrong end of the boulevard but I had no way of telling. All I knew was that I dared not turn off the avenue to explore because I was sure to lose my way and be unable to get back to the stadium. I would just keep track of the mileage so when I started back I would know exactly how far to go. So on I went. And behold, I was in Hollywood! There was Sunset and Vine. Where Lana Turner was discovered! I had no one to tell about this except Charlie, our Siamese cat, who was right on my shoulder. So I told him. And there was an enormous statue of Bullwinkle

Moose! I showed that to Charlie. I don't believe he marveled at it but I did. I was really in the cloudland I had so often dreamed about! And there was the very drugstore where Lana worked before fame found her! I showed that to Charlie too. But Charlie hardly blinked.

By this time we had come eight miles and I knew we had better start back. But the greatest thrill awaited me! (Please remember I was still a small-town girl from Indiana with a sprinkle of hayseed still clinging to her hair.) I stopped at a traffic light and glanced idly at the big car that drew up beside me. It was a Rolls-Royce! That *had* to be carrying someone famous! I had already seen a well-dressed lady that, I told myself and Charlie, just *had* to be Doris Day. Now I tried to make out, through the tinted glass, what manner of other-world denizen might be breathing the same air as Charlie and I were sharing. I peered close. That gaunt face. That lank hair. It was Tiny Tim! In the flesh! A real honest-to-Sam Goldwyn movie star! He spared me one sly little smile and the car pulled away. Now I just *had* to get back to share this thrill with Tommy. There were big signs along the boulevard that said "STADIUM," so I found my way without trouble.

Back at the stadium I had another hour to wait, with only Charlie for company, before Tommy appeared. When he came to the parking lot he was wearing a grin that would have lighted the place in the dark. He was sporting a Dodger cap and carrying a consignment of literature—yearbooks and enough other stuff to fill a briefcase. A photographer had come with him and his face lit up when he saw me.

"This your wife?" Tommy allowed that it was. Without further preliminaries the photographer put the Dodger hat on my head and posed us both alongside the car. Tommy, I could tell, was just athrob with happiness. He led me about to show me the beauties of the new plant. I had never in my life seen a stadium so splendid, nor grass so green. And this was our home! Oh I was so glad to be here! And Tommy rattled on like a small boy about the wonderful men he had met—Peter

O'Malley, Al Campanis. And when my turn came to meet them I agreed that they were just the finest and kindest baseball people I had ever known. (Actually my acquaintanceship in upper baseball circles was limited indeed. I had stayed for a while in a hotel room across the hall from one baseball executive who, whatever his fine personal qualities, was a hopeless—and yes, a disgusting—drunk.) But when I met these two they welcomed me as if they were about to sign me to a contract too. And I think they did count me included in the deal, for these men, unlike most baseball executives of that day, wanted their players to lead happy lives—not just in the clubhouse but at home, on the sound business principle farmers in Indiana were guided by too: that contented cows give sweeter milk. So the wives were included in all club functions and welcomed on road trips. And that is the chief reason that I fell in love with the Dodgers. Much later, after meeting Buzzy Bavasi, I fell in love with the Angels, too.

But before Tommy had quite finished telling me all about the Dodgers I had to tell him *my* thrilling story. *I* had seen Tiny Tim! Almost close enough to touch. Tommy laughed. But he was happy all the same that I had had my wish fulfilled of actually seeing a star in Hollywood, close up. And he was himself so charged up, so eager to begin his Dodger career, that he wanted to begin at once. And it was only December! From that time on, it seemed the Dodger management took special pains to make me feel a part of the organization. They would call up to check on our comfort. They remembered us at Christmas. They made it clear that I was expected—and would be heartily welcomed—at spring training in Vero Beach.

I contrast this treatment sometimes with the business-is-business feeling that seemed to color all dealings with the Yankees. Although I cannot say I was reluctant for Tommy to come to New York. And if all our dealings with the Yankees had been with Al Rosen I'd never have wanted them to end, for he was a warm, outgoing man who seemed honestly glad to have me present at all negotiations. Not that the rest of the organization, at the start certainly, before Tommy had decided among the Yankees, Kansas City and Cincinnati, were not exceedingly kind to me, for George Steinbrenner and everyone else wooed me as if I were Howard Hughes's or Paul Getty's sole unmarried daughter. I simply *had* to come to New York, they told me. But I was one week short of being nine months pregnant and I was as big as the Goodyear blimp, or felt as big. I dared not leave my doctor.

"Bring him with you!" they insisted. "We'll put him up!"

And when my doctor explained that he could not leave his practice even for George Steinbrenner, they insisted they would have a hospital room ready, an ambulance if need be, so that I'd have the best care in the world. Well, I did want very much to go to New York with Tommy because I think he always needed moral support in negotiations, and he wanted me to go. He was very reluctant to be away from me at such a time. But I was so *big*. At that point in pregnancy, as most women know, you feel as if you have been blown up right to the point of explosion. You cannot walk properly. You cannot sit gracefully. And besides, I was scared at the thought of giving birth on the plane, for I had no desire to name my child TWA John. So I talked to the doctor and he said he thought I might well make the trip. He said he would check me the morning of the flight and if he found I had five hours to spare, he would agree to let me go. But I must not sit down the whole flight. I should walk up and down the aisle as much as possible during the flight. Next Tommy checked with the airline to learn if I would be allowed on the plane. Oh, yes, they told me, but if she goes into labor our policy is to land the plane immediately and have you seek hospitalization on the ground. Well, that, I decided, was a chance I would have to take.

So off we went to New York. And the eyes of the stewardess very nearly started from her head when she asked me sweetly how soon I expected and I replied "Five days." I think she had visions of performing her midwife act in mid-air. She did not dare ask what on earth had prompted me to take a chance like this or I might have told her that I found participation in these free-agency negotiations among the most thrilling experiences I had known. What a change it made in our lives to find so many people setting out to win us to their side, competing with each other in courting our favor, in offering blessings of every sort, thinking up new acts of kindness and generosity, in just so obviously *wanting* us. It was flattery of the most satisfying sort.

Well, I did not have little Taylor on the plane or on the ground in Minnesota. We arrived safely in New York with Tommy's attorney, Bob Cohen, and his wife, to be greeted at the airport by the very top brass of the New York Yankees. I took to Al Rosen at once. He was so gracious, so sincerely concerned with my comfort, and so obviously pleased that I had managed to accompany Tommy. I won't say that George Steinbrenner wasn't nice. But he was business-nice and I got no feeling of warmth from him at all. I laugh now at his first impression on me, for he reminded me of a rooster, clucking in his rapid, chopped-off-sentence manner, and really strutting ahead of us up the long ramp to the TWA club restaurant. In later meetings, I never could get the chicken image out of my mind. But he was nice at this meeting and I really drank up all the admiring things he said about Tommy. I really have an insatiable appetite for flattery—as long as it's applied to my husband. And George was almost humble as he tried to sell Tommy on the Yankees, trying hard not to make it sound like bragging but listing all the advantages of the city, of the Yankee operation, of the stadium, of the team. Al Rosen meanwhile was doing his best to make me comfortable. He obviously knew that sitting a long time in one position was hard work for a pregnant lady. Then up popped George, clucking out phrases about having to catch a plane to Tampa.

"But you and Al finish up the business. Get this over with. Get you signed. Have a nice dinner. Then relax."

"Wait," said Bob Cohen. "There are still some things we have to work out. We just didn't come here to sign."

You might have thought Bob had pulled out a handful of George's tail feathers, for he actually squawked. "WHAT?!!" He strutted quickly back. "You didn't come to *sign*?!"

"No. We promised to get back to Kansas City and Cincinnati. They're waiting to hear from us."

George jumped again.

"I thought you came here to sign!"

"No, George. We just talked to you on the phone. We didn't come here to sign. We came here to talk."

"Well, Al," said George. "You've got work to do. You've got a lot of talking to do. Better get busy." Then off he scurried like a frightened hen.

This was not really my first meeting with George. I had met him once before at the World Series in Los Angeles after Tommy had beaten the Yankees in the first game. The Dodgers (and this is another sample of the "class" with which they operate) had a hospitality room at their stadium where they entertained members of both teams. There may be other clubs in the league who offer hospitality to the enemy in this manner, but I don't know who they are. After the game, many of the Yankee players with their wives came up to the room to help devour the great food and drink that the Dodgers offered, while the Dodgers' wives, me included, acted as hostesses and went about introducing ourselves to the New York folk. I was so star-struck at that moment, so exalted from having watched Tommy pitch a beautiful game, that everyone I met seemed more dazzling than the one before. Norma King, Clyde King's wife—a goddess! Arlene, Elston Howard's wife—a queen! Ginger Nettles—an angel! Catfish Hunter's wife, Lou Piniella's wife—absolute darlings! And then my eye fell on George Steinbrenner. Of course I had heard of George from a dozen sources, and had read stories about him in all the papers. A real "character"! So I hastened to introduce myself: "I'm Sally John. Tommy John's wife. I want to welcome you to Dodger Stadium."

George drew himself up and his eyes grew wide.

"Oh-HOH! Tommy John! Well your husband pitched one hell of a game tonight! Yes sir!" He shook his head and then seemed to be talking to himself, for his voice dropped to a mutter, or to a low clucking: "He ought to be with the *Yankees* next year!" I suppose if I had wanted to be technical I'd have called that tampering. Tommy was not a free agent—yet. But I was in no mood to start counting anyone's sins, for George went on—and on. Tommy was a great pitcher. What a hell of a job he did. Then I met George's wife Joanne, a beautiful lady, and a brilliant lady too, as I was to learn later. Whatever faults George may possess, his lovely wife more than compensates for them, even persuades you that there must be a really fine side to George, regardless of how he may look sometimes to those he deals with. Joanne spoke of her children—in college! In *college*! But she looked like a *girl*! Is this what happens to a baseball wife—that she remains forever young? And Joanne was really "into" baseball, full of confidence in a comeback for the Yankees. How could George have kept this paragon out of public view so long?

When I told Tommy what George had muttered, Tommy was delighted, tampering or no tampering. He had already just about made up his mind to free agency and this brightened his horizons considerably. And both of us decided then that there was a George Steinbrenner the public did not know—a gentler man, a less flamboyant figure, and, of course, a fine judge of pitching ability.

So the George I met at the airport that day was a disappointment to me. There was an air of insincerity about him, a suggestion that he was putting on an act about his manifold operations that hardly left him time to be polite. So I was a little scared of what might come of this. But I thought it best to keep my doubts to myself. Bob and his wife Joan, Tommy and I were then transported in a long black limousine, like Asian diplomats, to the Plaza Hotel where a magnificent suite awaited us, adorned with great bouquets of flowers and a king-size box of candy. Joanie and I, at least, were rendered so dreamy-eyed by this sort of lavish courtship that we might have signed any paper George Steinbrenner put in front of us. But Tommy and Bob remained cool.

In the early evening, there was another limousine to bundle us all to the "21" Club, famed haunt of the famous, where we were buttered up further by the warm attentions of the staff, and where Al and Rita Rosen awaited us to resume the Yankees' wooing. No serious business was discussed at dinner but we were given a tempting sample of Yankee openhandedness and the amenities available in New York to George Steinbrenner's chosen. We were even treated to a serenade—by the Yale Whiffenpoofs. To a small-town girl, it was like a fairy tale. And Al Rosen's soothing recital of all the good things that could happen if Tommy joined the Yankees and we moved to New York just enhanced the fairy-tale atmosphere. But there was one advantage that hadn't been mentioned and it was one that I had made up my mind to make sure about. In Los Angeles, the players' wives were usually welcomed on the Dodger jet, even on the longer trips. How about *that*?

Al Rosen had to stop and think for a moment. The Yankees had no private jet. And I think he may have wondered whether I customarily went trekking with Tommy when I was about to give birth. But like the gentleman he is, he gave me a hearty answer:

"Sally, if Tommy signs with the Yankees, you can go on a road trip whenever you want to!"

If Tommy signs with the Yankees. This was not the first time this question had been posed. Right after the World Series, Thurman Munson had asked Tommy if he planned to try free agency and Tommy allowed that he probably would.

"Come with the Yankees," said Thurman. "We *need* you!" Reggie Jackson expressed the same feeling, saying: "Yankee Stadium is *made* for you, Tommy!"

Later, in Las Vegas, where Tommy and I had been invited to participate in a testimonial dinner for Joe Louis (and where my heart was fluttered once more to find Tommy and me seated on the dais, not with Tiny Tim, but with the likes of Robert Redford, Ryan O'Neal, Angie Dickinson, and Muhammad Ali) we met Joe Torre, who was managing the Mets then and who gave us a strong sales pitch on the advantages of living in New York. But I think what probably moved us most was the ungentle persuasion of Howard Cosell. Here was another in my gallery of "characters" whom I had longed to meet. Of course, I had heard him badmouthed by TV and news people, but that only sharpened my urge to meet him and make up my own mind about his nature. Howard sighted Tommy early in the evening and greeted him in typical TV fashion, with heavy emphasis on every third or fourth word:

"*Tom*-my *John*! Well, *what's* it going to *be*! *Who* are you going to *sign* with? If you *ask* me there's only *one* place to *play*! The *New* York *Yankees*!"

I was standing at Tommy's side, with my eyes fixed on Howard, who, at that stage of my career, was probably one of the fifteen wonders of my world. Howard looked at me in his intense way, and without waiting for any reply from Tommy, he exclaimed: "You're beautiful!" Me, all swollen up to cow-size! With that remark, Howard won my heart. (And I should explain right here that he's in no danger of losing it.) "*When* is your baby *due*?" Howard went on. "Well, you've *got* to *make* up your mind *pretty soon, haven't* you? You'd *better* have that *baby* in New *York*. The *greatest* city *in* the *world*. If it's *made*, manufactured, or *bought*, it's in *New* York. Tommy, you're a *star* already! *Come* to New *York* and you'll be a *superstar*!" I know people say that Howard talks this way to everyone but I chose to believe he meant it and I absorbed his every word about the marvels of life in his favorite city. I know Tommy did too, and I know that Howard's presentation, and his obviously sincere desire to have us come to be his near-neighbors in this greatest of all cities, had much to do with Tommy's decision to take the Yankee offer without even visiting the clubs at Kansas City and Cincinnati. (I do sometimes wish he had gone there to talk at least.) Howard continued to court us all evening, as we kept running into him while we made the rounds. He asked me where I thought Tommy was going and I told him that Cincinnati sounded good, not only because it was close to home but because Tommy liked the park—and the grass infield, which had an advantage for a sinker-ball pitcher. Howard would hear none of this. He assured Tommy he could win twenty games for the Yankees and be on a World Series *winner*. Besides, "Al *Rosen* is a *dream. You'll* just *love* him." And the Yankee infielders would simply eat up those ground balls that Tommy throws. So by the time we had that dinner with Al Rosen, we really needed no more selling on New York as a place to play. All that remained was the contract.

Tommy and I and Bob and Joanie all went back to the Plaza with Al Rosen, where the men settled right down to negotiate. So Joanie and I retreated to the bedroom where we got into pajamas and robe and sat to watch TV while the talk went on in the next room. It was midnight. It was one o'clock. Then it was two o'clock and we could hold out no longer. We walked in on the men and they were still at it. A few things to settle about the strike clause and stuff, Tommy explained. So we retreated to the TV. Finally—it must have been getting close to dawn—Tommy and Bob came in, looking as if they had escaped from a raid on an all-night poker game—shirttails out, ties yanked free of their necks, collars open, sleeves rolled up, eyes bleary, hair in tussocks. But, they told us triumphantly, they had a deal! A few technicalities to be worked out with George Steinbrenner but once that was done, they had a deal for sure. What about

Cincinnati and Kansas City? Oh, they got them on the phone and they could not top the Yankee offer. So Al Rosen went home happy and after I had called my mom and my sister to break the news to them before they could hear it on the air, we went happily to bed.

Next day the Yankees scheduled a press conference about eleven o'clock and again the big limousine appeared to carry all four of us to the stadium. The stadium seemed like the capital of the baseball world with all those enormous pictures of bygone stars—Babe Ruth, Joe DiMaggio and the other hallowed names that I had heard of but never realized had all played here. And now *Tommy* would join these demigods. Cedric Tallis and Al Rosen were there to lead us to George Steinbrenner's office. George was not on hand so I had time to goggle at the appointments in his office—silver baseballs, crystal baseballs, sketches of baseball action, paintings of baseball players, prints of ancient baseball games. And then, before any of the press arrived, who should walk in, wearing a Cosell-size grin, but Howard himself. Without preliminaries he hugged us both and I could only gasp: "What are *you* doing here?"

"Why, Tommy John signing with the Yankees? I wouldn't miss it for the world! This is a big day in my life! And speaking of big days, what are you doing for lunch? Let me take you to 'Twenty-One' and treat you to lunch."

'Twenty-One'? This must be the Howard Johnson of the VIPs. The small-town girl inside me almost burst out: "Oh, yes. We've been there!" But I silenced her. The press having arrived, the conference began. During the formalities, Howard stood grinning over us all—so sincerely delighted at having Tommy with the Yankees that he might have been the man who had promoted the whole deal, as in a way he was. As the questions and answers proceeded, Bob and Tommy advanced my education by pointing out the good guys and reputed bad guys among the reporters and columnists. They all looked like good guys to me. Anyway, I liked Tommy's philosophy: "If you do good, they'll write good things about you. If you do bad, they'll write bad things about you. And that's the way it's supposed to be."

After that, it was time for photographs, and the picture-makers decided they wanted to pose me with Tommy. Me, with my misshapen form? Oh yes, indeed. So I insisted they picture me only from the chest up. Instead, they made a sort of maternity garment out of a full-size Yankee uniform top and took us out on the pitching mound to pose. It was freezing out there, but I was numb from excitement. After that, of the two hundred or more people who came to the conference, it seemed that everyone had a few more questions to ask. Then there was the big limousine again, but this time it was Howard Cosell's, come to whisk us all away to the "21" Club, where we were once more greeted like royalty and treated to Howard's enticing descriptions of the advantages of dwelling in New York. "New York will love Sally and Tommy John!" he declared. I think he was right, for New York did indeed take us into her arms when we went there to stay. I wanted that lunch to go on forever. But it was getting toward dinner time and we had a plane to catch. And when we reached the airport and boarded the plane we waited and waited and waited. I began to get nervous. More than nervous. I began to get strange pains. The beginning of labor? I had no fear really of having my baby in New York. But I still felt uneasy about having it on an airplane. Should we get another plane? There were a dozen planes going to Los Angeles about this time. No. It can't be much longer. It was *much* longer. By the time they had repaired the rubber bands or whatever it was that had broken on the plane, we must have been sitting there more than two hours, for we landed in Los Angeles eight and a half long, uneasy hours after we had boarded the plane. The expected baby, fortunately, waited until we had been home for a few days or so before he decided to make his landing. And that was how Travis came into the world on December 6, 1978. In a sense, he was born a Yankee.

Tommy:

I like to think of myself (who doesn't?) as a calm and reasonable man. But I am not altogether without emotions. I have even been known to blow my stack under certain circumstances—usually for being taken out of a ball game. And my anger is mostly directed against myself, or against the fates that have somehow misused me. Once, while I was pitching for the White Sox, I screwed up rather badly on the mound and celebrated the occasion, as I was headed unwillingly for the showers and found a large steel locker along my path waiting for someone to attack, by fetching it a solid boot in the front door. I didn't know this ahead of time but inside the locker there was about $100,000 worth of photographic equipment—lenses, cameras and appurtenances—that took a good rattling around. Happily, no real damage was done.

(Incidentally, I once laughed out loud when I was lifted, probably the only time I ever reacted that way. This was in Chicago, too, when I was coming back after a serious illness. I just had to laugh that time because of the way Eddie Stanky signaled his decision. He came walking to the mound carrying *my warm-up jacket* over his shoulder. I had never in my life in baseball been offered a hint so broad. "I presume I am coming out," I said. And Eddie agreed that that was a fair assumption.)

When I was with the Dodgers I was twice removed from a game that I was winning 2 to 1. Once I was beating Pittsburgh, and Alston, in keeping with his apparent notion that I could never pitch more than seven innings, pinch-hit for me in the seventh. That time I found the trainer's plastic bucket in my path as I clumped toward the clubhouse and I tried a place-kick on that. My foot went right through the plastic and the bucket went higher than Killian's kite. Afterward, I heard Bill Buhler, the trainer, and one of the best guys who ever lived, complaining to someone that "Tommy broke my bucket!" So I went out and bought one of those little yellow jobs kids use to play in the sand with. I tied a pretty pink ribbon on it and carried it in to Bill.

The next time I was beating Philadelphia 2 to 1 and again Alston pinch-hit for me in the seventh. This time, there was no bucket to kick so I grabbed a bag of slightly used baseballs and busted that against something. Baseballs flew all around the area as if someone has smashed a gumball machine.

But I lost my cool only once in a ball game when I was with the Yankees and that was on the very first night I pitched after Travis's injury. As I have already explained, everything seemed to go wrong that night, not only with my pitching but with the whole club, who seemed to determined to match my own futility. So when I came out in the fifth or sixth I was ticked at the entire situation but mostly at myself. When I saw before me the telephone that Yogi used to get word from our "scouts" in the press box on how to move the fielders, I laid hold of that innocent instrument and yanked it clean off the wall. "You guys aren't getting any good out of this anyway!" I explained and handed the rootless phone to Yogi. Yogi covered for me by holding the dead phone to his ear now and then so George Steinbrenner would not observe that communications had been cut off.

This is leading up to saying I think I showed plenty of patience in my dealings with George Steinbrenner, despite provocations. Maybe this was because I always felt George had a "better" side that could be appealed to in a crisis and that, when we weren't talking business, he was a good friend and pleasant companion. But his dealings eventually became so devious that it would have taken far saintlier folk than

Sally and I to have suffered his treatment without blowing up.

Unhappily enough, my estrangement from the Yankees began in a series of petty irritations while Travis was still in the hospital. We were staying in a hotel room reserved for us by the Yankees in the name of Jerry Murphy, Yankee assistant administrator. I expected to pay the bill however, which I thought would be presented when we checked out. But we had been there only two weeks when I ran into Ed Broderick, attorney for the Yankees, at the stadium and he asked me what I planned to do about the hotel bill. I told him I planned to pay it when I checked out. But they already had the bill, made out to the Yankees, and Ed acted as if I tried to slip something over on them. Then a bit later he asked me flatly if they were "going to get stuck with this limo bill." That singed me a little because I hadn't wanted any limo and the Yankees—and I supposed George himself—had offered to provide it, despite my protests. And the bill was about $800. For a trip to the hospital in the morning and a return of a few blocks at night. I fixed this by calling the owner of the limousine service, Bill Fugazy, and asking what could be done. Bill said apparently the driver had been charging for a full day and then taking off and working for his own pocket in between, as drivers had been known to do before. Bill told me he would "take care of the bill"—a mighty generous gesture for which I thanked him most earnestly. But my neck was still red from the suggestion that I was planning to stick anyone with this expense.

I offered to pay the hotel bill. In fact, I had written out a check and given it to the cashier. But in between, Bob Cohen, who was given to more tough talk than I was, had told George: "If you have any class, you'll pick up Tommy's hotel bill." George, who had often shown plenty of class, ordered the hotel to take no money from anyone but the Yankees. I really think this was a case of the people in the lower echelon trying to act the way they thought George would have acted. Only this time they got the wrong reading.

In my contract negotiations, which we started right after Travis got home, no one had to do any mind reading, because we dealt directly with George. Bob and I had decided to start working on the 1983 contract in the fall of 1981 so we would have plenty of leeway for negotiations. I had had an average year and I expected some vigorous negotiating sessions. But George sent me a contract with a cut of total salary of more than 20 percent. This was in violation of the Basic Agreement between the Players' Association and the club owners and naturally we balked. But George told Bob Cohen that he didn't agree with our figures and that the offer stood. At Bob's suggestion, we filed a default notice with the Players' Association office. Then George came back with a really good offer—a three-year contract (which was what I asked for) at a generous salary. I had hardly got through scolding myself for ever thinking ill of George when I got word from Bob Cohen that George had called to say he was "taking that offer off the table" and that it was a one-year contract or nothing.

For a long time then, Bob tried to reach George to talk this deal over but he never could connect. He would call and find George "out." He would ask for George to call back and George would invariably call at the very hours Bob had said he would be out of the office and in court. When George doesn't want any phone calls, he is impossible to reach. Meanwhile, the year was running out and we were getting closer to spring training time. I personally called George in Florida and after some growling, he took back the one-year deal and offered a two-year contract—but still at an unacceptable amount.

The Yankees went into spring training very early in February that year but I refused to report. I was not going down to risk injury when I did not have a valid contract to protect me. By this time Bob and George had got to snarling at each other so much there was little hope of their seeing eye to eye on anything. We had filed for salary arbitration and seemed headed for a collision. I decided to call George again myself. I had been working out regularly at home and felt ready to step right into the spring training regime with the rest of the team.

George answered my call in his usual friendly way and when I suggested that Sally and I come down and talk things over with him at dinner he agreed at once.

"See you tonight then," he said.

Soon afterward Bill Bergesch, vice-president of the Yankees, called me from the Yankee office to say that he had made plane reservations for us and that it was all arranged for me to "start working out tomorrow."

"I'm not going down to work out," I told him. "I won't work out without a contract."

Next event was a call from George.

"If you're just coming down to have dinner and talk about your contract," said George, "forget it! If you're ready to work out with the club, okay. I don't want to talk to you and Sally over dinner if you aren't going to report for spring training."

That plane took off without us and negotiations were back where they had started. Our arbitration hearing was only a week off. Ron Guidry, Dave Righetti, and I were still the meat of the Yankee pitching staff, and it seemed crazy for George to be so stiff-necked about talking. It was ridiculous for him to call this way and say we "didn't have anything to talk about."

On February 11 I called George again, for I could not believe that we could not come to some sort of understanding. This time George was all sweet reason. Almost at once he made a proposal that sounded like something we could agree on quickly. We made a conference call with Bob Cohen, George, and me on the phone, and Sally taking notes. We talked out some details and agreed on all the general outlines.

"I guess that covers everything," said George, "unless you have something else on your mind."

Sally broke in to explain that we wanted very much to move out of our multi-level house to a one-story place where there would be no more upstairs windows for kids to fall out of and wondered if George would lend us the cash for a down payment, to be repaid when we sold our present house.

"What about $200,000?" said George.

Sally and I agreed that would be just right. But Sally could not resist a slight rib.

"Interest free?" she inquired.

George laughed.

"Not so's you'd notice it. But I'll charge whatever it is I charge the other guys. I think it's around ten percent." (George knew exactly what percent it was!)

So that was agreed on and the talk was over.

But soon after that there were further personality clashes between Bob Cohen and George. Even though the package they had fashioned was pretty close to what we could agree to, we still could not close the deal. The arbitration was scheduled for February 21, and George and I admitted we wanted to avoid arbitration and suggested to Bob that we "get together and straighten out these details." After that, Bob could not get George on the phone, nor would he return Bob's calls. I decided to try again.

I know it was Valentine's Day when I called because I remember asking George if Joanne, George's wife, had given him a pair of shorts with hearts on them as a Valentine's Day present. George laughed and we talked like old friends. In a few minutes we were in full agreement and we got Bob in on a conference call with Sally again taking notes. Then we agree? George said we did. Remember about the $200,000 loan? "Yes, I promised that. We'll put that in the contract."

So I packed up at once and took off for spring training where all was sweetness and light. Bob and I visited George in his trailer-office to work out some cranky details on guarantees—stuff about my being disabled from use of drugs or alcohol or being disabled in an auto accident when my driving ability was impaired by drink or drugs. I had no plans along those lines so there was really nothing to argue about. But one point from my old contract remained unsettled. I had been paid during the strike because of the strike pay clause in my contract. For me to receive these payments, I had to file a default notice at each pay period. The Yankees would pay under protest, and the entire matter had to be settled at a hearing before an impartial arbitrator.

Bob asked George about the strike arbitration.

"My people tell me I don't have any case on that score," said George, "so we're dropping it."

Fine. There was nothing more to negotiate on and I was ready for a good season. I signed the contract and went to work.

Six weeks later I had heard nothing about calling off the arbitration on the strike pay, and Bob called George.

"Oh, that's out of my hands," said George. "That's got to come from Ray Grebey." (Grebey was the representative of the club owners.) I called Marvin Miller. The Players' Association had never heard from Grebey. Marvin Miller then called Grebey. No, that's not my province. You'll have to get George to drop that. So we got back to George. Oh, no, says George. That's Grebey's area. You have to settle with him. "But I had your personal word the case would be dropped." "I can't help that. It's out of my hands."

As a result of all this, the arbitration hearing was still scheduled.

Present at the hearing, held at the Federal Mediation offices in New York City, were Ray Grebey, Barry Rona—who is Grebey's counsel—Peter Alkalay, and Ed Broderick for the Yankees; and, on our side, Marvin Miller, Don Fehr, Players' Association counsel, Bob Cohen, and me. An arbitration hearing proceeds like a court trial, with witnesses from both sides who, after presenting testimony, can be cross-examined by opposing counsel.

Bob Cohen was our first witness. He was on the stand for almost an hour of direct- and cross-examination. After Bob's testimony, the Yankees asked for a recess, during which Grebey, Rona, Alkalay, and Broderick caucused. When they returned to the hearing room they announced they had no defense to offer at that time. The hearing was adjourned and the arbitrator's decision is still pending.

That little bit of harassment really finished me with George, I believe, for there was no pretending that it was Grebey or Alkalay or Broderick who had insisted on this hearing. It was George! He had already admitted he had no case, yet he put us through all this needless travel and expense just to recover a few drops of revenge.

Soon after that we started looking for a new house and we ran into more typical Steinbrenner evasion, obfuscation, contradiction and pettifogging. We had put our house up for sale and I felt it was time to ask for that loan so we could make a deal on a new one. But when I asked Dave Weidler, the Yankee comptroller, for the money I was told that they didn't have it. You know, unexpected expenditure, bonuses, player purchases and all that. Well, when would they have it—next week? Can't say. Two weeks? Can't be sure. Maybe never? I don't know. Well, when? When George releases the money.

Once more I was on the telephone to Marvin Miller. (The Players' Association is always there to hear a complaint from a ballplayer, and more often than not the matter can be settled in a phone call.) Marvin connected me with Peter Rose (no kin to the mighty hitter), counsel for the Association, and I spelled out to him the details of my latest problem with the Yankees. Peter Rose wrote to the Yankees, asserting our claim.

He was told in response that I had failed to fulfill a number of requirements—that I had not shown evidence of a *bona fide* attempt to sell the house, no list of agents who were offering it, no indication of what price was being asked and how the price compared with comparable properties in the neighborhood, no proof even of any effort to buy a new house. (Not a single one of these "requirements" was listed in the contract.)

Ed Broderick, Yankee attorney, even wrote a letter to Rose in which he did more than hint that I had engaged in serious misrepresentations—that I really wanted the money to buy an extra house in Florida or California, that I had no intention of selling my present house and that, by clear implication, my plea that I wanted a one-level house for the safety of the kids was just a fairy tale. This was cheap-shot enough. But, through what I would like to believe was inadvertence, some of these accusations began to filter into the newspapers where one or two of the consistently pro-owner commentators accepted them as solemn truths that were just added evidence, if any were needed, of Tommy John's insatiable greed.

I did meet Ed Broderick after this and I asked him how he could bring himself to utter the sort of snide near-libel his letter contained. Said he: "I just do what I'm told." And so, of course, do all the rest of George's minions if they want to stay on the payroll. I hope I am not being paranoid in interpreting this move of George's as part of his campaign either to punish me for a mediocre season on the mound or to goad me into better performance. There were stories current about this time that George was in default on other fronts and it was suggested in print that perhaps the Yankees were pinched between high salaries and poor gate receipts or that George was getting ready to sell out.

One day Jane Gross, a sportswriter for the *New York Times*, asked me if I would comment on a quote she had just received from Bill Bergesch.

"Sure," I said. And Jane read me the quote:

"Tommy should be more grateful to George Steinbrenner

and the Yankees for all they did for him last year when he had his troubles. He should just go to the bullpen and shut up."

I was honestly dumbfounded! Bergesch said *that*? I told Jane Gross that I had expressed my gratitude at length in a personal letter to George. Was there some other gesture I was supposed to make? I knew, of course, that George has always liked to have people "in his pocket," so they will do as he says and shut up about it. But that was not for me!

"My troubles," I told Jane, "did the Yankees no harm. Actually, all the press coverage and Travis's appearance at the stadium that night to throw out the first ball at the play-offs brought them a ton of publicity. I don't believe Bill Bergesch ever dreamed up a statement like that. That was George Steinbrenner talking through Bergesch. And Bergesch is no different from Ed Broderick, who told me 'we do as we're told.' "

I stewed over this comment all through the game and decided I would have to confront Bill Bergesch to learn if he *really* had said it. I found him in the clubhouse, feeding his face at the food table, and asked if I could talk to him in private. He agreed cheerfully enough and we went into the only room available—the laundry room. I could not get the door closed tightly, so I imagine most of what was said became public property.

Of course, he flatly denied my accusation at once. Even when I explained what I had learned from Jane Gross, he continued to insist he had been misquoted. Although I had come in with the idea of offering him, in a controlled manner, a very cold assessment of his character, I almost immediately felt the stopper blow off the stack. I am not exactly sure what I said but I am afraid I used some words that I ordinarily try to avoid. And I am sure I called him everything except a human being. Afterward I was ashamed to realize that I had been hoping all along that he would make some move—a slight push, or a tap on the arm—that would have justified my getting both hands on his throat. It really didn't matter so much what he might have said about me. But when he tried to use Travis's misfortune to justify Steinbrenner's petty persecutions, he had stepped over the limit of what I allow.

When the discussion ended, with Bill still insisting he had been grievously "misquoted" and me not believing a word of what he said, I went out to my locker, too upset to sit still. A whole flock of reporters converged on me.

"What was that all about? What'd he say? What happened in there?"

I told them, as calmly as I could, just what Jane Gross had reported to me. The reporters, every last one of them, seemed as shocked as I had been. Would Bergesch, would Steinbrenner, would the *Yankees*, stoop *that* low?

I could not trust myself to choke down my wrath much longer, so I excused myself from the clubhouse, went back to the hotel, and—as I usually do when I need some sensible advice—called Sally. She was every bit as horrified as I was, and I think for the first time she began to understand what the *real* George Steinbrenner was like: tough, self-centered, and crafty.

After Sally and I had hashed the matter over at length and I felt able to talk more coolly about it, I called Bob Cohen, told him the story, and urged him to intensify his efforts to persuade the Yankees to trade me. I had had enough.

But Steinbrenner had one more humiliation to lay on me, and this one might well have put an end to my pitching career. For Gene Michael began to schedule my mound appearances in a way that almost seemed deliberately designed to shatter my concentration and my self-confidence. I would pitch every five days, then there might be a ten-day gap, then an eight-day layoff, then a two-day layoff, then a six-day hiatus. I am convinced Gene Michael never selected this schedule on his own, for no sane manager would misuse one of his top three pitchers in this manner without orders from the club deity. And my resentment against George deepened when Michael came to me one day and announced he was shifting me to the bullpen.

"What for?" I inquired.

Gene offered me that little smirking smile of his that never fails to raise the hair on my neck, and spake thus:

"Because it will do you good."

Was I a sixth-grader who was being sent back to the fifth grade to get a better grasp of fractions, for Pete's sake? Could this guy Michael really present himself as a judge of pitching skills? Who ever told him he knew how a pitcher can work himself out of a slump? If Clyde King, or any of the very few who know as much about pitching as Clyde does, should tell me I was losing my skills or needed a long layoff, I would accept the decision as worth taking seriously. But Gene Michael? I am not sure he has ever been able to decide between a fork and a spoon or make a positive distinction between spit and Shinola.

After that, in Texas, came the final nail in the coffin, or straw on the camel's back, or spark that set off the powder train. I was working out in the bullpen, feeling loose and limber in the Texas sun, and we were hanging on to a slim lead against the Rangers. Then word came from the dugout that if the Rangers should tie, or grab a small lead, Righetti should come in. But if the Rangers piled up a big lead, then the choice was T.J. So now I had descended to the status of a kid pitcher who could not be trusted to hang on to a lead but would be used just to hold the franchise while we coasted to defeat. I looked at Jeff Torborg, boss of the bullpen.

"I guess that tells me where I stand with the Yankees."

Jeff pulled his mouth around a little and said nothing. He had learned diplomacy in a hard school.

With all this, plus the mean-spirited shenanigans concerning the loan, I became convinced that I wanted nothing more from the Yankees except to leave. In a TV interview with Howard Cosell, I recalled a statement George Steinbrenner had made to the assembled squad early in the season. If anybody present, he said, ever felt that he could not put out his best for the Yankees and wanted to be traded, that player just had to let George know and he would be traded instantly. So now, I told Howard, I'm calling George's bluff! I want to be traded. I have a no-trade clause in my contract but I'm ready to waive that. I'll give George the names of three or four clubs to which I'd like to be traded and I'll agree to the deal without any bonus or advance or premium of any sort. (The Yanks had had to pay John Mayberry about $200,000 to get him to agree to a trade. And they had been balked in trying to trade Oscar Gamble when Oscar wanted closer to a million dollars to agree.) As a matter of fact, I believe, although I did not say this to Howard Cosell, that if I had remained another two years—maybe only one more year—with the Yankees, I'd have been out of baseball for keeps.

As it worked out, after a lot of false moves on George's part concerning the physical condition of the player I was to be traded for, I wound up with my first choice of clubs—the California Angels. And my very first intimation that I had truly found a home came in an unsought decision by my new boss, Buzzy Bavasi, to extend my contract for three years. That, in case you are not familiar with baseball contracts, is an unheard-of concession. But Buzzy, when he was questioned about it, just said that he wished Sally and I had been with him for the ten previous years and now he wanted to make sure I would not stray from the fold again.

So here I am and here I stay. Maybe I'll move on, after I can no longer pitch, to some job in baseball administration, because that's where I want to finish off my working years. But as long as I can win baseball games with my head and arm, I want to win them for Buzzy, Gene Autry, and the Angels.

It may be, of course, that my ideas are a bit too far-out for today's club owners. But I think baseball is undergoing an upheaval now. It used to be that men could get by in a baseball front office with not much more to qualify them than a lot of friends in the TV and newspaper world, a cheery manner, a willingness to do as bid, and a capacity for strong drink. In those days, when baseball players were "property," there was not much need to appraise the true worth of a player or even negotiate with any skill, let alone deal in salary figures that total more than the entire payroll of a ball club of a quarter century ago. As a student of mathematics and baseball, I am used to figures with a lot of commas in them. And as a player who has known baseball both before and after free agency, I think I am able to distinguish what is worth conserving in both worlds.

For one thing, I do not believe it is free agency that is really storing up headaches for the baseball clubs. Ballplayers will always be able to command what they are worth at the box office, just as other entertainment stars do. The real frog in the turbine is salary arbitration, which too often leaves a baseball club with a player for whom no better job can be found then, as Red Smith put it, counting the dugouts, and who still draws a salary five or six times what they pay to the manager. I would like to see some incentives added to the pay system, so that players who help most in winning baseball games will pick up the fattest pay envelopes. For, on every club, to balance whatever players may be riding the bench at high salaries, there are workhorses who save game after game (George Frazier of the Yankees is a prime example) and yet draw salaries comparable to the groundskeeper's or the front-office attorney's.

Baseball players need incentives to insure their concentration on the game. It has been my observation that too many of the new ballplayers, who are on an average less skillful than the old-timers just because the available talent has to be spread among so many more clubs, are far more concerned about the fit of their new skintight uniforms than they are with putting the team into the play-offs. (I talked to one young man not long ago who, after bitching about his uniform, allowed frankly that he had "just as soon" be playing back in Triple A. I don't think anyone can play winning baseball with that attitude, commendable as it might be in some less competitive sphere.)

But my own attitude toward baseball has changed since Travis's accident. I find it difficult to believe that God put me here primarily to play baseball. I think I serve Him best when I concern myself first with the well-being of my family, and love Him best when I love those who are nearest to me. And while I know I never put baseball ahead of my family, I sometimes rated them too nearly on a par. Now there is no doubt whatever. For instance, I would not accept a manager's job when my playing days are over, or any job that required my separation from Sally and the kids for extended periods. Baseball, I know, has, as players are constantly avowing, been very good to us, has enabled us to enjoy comforts we might never have known and earned us places in a world that might have seemed far out of reach to us. It has also enabled us to extend help to hundreds of the poor, the aged, and the ailing, to help finance the search for cures for the ailments that destroy so many young lives—and thus to lay up for all of us treasures in Heaven. But without Sally and the kids, baseball would be just a pleasant game to me. Much as I love it, and thrilled as I am by it whether I am winning or losing, it still cannot ever woo me away from my abiding devotion to my family and to the God who has blessed me with their presence.

Now I am with the baseball club that I hope to remain a part of for as long as I can contribute to their cause. I have been reunited with Reggie Jackson, one of my best friends in baseball, and we have an owner whose word can be relied on and whose interest in his ballplayers extends beyond their performance on the field.

My only regret so far is that I failed to get the Angels into the World Series. Losing the second game I pitched in the play-offs was something I suppose I should have foreseen, not because Gene Mauch put me in with insufficient rest, as some writers said, but because I succumbed once more to a weakness in my nature I have been long aware of. I call it my fishbowl syndrome. Every now and then, throughout my career, I have found myself reacting in an adverse way to pressure I put on myself when there is a tremendous public buildup to some one game. I felt it in that first game I worked in after Travis's accident. I felt it again in the play-off game in New York when Travis threw out the first ball and I had been held back from my normal start so I could pitch that game.

Most of the time, if I have notice enough of what's coming, I can go through my long mental and, I suppose, psychological workout, so that I am impervious to the pressure at game time. But these three times, the buildup was so sudden that I simply did not prepare myself—or it may be that I was able to persuade myself I had "outgrown" that weakness. Anyway, what happens in these circumstances is that I try to pitch "too fine." I try to pitch to spots, to force the ball to go to the very area where I think it must, instead of simply flipping the ball for the strike zone and letting the movement take care of itself. But at least in all of these losses, I learn a little more about myself, so that, by the time I am Gaylord Perry's age and I am asked to pitch out of turn and under some tremendous pressure from media and fans, I can just take two deep breaths and be ready.

Sally:

I cannot play baseball. I never want to play baseball. I don't even aspire to being an umpire or a coach. Club owner I might accept. But what I am best at is holding this baseball family together. And that makes me, I think, an important part of Tommy's success. Buzzy Bavasi, I am sure, agrees with me on that, for he is one club executive who shares the view that the baseball wife deserves some consideration.

That is my idea of "equality of the sexes." Each of us has a job to do, each of us is peculiarly fitted to do that job better than the other spouse is. And each of us deserves equal rewards—not in income alone, but in authority within the family, in standing in the eyes of the employer, and in dignity in the eyes of the public. Most married women, I believe, would go along with a plan like that. I think if it were possible to take a plebiscite of *all* women, most of them would vote for equal wages for equal work, for equal chances of advancement, for equal opportunities in the professions, and for a square deal in marriage—and would not waste a single breath in a struggle for admittance to male locker rooms (what would happen I wonder if male reporters demanded access to girls' dressing rooms?), for abolition of male "sanctuaries," for being identified as "persons" (as in chairperson, personkind, and the Isle of Person) and for unisex toilets.

Of course my lot, as the wife of a very well-paid athlete, is not that of the average woman. But to do the job as I want it done—to hold the family together spiritually and physically, to provide an enjoyable home atmosphere for husband and kids—I have to work hard and work steadily, sometimes under extremely trying conditions—although never of course under the desperate circumstances many less fortunate know. Still, to travel all over the country, with one or two, or even four children under my wing, just so that they (and I) can spend extra time with their father, to keep him from becoming a stranger to his kids, that is often no job for a lady given to feeling sorry for herself. Trying to keep the peace when one little boy is at the point of wetting his pants, another child is getting into a poke-and-slap affair with a kid in the seat ahead, and a third requires immediate nourishment is, to my mind, every bit as nerve-straining an experience as pitching a doubleheader. Yet I think the result is more than worth the strain. Tommy gets real comfort from having the little ones close when he is far from home, the kids take special pride in seeing Tommy in action and relish his love and attention at bedtime.

It is not always possible to take all four children at once on a road trip. But I try to give them turns, as school and other commitments allow, so that their relationship with their father will be as nearly normal as can be arranged. I try in other ways too to keep the kids conscious of Tommy's presence. If you were to visit our house you might go away with the notion that there lives a real egomaniac—photos of Tommy John, paintings of Tommy John, drawings of Tommy John, cartoons of Tommy John, along with plaques and prizes of every design adorn nearly every wall, shelf, and alcove. But that, to me, is a way of keeping Tommy's presence, and his position as part of the family, in the kids' minds every day of the year. Baseball players must be away from home at frequent long intervals through the eight months of the season, and more than a few baseball families have cracked up under the strain of these separations. I sympathize with the baseball wife I talked with not long ago who told me that *never* again would she move her family to keep up with her husband should he be traded once more. The kids were happy in their schools and with their friends. She had settled into the community, had friends she did not want to lose, and had made a life for herself in local organizations.

"If he wants to go out to the Coast," she declared, "let him go! The kids and I stay *here*!"

That seems a natural and certainly forgivable reaction. But it will never be mine. Kids, I have observed, adjust easily to change in environment as long as the home is stable and happy. I perhaps do not adjust quite so easily. But adjustments being part of baseball, then they are part of my job just as they are part of Tommy's. There is a job in television and public relations that I would like to try and maybe even a "career" I might succeed in. But never at the cost of the family. My kids will be raised by their parents, not by grandparents or nursemaids. And while Baseball continues to provide us with comforts and even luxuries, I will give back to Baseball as much as is required.

Come to think of it, I am perhaps one of the few women who have ever made a "mound appearance" in professional baseball—and I did it twice. And both times I was noticeably, even alarmingly, pregnant. The first time I have already told about, when I had my picture taken with Tommy after he signed with the Yankees. The second time was also at Yankee Stadium, before one of the largest crowds in the history of the new plant. That was the night when Travis (and I bless George Steinbrenner for this) was asked to throw out the first ball, less than a month after his release from the hospital, in the Eastern Division play-offs against Milwaukee. Tommy was scheduled to pitch that night so he was not going to be able to escort Travis to the mound. We thought of asking Reggie Jackson. But would that be an imposition—to ask Reggie to perform in the ceremony and then trot all the way out to right field so the game could begin? Well, Tommy decided to ask him.

"Tommy," said Reggie, with tears in his eyes—and I should have known he would react this way—"I would consider that the greatest honor of my career." So Reggie and Travis and I stood waiting by the dugout as the preliminaries were completed. And Reggie said to me suddenly, "Listen. You have to go with me, you know."

I actually gasped at the idea.

"But I'm too emotional! I'll look dreadful out there!"

"Well, you don't think I'm going out there all by myself, do you? No way!"

At that very moment the introductions began and Reggie grabbed my arm, took Travis by the hand, and started off. Unless I wanted to create a scene that would set the whole house to laughing, I had to trot along.

Travis, who surely must have some trace of ham in his makeup, put us both to shame by the way he reacted to the thunderous welcome. Reggie pointed out to Travis his picture on the screen in center field. Travis saw himself walking out with Reggie and Mommy. He looked this way and that, like a parading politician, and waved his hand to everyone. On the mound, with the cameras rolling, with Rick Cerone crouched a few yards away to take the throw, Travis took his position on the mound as if he were truly going to start the game in Tommy's place. He held the ball in both hands, looked over one shoulder as if to check the runner at first base and then actually smoked the ball on a line to Rick. The applause that greeted this beat down on us like an avalanche. It was as if Reggie had hit his third home run in a row. And Travis reveled in it. Reggie hoisted Travis to his shoulder to show him where the big television scene was displaying the whole group of us, bigger than life.

"That's you!" Reggie told him. And Travis joyfully greeted himself with an arm's length salute.

That joyous aftermath of the dreadful accident that nearly destroyed our lives is one I never tire of reliving. But they were precious words to me. Precious because they told me not only that my little boy could talk but that he was *normal*. That he was a little boy again, and that if there was hunger in his stomach there was love in his heart. I did not have to *hear* the words I had been longing for. I knew they were there. I knew that the moment would come soon when he would tell me, just as earnestly as he had told me countless times when he was well: "I love you so-o-o-o much!" Only, in those days, he pronounced it "wuv." And there is another moment, so long looked forward to, so vividly imagined, and so replete with tears and laughter that it already outshines in my memory many of the terrifying hours we lived through the summer of 1981.

Beginning with the first signs of returning consciousness, I yearned for the moment when Travis would utter his first words after those never-ending days of silence. Because I knew exactly what he would say when he finally found his tongue again. He would say what he always said when I left him at night, when I greeted him in the morning, when we were saying good-bye for only an hour or two. He would look deep into my face and tell me: "I love you so-o-o-o much, Mommy!"

When finally Travis could walk and could understand what we said to him and could perform the little tasks we asked him to, I kept holding him close, to hear those words again.

The day did come when he suddenly looked at me with his lips working. I could just see those words trying to form themselves in his throat, struggling to be free. They were on the very surface of his lips and I could *feel* them taking shape there. I caught him up and held him close so his mouth was almost against my ear. I was beginning to cry with happiness. Then the words burst out at last, without a stammer:

"I'm hungry!"

Famous first words.

It will always remain in my mind as one of the most magnificent moments in my experience—not for my part in it. Not at all. Not even because Travis appeared before more than a hundred million television watchers to help them all share my own joy at his return to the world. I think it was magnificent because of Reggie Jackson.

It is almost unheard of for a professional baseball player to get involved so selflessly in the tribulations of a teammate. While ballplayers will offer sympathy and even financial help to teammates in trouble and will often share their joys, most of them have learned through experience that baseball friendships are subject to sudden and permanent disruption and that bitter rivalries can develop almost overnight. So they tend to hold themselves at arm's length from one another's woes. But Reggie had acted from the beginning as if our troubles were his own. And in this special moment of public rejoicing, he eagerly accepted the position of second-fiddle to a happy little boy. Reggie loves limelight as much as any performer does. But this time he took care to see that it was centered on Travis and that Travis savored it all. That vision of Travis joyously perched on Reggie's shoulder while the whole baseball world seemed to rejoice in his recovery will be held in my heart forever.

INDEX